THE CALIFORNIA PROGRESSIVES

Professor George E. Mowry was born in Washington, D.C., and studied at Miami University (Ohio) and the University of Wisconsin. He is the author of *Theodore Roosevelt and the Progressive Movement* and *A Short History of American Democracy*. He is at present Professor of American History at the University of California, Los Angeles.

THE

CALIFORNIA

PROGRESSIVES

by

GEORGE E. MOWRY

Q

QUADRANGLE PAPERBACKS

Quadrangle Books / Chicago

PREFACE

In many ways the progressive movement that swept throughout the United States from 1900 to 1916 in the name of reform was a paradoxical social phenomenon. Since it was bipartisan, its origins obviously were not political in the narrow sense of the term. Since it came of age in a period of relative prosperity, and since most of its leaders were recruited from the middle or upper economic classes, its motivation did not appear to be economic in character, again in a narrow sense. Many very wealthy men contributed to the progressive movement. From Theodore Roosevelt and Woodrow Wilson down through all the levels of local government, most progressive leaders had been violently opposed to the nineteenth-century agrarian radicalism of William Jennings Bryan and the Populists. Yet these same Progressives, in the years between 1900 and 1916, enacted most of the reforms that had been sponsored previously by the Bryan Democrats and the farmer Populists. In the light of these seemingly contradictory facts the bewildered student of history might well ask just who were the Progressives, what prompted them to act, what were they trying to do, and where did they think they were going?

After attempting for ten years to answer these questions by a study of national progressivism, I concluded that for real insight into the movement one had to study it as it developed from the grassroots in the several states. Hence this book on California, which I hope may throw as much light upon the nature of national progressivism and recent American "liberalism" as it may upon the history of the state. I also hope that the book may say something not entirely insignificant about the more general problem of why American reform movements start and why they die.

The intelligent reader will not have gone very far through the pages of this book until he realizes that there is an unfortunate lack of references to the personal papers of the men who defended the status quo in California. Had these papers been available, this story might have been modified here and there. I have tried without any appreciable success to obtain such papers. The men who supported the rule of the Southern Pacific railroad and who were opposed to the democratization of state government either have not kept their papers or have been reluctant to place them at the disposal of the student. Like so many recent histories, consequently, this one is probably biased toward the "progressive-liberal" position. Not because it was willed so; but because a historian is no better than his sources.

Had it not been for the great kindness of many California Progressives still living and for many public institutions, together with the helpful and generous people who run them, this book would have been impossible. Edward A. Dickson, the late Chester Rowell, Marshall Stimson, Robert Waring, and Franklin Hichborn were particularly helpful with both their personal manuscripts and their time. My thanks are due to Professor Sherman Kent for permission to use his father's papers, as well as to the libraries of Stanford University, the University of California, Yale University, the City of Los Angeles, the State University of Iowa, the John Randolph and Dora Haynes Foundation of Los Angeles, and to the Library of Congress. Finally, there is no adequate way to thank my second head and my third arm—my wife.

G. E. M.

CONTENTS

Illustrations

CHAPTER I

The Southern Pacific's California

*

In 1900, as the century turned, Californians might well have been proud as they compared their lot with that of their fellow citizens east of the Sierra Nevada. It was a good land, this west land, with its cloud-shadowed foothills, gray, granite piles of mountains, long, rich, sometimes vineclad valleys, strange deserts, and its coast, fogged and grimly scarped to the north, and bright and smooth-sanded to the south. And over its entire length hung Vachel Lindsay's ten gold suns, "when all other lands had one."

Californians could also be proud of San Francisco at the turn of the century, that gay, lusty city by the bay, the city where, Ambrose Bierce said captiously, nobody thought. Home of the bonanza kings and the fabulous Palace Hotel, of famous cafés and glittering theaters, of the roistering Barbary Coast and the more seductive cocktail route up Market Street, it was the "Paris of the West," where most of its 350,000 citizens of all shades of skin had shaken off their Puritan heritage and were busy enjoying themselves. In its bistros Kipling and Stevenson were still a subject of conversation. Frank Norris had just written the third of his powerful novels, and across San Francisco Bay Jack London had sold his first story to the *Atlantic Monthly*. Ambrose Bierce bitterly stalked its streets and dominated its journals. There, Arnold Genthe, Wallace Irwin, and a host of lesser creators worked. And there California's best known poet, George Sterling, the legend goes, pursued Bierce, women, and drink.

In spite of all its natural grandeur and human color, not a few Californians were a little troubled in 1900 with the development of their commonwealth. For the state as a whole had

1

not lived up to its golden promises of the 'fifties and the 'eighties, when people had virtually poured across its boundaries. During the troublesome 'nineties, in fact, the population of California increased at just a little higher rate than the average for the rest of the nation, an increase so slow that it would take years, it seemed, before the state's great raw areas would be developed into the patterns of a mature civilization. At the turn of the century, notwithstanding the growing citrus culture, California was sparsely populated for its size and depended upon a traditional commercial, extractive, and agricultural economy. Far removed from other population and cultural centers of the country, its inhabitants felt their isolation. Writing at the start of the new century, Benjamin Ide Wheeler, president of the state university, described California as a backwater "where few people come except the very rich, and they only to stay a few months during the winter." The New York papers, he observed, never mentioned the state except to record "an earthquake, a murder, or a birth of a two-headed calf."

In contrast to this somber review of the past, however, Wheeler held forth great hope for the future, predicting that the state would soon lose its provincialism in a burst of material and intellectual activity that would amaze its sister commonwealths along the Atlantic seaboard.[1] He lived to see the basic elements evolve which were necessary for that period of unparalleled expansion and construction. In the first two decades of the twentieth century, critical developments in high-speed transportation, large-scale irrigation, and the subtropical fruit, vegetable, petroleum, and movie industries, all took place. These, together with the unrivaled climate, formed the material substructure for the modern state.

In the piping times immediately following the Spanish-American War, three international shipping lines were established, connecting San Francisco to the Orient, to Great Britain, and to Germany. By the time the Panama Canal was opened, six lines with regular service were opening the windows of the world to the state. More than matching the increase in sea-borne traffic was the development of railroad facilities within and to the state. In 1901 the Southern Pacific completed its coast line, and four years later Los Angeles was directly tied by steel rails to Salt Lake City and the East. On August 22, 1910, the first Western Pacific passenger train arrived in Oakland from the East, thus completing California's network of major railroads. Perhaps even more eloquent of the future was the arrival in New York in 1903 of the first automobile driven across the continent. (Eight years later the first transcontinental flight was made to Pasadena.) It took the automobile fifty-two days to make the trip. But by 1909, of the approximately thirty thousand owners of the new horseless carriages in California, five hundred and thirty-nine had been convicted of fast driving. Clearly, technology was rapidly ending the era when the state was remote from the rest of the country.[2]

Before California could comfortably take care of the many newcomers to her lands and cities, however, a solution had to be found to the old problem of inadequate water. For precisely in that part of the state where the lands were most tillable, water was least available. In the southern part of the San Joaquin Valley and almost everywhere south of the Tehachapi, the desert had to be conquered and driven back by water before man and crops could sustain themselves. Thousands of powered pumps were in operation by 1900, but already by that time the water table was rapidly falling and a new source of water had to be found. Simple irrigation was old in California, and in 1886, at the completion of the Gage canal system near Los Angeles, the possibilities of moving water artificially on a large scale were first realized. It was not until the new century, though, that water diversion on a herculean scale was tried and proved feasible. Colorado River water made the Imperial Valley first bloom in 1901. Lesser projects in the San Joaquin Valley and the great Owens River aqueduct made the present Los Angeles region possible. By 1916 more than three million acres were irrigated in the

3

state, the overwhelming proportion of which lay south of Sacramento.[3]

In the 1890's California had been the second largest wheat producing state in the union, but with the advent of expensive irrigation projects the yellow grain could no longer be grown economically on the resulting high-cost land. During the first decade of the new century the acreage planted in cereals in the state decreased by 50 per cent, and by 1920 most of the San Joaquin great wheat ranches had fallen prey not to Frank Norris' Octopus but to fruit, nut, and vegetable farming. In 1901, the California Bureau of Labor Statistics was still relating the state's seasonal unemployment problem to the yearly cycle of grain and hay crops; ten years later the bureau emphasized the connection between transient labor supply and the harvesting of citrus and orchard fruits.[4]

By 1900 table, raisin, and wine grapes were all important crops in California together with figs and the more common orchard fruits and nuts. With grapefruit, dates, and avocados introduced in the first decade of the new century, they represented by 1910 a sizable part of the state's total cash income from agricultural produce. But by any measurement the most important as well as the most spectacular of the state's products was the orange—a veritable golden apple. First shipped in quantities from the state in the 'eighties, by 1900 the orange crop had passed the cash returns from gold. Within the next two decades the receipts from both the orange and lemon crop were to double and double again. The introduction of the seedless orange and the refrigerator car, plus the extensive irrigation projects, had given to southern California her first great money crop. The organization of the California Fruit Growers' Exchange in 1905, assuring the citrus producer of a controlled and "rationalized" market, made the industry a big business.[5] Within ten years the approximately fifteen thousand members of the exchange, mostly located in the five counties of Los Angeles, San Bernardino, Tulare, Riverside, and Orange, were using more than thirty thousand laborers and collecting free on board receipts of over $27,000,000 annually. Though not as much publicized in the scale of their operations, similar organizations for the raisin, almond, and other produce growers resulted in comparable financial returns. In 1919, at the request of the attorney general, the Federal Trade Commission investigated the Raisin Growers' Association and reported that the "price fixed by the Raisin Company for the 1919 crop was in excess of fair and reasonable price." [6] Irrespective of the reasonableness of the returns, the expectancy of such golden profits was the essential motive force in the great expansion of California agriculture in the twentieth century. People poured across the state's boundaries to invest either their capital or their labor in the high-priced irrigated fields.

Though fruit growing was one of the major reasons for the growth of twentieth-century California, petroleum production and its derivatives were probably even more important. The presence of oil in the state had been known for a long time before 1900. It had first been accidentally discovered in 1838, and by mid-century Andrés Pico was supplying it to the San Fernando Mission for illuminating purposes. But until the 'nineties the inadequacy of drilling methods and the lack of a market made it a subject of vocal instead of financial speculation. Then oil-burning engines, combined with more efficient drilling equipment, opened a new future. In the summer of 1898 Canfield and Chanslor went down more than a thousand feet to bring in a 1,200 barrel well, and the great oil boom was on. Production doubled in the next two years, and in the first decade of the twentieth century every succeeding year saw the figures mount skyward. To the older Ventura, Newhall, Los Angeles, and Sunset districts were added the great Coalinga, Kern, McKittrick, and Midway fields. When practically worthless desert land jumped in price in a matter of weeks to thousands of dollars per acre, Los Angeles, the urban heart of the oil boom, became slightly hysterical. As new oil companies sprang up daily, and as merchants gave a share of oil stock with every purchase of more than three dollars, fortunes exchanged hands overnight. Above all this

5

profit and loss, the one overpowering fact stood out—California oil production jumped from four million barrels in 1900 to more than seventy-seven million in 1910, almost a twenty-fold increase. The present skyline of downtown Los Angeles, punctuated sharply by the home offices of the great oil firms, is eloquent testimony to petroleum's part in the building of the modern state.[7]

The profits from the flow of oil alone, however, did not reflect the complete influence of the black oleaginous substance on the state. In a land barren of coal, oil and the development of hydroelectric resources constituted the power potential desperately needed to convert California from an agricultural and commercial community to a complex industrial society. That translation was to take time. In the first decade of the twentieth century, industry was already well on its way. Although the 100 per cent increase in the value of manufactured products from 1899 to 1909 was largely due to the expansion of the traditional lumber, smelting, slaughtering, and canning industries, hundreds of newer products had already gained a foothold in the industrial register of the state. Not the least of these, measured either in influence or in gross profits, was moving pictures. As Cleland points out, California weather and the possible desire to break a monopoly hold over the movie industry, encouraged the first movie promoters to settle in Hollywood sometime after 1901, there to grind out the fabulous product that was to cause so many startling changes in American tastes, dress, morals, and even language. The makers and owners of the silent films followed what seemed to be a set California pattern in the early years of the twentieth century. Within three or four years, many of the early companies which had started on a financial shoestring of a few thousand dollars were capitalized in the millions.[8]

With the climate so pleasant and profits so plentiful, mass immigration into the state was inevitable. After this natural movement was spurred on by the Los Angeles Chamber of Commerce, the result was intensified to startling proportions.

The peak of this great flood of moving humanity did not reach the Pacific shores until the 'twenties. But already in the first decade of the century its waters had begun to rise. In the preceding few years the state's population had jumped only moderately; it now registered a 60 per cent increase in one decade. Consequently, in 1910, native-born Californians were still as much of a minority in the population as they had been when the state was first organized.

More important to the future of the commonwealth than the gross numbers of the newcomers was their over-all character. A close student of California immigration has pointed out that the average immigrant into California after 1900, while still young, was at least six years older than the one who had come in the 'eighties. He brought more wealth with him into the state. Probably more important, this average wayfarer had changed both his place of origin and his final destination. Whereas before he had come from New York, Illinois, Pennsylvania, or Ohio, now in the twentieth century he made his farewells in the central Middle West. Instead of settling in northern California, he was now finding a home in the San Joaquin Valley, or more likely south of the Tehachapi and Tejon passes.[9] By 1890, it has been estimated, 45 per cent of California's population originated in the Middle West. By 1900 and 1910 that figure had increased to 50 and 60 per cent respectively. Since most of southern California's population was made up in 1910 of recent immigrant stock, the Middle Western influence there was proportionately stronger than in the state as a whole. And in the wake of these Middle Westerners followed the traditions of populism, Protestant morality, and progressivism.[10]

The influx of this new stock into the southern part of the state made southern California a major population area. In 1900 the eleven counties south of the Tehachapi had a population of only 350,000, or less than one-third that of the north; by 1920 the figure had grown to more than 1,400,000, or only a little less than three-quarters of the north's 2,000,000. Within the same period Los Angeles became the largest city in the state. As this new stream of population flooded the south, it served to intensify a sectionalism in the state that had existed since the days of the gold rush.

Geography and distance probably first accounted for the separatism of the two sections in the state which was manifest during the first state constitutional convention in the proposal to split the territory into two states. Later, the changing character of the population in the two sections, and the difference in their social attitudes emphasized this original divergence. By 1900 San Francisco was heavily Catholic, the south predominantly Protestant.[11] Although both sections of the state contained sizable foreign groups, the minorities in San Francisco, possibly because of the religious pattern or perhaps because of the strength of organized labor, were usually more influential in civic life than were comparable groups in the south. At any rate, in the early years of the twentieth century, southern California was inclined to be stricter on moral issues than was the north, but more liberal in purely political experiments. A proposal for woman suffrage was defeated by northern votes in 1896. At the same time, San Francisco's divorce rate was appreciably higher than that of Los Angeles. In 1911 there was one divorce to every five marriages in the bay city; the comparable rate in Los Angeles was but one to eight.[12]

The rapid growth of the southern part of the state increased southern California's demand for an equitable place in the commonwealth's political life. Since the founding of California, San Francisco and the north had practically dominated the state government. But with the rising southern population, the demand by Los Angeles and its hinterland for a fair representation in the state legislature and in Congress was an issue always close to the surface in state politics. During the first two decades of the new century, however, this sectional political issue was far overshadowed by two other great struggles for power which cut across all regional boundaries. One of these centered around the rise of an increasingly politically conscious laboring class in urban California. But within the early years of the century the labor issue, while

8

extremely important, was always secondary from the viewpoint of the entire state to the struggle to free the state from corporate rule. California, like so many of her sister commonwealths at the turn of the century, had only the shadow of representative government, while the real substance of power resided largely in the Southern Pacific Railroad Company. To a degree perhaps unparalleled in the nation, the Southern Pacific and a web of associated economic interests ruled the state.

Given the original conditions of constructing and financing California's first transcontinental railroad, the events that followed seemed almost to pursue a natural law. Like so many other great railroad builders, the Big Four had not created the Central Pacific, predecessor of the Southern Pacific, for the purpose of operating an efficient and profitable railroad. That was incidental to their real design of amassing fortunes out of its construction. Once completed, the Central Pacific was so overcapitalized that profits from operations seemed extremely remote. Unable to sell this "streak of rust entirely surrounded with water" because of a conspicuous lack of would-be purchasers, the original constructors were virtually forced to operate the road and to wring every possible cent from the rate-paying public. This seemed to be the only way the railroad could possibly enhance the fortunes of its controllers and partly service its great debt. Consequently, from the first day of operation the company adopted the principle of charging all the traffic would bear. In extending its lines, the railroad regularly forced towns on a prospective course to pay a heavy tribute. On the threat of building around Los Angeles, the city was forced to cede to the Southern Pacific a franchise intended for a competing railroad, a sixty-acre tract for a depot, and a bonus of $600,000. Once in operation, railroad agents demanded and obtained the right to inspect the books of private companies. When a concern's rate of profits went up, so did railroad rates upon the commodities it shipped. In agricultural regions rates varied with the market price of the products raised. Only rarely were rate favors

9

given, and these usually to large corporations. In the 'nineties for example, when the Standard Oil Company wanted to make a shipment, the rates along the way were suddenly lowered and then raised again to the original level when Standard Oil had finished its shipment.[13]

To insure the future success of such highbinding tactics, the Central Pacific–Southern Pacific rapidly achieved a monopoly over most of the state's transportation facilities, a combine that eventually included in the early 'eighties not only 85 per cent of the railroad mileage of the state but also river and ocean shipping lines, ferry service, and urban transportation facilities. In achieving this powerful position, the railroad ignored all other interests of the commonwealth. Quick to war against possible competitors by land, it also lobbied against the proposed Nicaragua and Panama canals. For years its almost absolute control of the Oakland waterfront stunted the commercial development of that city and prevented any competition to the railroad's ferry service in the cross-bay haul. After the city of Oakland, under Mayor Pardee, claimed the shore rights at the foot of its main street, Broadway, the railroad fenced off the area by driving huge piles between its property and deep water. When an intrepid coal merchant sought to establish a nickel ferry service across San Francisco Bay, the company attempted to destroy the service by blocking his wharves with company trams, ramming his boats, and covering his passengers with coal dust released from near-by bunkers.[14]

In Los Angeles the situation was substantially the same. Since the railroad company had acquired possession of the waterfront at Santa Monica, it fought the development of a municipal harbor at near-by San Pedro. In spite of the report of a board of army engineers that the San Pedro site was preferable, railroad pressure brought upon Congress and executive departments was sufficient to stop the municipal harbor development for six long years. Similar obstructions were placed in the way of the development of competing railroads. It was not until 1900 that the Santa Fe reached

10

Point Richmond on San Francisco Bay. Even then the Southern Pacific held a vise-like transportation monopoly on a major part of the state. Along the entire coast north of Los Angeles, on the direct routes east from San Francisco, and in practically all the territory north of the capital city, Sacramento, the Southern Pacific and its subsidiaries reigned in solitary grandeur.

The long tentacles of the railroad company were entwined around many other California resources. Under one of the provisions of its original charters the federal government had granted the Central Pacific more than 10,000,000 acres of land from the public domain. This and subsequent grants made the company the largest landowner in both California and Nevada. Much of the land was of course later sold to farmers, but as late as 1916 the California State Commission of Immigration and Housing reported that the Southern Pacific owned more than half of one of the state's largest counties and major parts of many more.[15] What proportion of the state's lumber, mineral, and petroleum wealth was contained in these millions of acres is unknown. But it is reasonable to suppose that in all its gigantic land deals, Southern Pacific officials were not unmindful of these nonagricultural possibilities. In May, 1912, Attorney General Wickersham entered suit against the railroad to recover for the government oil lands in California valued at $15,000,000, which he deposed had been fraudulently secured under the guise of an agricultural grant.[16]

Accustomed to such cavalier treatment of public authorities, the railroad was downright ruthless in its dealings with private individuals, irrespective of whether they were merchants and shippers, laborers on its lines, or farmers seeking to purchase its lands. The story of Mussel Slough in what is now the Lucerne Valley, where five ranchers died in 1877 seeking to protect their land from the grasp of the railroad, was an often-told tale even before Frank Norris centered his novel around it. To tens of thousands of Californians, Norris' description of the iron grip of the Southern Pacific on the ranchers of Mussel Slough was more than a literary exercise; it was a part of their own biographies.

As the last step in securing their hold over California, the managers of the Southern Pacific early sought to control the government of the state. Without political power, their exorbitant rate structure, transportation monopoly, and grasp on much of the state's resources would be in constant danger from an aroused electorate. The path of the Big Four, therefore, led almost inexorably from the first fraudulent construction contracts, through a bankrupt railroad, to the state legislature and the Supreme Court bench. In the nineteenth century, the way was not very difficult. This was primarily because of the railroad's own great wealth and power, the lack of any business, farmer, or labor organization of comparable size and influence that might have challenged its strength, and last, but not least, the corruptibility of a multitude of Californians. As in many western states of the time, the railroad so far overshadowed any possible competitors in point of number of men employed, invested capital, and value to a community, that it stood alone in terms of crude social power. Enlistment in its service was one of the more certain ways to wealth and power. During the latter half of the nineteenth century, that interesting age of private Victorian primness and great public corruption, Californians were certainly no models of public virtue. Sired by reckless and daring men with the glint of sudden fortune in their eyes, the state had attracted "the blood of all lands and the law of none!" Long before the Central Pacific was chartered, the first California legislature had been called the session of a thousand drinks. Along with the great corruptionists of the Central Pacific–Southern Pacific, with their easy public morals and open purses, there existed a host of willing and even expectant corruptibles all over the state. Every Huntington, Crocker, Hopkins, and Stanford had hundreds of purchasable smaller counterparts in editors, jurists, legislators, and city councilmen. The point is that the Big Four did not corrupt the state; it corrupted itself. Collis P. Huntington and his aides were but the most skillful and forceful practitioners of a much practiced art. And while many men cried woe alas, many men indulged.

In this atmosphere it was relatively easy for the railroad company to purchase a good part of the press and muzzle public opinion. Where the Southern Pacific led, lesser companies could safely follow. Before Fremont Older became a reformer, his paper regularly received a monthly subvention not only from the railroad but from the San Francisco gas and water companies as well.[17]

More important to the railroad than public opinion was sovereignty itself. Through means usual and unusual the Southern Pacific eventually organized a government within a government that James D. Phelan described as more powerful in normal times than the state government. In the 'eighties the famous Colton trial, on charges brought by the widow of a former associate of the Big Four, plainly indicated the enormous extent of the railroad's political power. Huntington's and General Colton's letters, produced as evidence, contained long lists of state and national officeholders who were little more than hired servants of the railroad, to be elevated or dismissed from public life according to their zeal in promoting the company's interest. The cost of obtaining passage of individual bills through Congress or the state legislature was frankly discussed. "The boys are very hungry," one Huntington letter ran, "and it will cost us considerable to be saved." [18] Others described the influence of the Southern Pacific with the state and federal judges. Supreme Court Justice Stephen J. Field was one such good and powerful friend. A personal associate of the Big Four, he had been elevated from the California Supreme Court to the highest bench in the land largely through their influence. And in leading the judicial assault on a narrow interpretation of the Fourteenth Amendment, he had done yeoman service in the interest not only of the railroad but of corporate wealth everywhere in the country. A letter from General Colton in 1885 clearly indicated that the judge's period of faithful service was not yet ended. Field would not sit on a case in California,

Colton wrote to Huntington, "but will reserve himself for his best effort (I have no doubt) in the final determination of the case at Washington before a full bench." [19] As for the state judiciary, it was the considered opinion of Dr. John R. Haynes that the Southern Pacific's domination of no other arm of state government was as complete or as pernicious.[20]

Among the lower levels of the government the influence of the railroad was often as potent as it was in Sacramento. The most exact testimony to the point came from Huntington himself. After rowing with Stanford and electing himself president of the road, the tough old capitalist indicted the previous company administration for the time and money spent on politics, which he felt had demoralized the company and wasted its resources needlessly. Promising that the road would withdraw from politics, Huntington went on to say: "Things have got to such a state that if a man wants to be a constable he thinks he has first got to come down to Fourth and Townsend streets to get permission." [21]

Even had Huntington wanted to withdraw from politics in 1890, which is dubious, by that time it was impossible. By 1890 the pattern had been set; the appetite for corruption had grown as it fed. So thoroughly had the Southern Pacific done its work that the entire state seemed to move on the lubricant of graft and privilege. Following the pattern set by the railroad, utility corporations, city street railways, the Royal Arch (the organization of the liquor dealers), gambling associations, and vice rings, together with more legitimate businesses, demanded extra legal privileges and protection. The politicians who supplied them, ranging from state legislators to city councilmen, and from jurists to the "plug-uglies" who delivered the votes on election day, also demanded their price as a vested right. The politician was well aware that penalties as well as favors could come out of the legislative hoppers. To keep the state "safe," William F. Herrin pointed out to Lincoln Steffens, the Southern Pacific was forced to allow all the little grafters and vice rings in the state to obtain their share of the public loot.[22]

Consequently, after Huntington became president of the railroad, there was little change in its political policies. And when E. H. Harriman followed Huntington at the opening of the new century, the railroad machine was, if anything, politically stronger than at any time in the past. At its apex stood William F. Herrin, chief counsel of the railroad until 1910 and afterwards vice-president. Born in the Rogue River country of Oregon, Herrin had come to San Francisco after graduating from law school. There he married a daughter of a judge, and with his father-in-law joined a law firm headed by United States Senator William M. Stewart of Nevada. His own great legal abilities and these important connections soon brought him into touch with the men who ran the Southern Pacific. So well did he serve the interests of the railroad that he survived every reorganization of the corporation, and 1900 found him not only chief counsel, but also head of what was popularly known as the "Southern Pacific Political Bureau."

From the railroad's home offices in San Francisco, Herrin's political influence extended over the state in both the Democratic and Republican parties. Asked once how the railroad had managed to keep California shackled so long, Herrin cynically replied, "because of its control of reform movements." [23] Aiding this powerful boss was Walter Parker, who headed the Southern Pacific machine in southern California. Affable and able, Parker also directed the Southern Pacific lobbying in conventions and in the legislature. Jeremiah T. Burke and George F. Hatton usually were found supporting his activities. Hatton had first come into political prominence by managing the political affairs of United States Senator George C. Perkins, and Jere Burke had started on his way up the Southern Pacific escalator as assistant secretary of the San Francisco Clearing House Association. Lobbying for the association in the legislature, he had become interested in the reorganization of street railways and subsequently became president of the San Jose interurban lines and tax attorney for the Southern Pacific.

Perhaps Dr. John R. Haynes was a little too inclusive in his statement that in the first decade of the new century, "From the village constable to the governor of the state, . . . the final selection of the peoples' officials lay with Mr. Herrin or his subordinates in the railroad machine." [24] Nevertheless, the public-spirited doctor, who dedicated the better part of his life to reform, had his point. The power of Herrin, Parker, Hatton, and Burke was evident in almost every party convention during the period and in practically every election. It was apparent in the nomination and election of Governor Henry T. Gage in 1898, and again in the selection of his successor, George C. Pardee. Although the railroad forces were originally for the renomination of Gage in the Republican convention of 1902, they switched to Pardee in order to beat a nonmachine man, Thomas Flint. Pardee later acknowledged that had it not been for the railroad, Flint would have won. He also confessed that the Republican platform of 1902 was drawn up by representatives of the Southern Pacific. [25]

The power of the railroad was also shown in the regular reëlection of United States Senator George C. Perkins. Former governor of the state and senator from 1893 to 1915, Perkins was notoriously a servant of the railroad. A common story of the day was that the senator had been in deep water only once in his life, while bathing at Monterey in 1906, and that on that occasion he had, appropriately, been rescued by a Standard Oil tanker. During the first years of the decade Perkins' colleague in the Senate was Thomas R. Bard, a consistent conservative but a man of independent mind, who refused to accept dictation from the machine. Therefore, even though supported by the powerful Los Angeles *Times,* Bard was defeated for the renomination by a more amenable candidate, Frank P. Flint, who gracefully admitted after his election that he owed his good fortune to Walter Parker. [26] What was true of the elections of governors and senators was also true in varying degrees of all elections, from lesser state offices down to city councils.

In affairs more directly concerned with the business of

transportation, some checks on the Southern Pacific's high-handed tactics of the past were supplied in the twentieth century by the Interstate Commerce Commission and by the competing Santa Fe and Western Pacific roads. But the commission had no power over intrastate shipments, and its decisions on interstate cases were contestable in the federal courts. For the individual shipper, moreover, the competition proved to be more apparent than real, since the newer roads all too often followed the precedents set by the Southern Pacific.

Around the turn of the century all the western roads refused to permit the citrus growers to route their own shipments, a scheme designed, the growers complained, to force them into using high-priced refrigerator car lines. Eventually the growers found that the precooling of refrigerator cars eliminated the need for re-icing in transit. The railroads, however, continued to charge the customary thirty-dollar fee for a service no longer rendered. An adjustment was secured only after the case had been fought twice through the Interstate Commerce Commission and the federal courts. But perhaps the most spectacular move of the Southern Pacific and other west coast railroads was in raising the freight rates on lemons immediately after the Payne-Aldrich tariff act had raised the duty against foreign fruit by fifty cents a hundred pounds. The customs rate had been increased to allow California growers to dominate the New York City markets to the exclusion of foreign shippers. According to experts, the raised freight rates destroyed about 50 per cent of the tariff's new effectiveness.[27]

The Southern Pacific's continued stranglehold on municipal politics in the twentieth century was well illustrated by its struggle to prevent the Western Pacific road from securing trackage rights in northern California. Undoubtedly at the Southern Pacific's behest, the Sacramento city council defeated a franchise granting the Western Pacific a right of way through the city. Only after the local merchants had threatened to recall the council did it approve a popular referendum

17

on the grant, which, needless to say, was adopted by a huge majority. Again at Oakland the dominant railroad attempted to throttle this new competitor. In the south, the Southern Pacific was still obstructing the development of the Los Angeles free harbor. And thus even as late as the spring of 1910, the people of California might still have echoed the words of Preseley, the young idealist in *The Octopus:* "They swindle a nation of a hundred million and call it Financiering; they levy a blackmail and call it Commerce; they corrupt a legislature and call it Politics; they bribe a judge and call it Law; they hire blacklegs to carry out their plans and call it Organization; they prostitute the honor of a state and call it Competition."

Many Californians, of course, had not watched the growth of the railroad's power with equanimity. They had protested vigorously even before the last spike had been driven to complete the Central Pacific. During the depression-ridden 1870's the Peoples' Independent Party, the followers of Dennis Kearney, and later the Grangers, all had sought to curb the growing political strength as well as the excessive rates of the railroad. These movements culminated in the state constitutional convention of 1879, when a railroad commission was created and given power to regulate rates and to prevent discrimination between shippers. But with the return of prosperous times the attacks upon the railroad lessened, and soon the great corporation was not only in control of the legislature but of the railroad commission as well. A serious study of rate regulation in the state, published in 1895, concluded that, "Not a single majority report has ever issued from the railroad commission of a nature unsatisfactory to the company the commission was established to control," and that the main result of the constitutional provision had been the creation of a new Southern Pacific literary bureau maintained at public expense. Twelve years later a similar study by the Commonwealth Club concurred in the judgment that the thirty-year experiment in attempting to regulate railroad rates had been a complete failure.[28]

With the return of hard times during the early 'nineties, another great popular movement against the Southern Pacific was launched. In despair of a political solution to the railroad problem, and caught between rapidly falling prices and extortionate railroad rates, the independent merchants and shippers of San Francisco organized the Traffic Association of California. By supporting the Atlantic and Pacific Steamship Company, a competitor to the Southern Pacific lines, the merchants won a temporary victory, forcing lower water rates from the dominant transportation monopoly. Two years later a similar group of independent merchants and capitalists, led by Mayor Sutro, Claus Spreckels, James D. Phelan, James Flood, and O. D. Baldwin, organized the Valley Railroad on a popular subscription basis. This "Peoples' Road," as it was sometimes called, reached Bakersfield in 1897. Sold to the Santa Fe the following year, it constituted an important link in providing an alternative railroad route from northern California to Chicago and the east coast.

Paralleling the shippers' attacks upon the railroad in the 'nineties were the efforts of the journalists and writers. Of foremost importance in this literary activity was Arthur McEwen, who had learned his journalism around the Comstock along with Bret Harte and Mark Twain. Editor of papers in Sacramento, Oakland, and San Francisco, he devoted a great part of his efforts to castigating the Southern Pacific. In 1894 he established Arthur McEwen's *Letter,* a weekly sheet, in the first edition of which he declared war upon the "associated villainies," a name that stuck to the Southern Pacific and its corporate political allies for the next twenty years.[29]

Forced to suspend publication of the *Letter* because of insufficient financial support, McEwen joined Hearst's *Examiner,* from which Ambrose Bierce was soon to launch his barbed shafts against the Southern Pacific's attempt to avoid paying its debt to the federal government. So sharp were Homer Davenport's antirailroad cartoons during that hectic struggle, that the California legislature passed a law in 1899 prohibiting the publication of certain types of political drawings. The legislature, acutely sensitive to the feelings of the railroad operators, probably had in mind a Davenport effort depicting a gross and grinning Huntington leading Governor Gage around on a leash. Simultaneously, the Los Angeles *Times* denounced the railroad for obstructing the development of the municipal harbor, and young Frank Norris published *The Octopus*. Whatever Norris' intention was in writing his story of wheat and the railroad, the reading public interpreted the novel as another assault on the Southern Pacific.

The results of this antirailroad activity in the 'nineties were extremely scanty. True, some shipping rates were temporarily reduced, the worst features of the funding bill were eliminated, and the Southern Pacific's attempt to thwart the development of the Los Angeles harbor was momentarily checked. But in 1898, the antirailroad candidate for governor, James G. Maguire, was soundly beaten, and at the turn of the century the railroad commission still sat in Sacramento in a state of masterful inactivity.

During the nineteenth century the periods of intense railroad opposition had closely coincided with bad economic conditions. In the hard times of the 'seventies and 'nineties criticism of the corporation was at a height. Through the relatively prosperous 'eighties it abated. If that cycle were to repeat itself, the bountiful times following the Spanish-American War promised nothing but success for the continued corporate control of California. For the first six years of the new century it seemed that the old correlation between prosperity and state subservience to the corporation might hold. In 1902 George C. Pardee, the railroad's candidate for governor, was elected. Two years later the Southern Pacific machine defeated United States Senator Thomas R. Bard in his fight for the Republican nomination. And at the 1906 state Republican convention at Santa Cruz the railroad politicos were so confident of their power that they made little attempt to hide their bartering of offices from either the newspapers or the general public.

Notwithstanding this unbroken row of victories for the machine, however, a closer look at California politics in the period reveals the first faint indications of the coming storm of revolt. From 1898 on, in every gubernatorial election, at least one strong antirailroad candidate was running on the Democratic ticket. During the violent swing toward Republicanism following the Bryan campaign, James G. Maguire, the "Little Giant," made a respectable showing against the railroad's Gage in 1898. Four years later Franklin K. Lane, an old associate of Arthur McEwen, came within an eyelash of defeating the machine-supported Pardee. And in 1906 Theodore A. Bell came extremely close to victory with a strong anti–Southern Pacific campaign.

Since these narrow Republican majorities in state elections came at a time when McKinley, Roosevelt, and Taft were carrying the state easily in national elections, it was evident that many California Republicans were actively dissatisfied with the character of the state party. At first, presumably, the majority of these dissident Republicans, who supported Lane in the state and Roosevelt nationally, were reform-minded men. But after 1904 their ranks were increased by many good conservative Republicans who bitterly resented the Southern Pacific's defeat of Senator Bard because the latter had not always followed the railroad's best interests at Washington.

This increasing opposition to the rule of the railroad in the early years of the twentieth century was in part due to the intensive propaganda campaign of the 'nineties. Another important factor in the rising criticism was the growing split between the interests of the Southern Pacific and those of the comparatively new industrial, commercial enterprises in the state. For many years the Southern Pacific had been a corporate giant living in a land of business pygmies. Now in the twentieth century, with the introduction of new industries and the consolidation of old ones, its relative size and social power did not bulk so large even in the business world. Although there existed a community of interests between the railroad and the large businesses of the state, there was also a sizable area of conflict that augured none too well for the continued political control of the once superdominant Southern Pacific.

Even more to the point, the new century found some of the railroad's natural opponents, who had hitherto been a weak collection of individuals, organizing and consolidating their strength. Among the farmers, the Southern California Fruit Growers' Association, the Deciduous Fruit Protective League, and other comparable combines were not without considerable strength. On another plane, the rapidly growing Los Angeles Chamber of Commerce forged a powerful social group out of what had been isolated and individualistic businessmen. The evolving labor unions also foreshadowed the relative decline in social power of the railroad, to say nothing of the rise of the Socialist party, whose vote was not insignificant by the end of the decade.

If the railroad's power within the state were to be limited, it was logical to assume that one of these newer organizations, with power and geographic spread somewhat comparable to the Southern Pacific's, would lead the movement. Paradoxically, that was not to be. The leadership in the battle against the railroad did not come from the ranks of organized business or agriculture or labor. Instead, it was seized by a group of supreme individualists, well educated and bound together by a particularistic point of view, a remembrance of things past, a new code of morality, and more than the normal dash, perhaps, of a sense of indignation and a desire for power. Many of them were not interested, initially, in planning a state-wide campaign against the railroad, but only in a limited struggle for the control of their home cities. The opening skirmishes of the crusade against the Southern Pacific were fought almost simultaneously within the urban confines of San Francisco and Los Angeles. Between the developments in the two cities there was at first little or no connection except for those broad compulsive movements of ideas and material facts that often control the destinies of men.

CHAPTER II

The Struggle for the Cities

*

Of all the units of democratic government in the world, Lord Bryce once observed, the large American city was perhaps the worst governed. Had the famous English authority on American government been dealing in particulars, he undoubtedly would have cited San Francisco as a case in point. In the years before the turn of the century, it mattered little whether the Democratic or Republican party ruled in the city by the bay; the results were the same. During the 'eighties the blind boss, Chris Buckley, followed an ancient pattern and impartially granted favors for a price to captains of industry and to masters of vice. Buckley and his Democratic machine ruled the city until 1891, when he left the state hurriedly as an industrious grand jury brought to light evidence of wholesale graft and fraud. The righteous citizens who had supported the investigation then turned to the Republican party in their quest for good government. Buckley was succeeded by the Republican boss, Daniel Burns, who, after his acquittal in a graft trial in 1894, also left the state for an extended stay. For a short interlude, with the election of Adolph Sutro, Populist candidate for mayor, the government of the city became respectable. But soon thereafter the city returned to its old ways. Men and reformers were transient; fraud, graft, and vice enduring.

Among the most persistent foes of this "California Tammany" during the 'nineties was James D. Phelan, a young liberal-minded wealthy financier and a member of a socially prominent family. Influenced by the works of Dr. Albert Shaw, Phelan came to the conclusion that the source of most civic corruption in the United States lay in the private ownership of municipal utilities. Once the demands of utility companies for franchises, higher rates, and stock-issuing permits were stopped, Phelan claimed, the corrupt nexus between city politicians and big business would disappear, and it would be easy to eradicate the corruption flowing from the vice and liquor interests. In 1897 Phelan ran for mayor of San Francisco on a program calling for a new charter that would enable the city to purchase the street railways, the water service, and the gas and electric facilities, then all privately owned. At the same time, the young reformer promised lower taxes. Supported by the San Francisco Merchants' Association, Phelan was handsomely elected, and two years later a new city charter was finally adopted. Among its provisions was one permitting the city to own and operate all utilities. A second greatly restricted the conditions under which franchises were to be granted to private owners in the future.[1]

Under Phelan, San Francisco achieved for a time quiet, honest, economical government, and fortune seemed to favor the reform administration. But in the summer of 1901 all civic unity disappeared in a tremendous struggle between capital and labor that was fought out on the city streets. The depression of the early 'nineties had left organized labor woefully weak in San Francisco. It recovered some of its strength during the Spanish-American War. Then, spurred by the rising cost of living, an evangelical fever of unionization swept through the laboring ranks. A strong central labor council was organized, and in January of 1901 the first convention of the California State Federation of Labor, with sixty-one unions represented, was held in San Francisco. Until that time only the skilled trades had managed to obtain agreements with employers. Now labor set about organizing all classes of workers and launched a campaign to make San Francisco a closed-shop town. The great struggle started on May 1, 1901, when the cooks and waiters left their jobs, demanding a closed shop. A week later the carriage and wagonmakers struck, followed shortly by the machinists and the teamsters.

24

Meanwhile, the recently organized Employers' Association had raised $200,000 to fight the strike and break the unions. Strikebreakers were brought into town by the carloads, and hundreds of special strike police were employed and paid from the employers' war chest. At this juncture eighteen unions, composing the City Front Federation, walked out in sympathy with their fellow workers, and San Francisco was confronted by what was virtually a general strike. With an estimated 60 per cent of the city's business closed, violence and death stalked the streets. The special police used clubs and guns; the teamsters broke the arms of "scab" workers with iron bars to insure against their driving again. But with the organized power of the city government against it, plus the financial strength of the Employers' Association, labor was finally forced to capitulate. The strike was settled on October 2, 1901, at the instance of Governor Gage, by a so-called compromise in which the employers were obviously the winners.[2]

Labor retired from the struggle extremely bitter against the employers and particularly against the reform government that had hired the special police and had instructed the regular force to protect the strikebreakers and quell violence. Never again did San Francisco union leaders completely trust the "goo-goos," as they called the business-minded reform element. In fact, with an election coming up in November, many of them in the last days of the strike, the building-trades leaders excluded, talked about a labor ticket. Into this super-heated situation stepped Abraham Ruef, with a positive genius for organizing the seamy side of politics. The "Curly Boss," as he later became known, had allied himself with the reform element immediately after his graduation from college and had once been a political companion of Franklin K. Lane. But reform politics were neither successful nor lucrative enough for Ruef. Soon he joined a more materialistic group, and in 1901 quickly perceived his chance to ride to power on the back of a labor party. As the main organizer of the Union Labor party, Ruef helped to select Eugene E. Schmitz as its

25

candidate for mayor and managed his successful campaign, so
that it was Ruef's money and brains which were largely responsible for labor's first major political victory.

The tall, bearded Eugene E. Schmitz was a striking figure
when he became mayor. Although he had once been leader of
an orchestra in a local theater, he was radical neither in his
dress nor in his politics. Formerly a conservative Republican,
he announced that it was his intention to take the Union Labor
party into the Republican fold once its aims had been attained. The new party was not an example of "class politics,"
he wrote, but rather a machine for economic justice. Labor
disputes, he asserted, should not be settled by police clubs but
rather by arbitration. The only other reform he was apparently interested in immediately after his election was the
public ownership of public utilities, since he believed that
private ownership promoted corruption.[3]

San Francisco did not get public-owned utilities during
Schmitz's three terms, but labor, at least in the first years of
his incumbency, prospered. During the streetcar strike of 1902
the labor press described the mayor's policy as "fare and fearless." [4] With the police "neutral," labor easily won the strike,
and later went on from victory to victory until San Francisco
became probably the tightest closed-shop town in the nation.
Meanwhile, as labor's star ascended, Ruef's climbed with it.
Drawing the strings of power into his own hands one by one,
Ruef rapidly became the real government of the city. Soon it
was common street knowledge that if one wanted to deal with
the government of San Francisco, one had better go straightway to the dark Curly Boss. This information was usually accompanied with the ugly rumor that almost anything could
be obtained at the city hall provided the price was right. As
early as 1903 the "muckraker" Ray Stannard Baker charged
Ruef and Schmitz, in a national magazine, with entering into
"conspiracies to mulct the public." Some months later Fremont Older, the crusading editor of the San Francisco *Bulletin* editorialized almost daily on the "boodlers" and
"grafters" who had taken over the city hall.[5]

With the election of 1905 in the offing, a grand alliance was rapidly formed against the Ruef-Schmitz regime. Older had already taken his position in the *Bulletin.* Soon he was supported by the good government forces under former Mayor Phelan. The city's employers, banded together in a Citizens' Alliance to finance a private police force, were implacable in their hatred of the labor boss. More money was forthcoming from the great public service corporations of the city, two of which in particular, the United Railroads and the Home Telephone Company, were in the market for new charters. Not until much later was it discovered that these two, as well as virtually every other utility corporation, had with fine impartiality given money to each side. The ranks of the anti-Ruef forces, however, became truly formidable when William F. Herrin, political head of the Southern Pacific, joined the group. Obviously, the labor machine in San Francisco had become too powerful even for the legendary, potent railroad.[6]

After many conferences the Democratic party graciously agreed to forego naming a candidate for mayor, and the heterogeneous group of reformers, reactionaries, idealists, and materialists consolidated their strength behind the Republican candidate, John S. Partridge. As the campaign developed, charges became painfully specific and tempers grew hot. Shortly before the election a young attorney, Francis J. Heney, openly charged Ruef with public corruption. "I will guarantee," Heney shouted, "that if I take charge of a grand jury in this city, it will return indictments against Ruef for grafting inside of a week." But even the combined weight of such charges plus the support of most of the city's newspapers and the Southern Pacific was not enough to produce victory. Schmitz was reëlected along with the entire group of union labor supervisors by a handsome majority. Ruef and graft apparently reigned supreme.

Its power confirmed, the labor machine soon found recent enemies ready to do business. Operating on the old political principle, "If you can't lick 'em, jine 'em," the Home Telephone Company, which had previously retained as council one of the chief lobbyists for the Southern Pacific, now employed Ruef. Even Herrin himself was shortly to purchase Ruef's support to nominate a governor. And where the Southern Pacific led, other corporations could safely follow.

Emboldened by such success, the Ruef-Schmitz regime lost all sense of proportion. Where before the elections its grafting operations had been cut after the Southern Pacific pattern, discreet and selective, it now became open and ubiquitous. Where once tribute had been covertly taken in larger franchises and kindred operations, and had affected the average citizen only indirectly, it was now assessed upon practically every municipal action. Moreover, where once it had been collected by the men at the top of the machine and systematically divided among the underlings, now many city officials were accepting the "easy money" directly.

Nearly all the eighteen supervisors elected in 1905 were poor and uneducated men. Sensing the opportunities for wealth, many of them soon set up in the business for themselves. So avid were they for quick returns that they were soon known as Ruef's "pack of hounds," the boss himself remarking that they were so hungry for graft they were ready "to eat the paint off of a house." [7] Everything had its price, from franchise "fees" to the sums extracted from prostitutes and dope peddlers. In the San Francisco tenderloin a regular schedule of protection fees was collected from houses of prostitution: five dollars a week by the policeman on the beat, fifteen by sergeants, twenty-five by the precinct captain, and seventy-five by the chief of police. The sums were correspondingly higher for the more pretentious houses and French restaurants in the heart of the city. The entire city administration apparently was off on a four-year drunken spree of boodling. Yet so confident were its leaders of their power to silence opposition that Mayor Schmitz, after a conference with William Herrin, announced in July, 1906, that he had been advised ". . . by those who are in a position to assure me that, if I desire it, I may have the Republican nomination for governor at the hands of the convention to assemble in September." [8]

In the spring and summer of 1906 the Ruef-Schmitz machine seemed impregnable. Following the great earthquake and fire of April 17, Mayor Schmitz displayed an unaccustomed leadership in restoring somewhat normal life to the stricken city, and won measurable applause. Almost immediately afterward, against the opposition of some of San Francisco's most powerful citizens, the supervisors granted a free charter to the United Railroads for the installation of an overhead trolley system in the expansion of the city's street railway system. For some time a sizable group of property owners, headed by James D. Phelan, Rudolph and Claus Spreckels, and Charles S. Wheeler, had protested that the overhead system would disfigure the city streets along which their property lay. When both the city and the president of the United Railroads, Patrick Calhoun, assumed a "public-be-damned attitude," the group organized the Municipal Street Railway Company and asked the supervisors for a charter to construct a railroad powered by an underground conduit. Soon after the petition of this group was summarily ignored, another charter was granted to the Home Telephone Company, again with no apparent benefits accruing to the city. In September Ruef occupied a most important position in the Republican state convention at Santa Cruz. The power of the Union Labor bosses seemed to be growing rapidly in 1906 and extending itself out into the state.

Seemingly at the top of its power in September, 1906, the Ruef-Schmitz plunderbund was, however, already beginning to crack apart. The first serious rift appeared on the inside of the organization. On September 11, 1906, a sensational story appeared in the San Francisco *Call* to the effect that William F. Herrin had paid Ruef $20,000 for delivering the San Francisco votes to the Southern Pacific machine candidate for the Republican gubernatorial nomination at Santa Cruz. According to the *Call*, the facts had been revealed by one of

Ruef's important lieutenants, who was indignant because the Curly Boss had divided neither the loot nor the patronage he had obtained at Santa Cruz. Soon thereafter it became known that at least three of Ruef's important men were at odds with the machine. But this schism among the spoilers would probably have been sealed had it not been for outside forces working against Ruef, and for a quirk of fate.

Months before the election of 1905 Fremont Older, editor of the *Bulletin*, had launched a one-man campaign to bring Ruef and his colleagues to book. During the election Older talked to Francis J. Heney about organizing a graft prosecution campaign. He estimated that a minimum of $100,000 would be needed before a successful investigation and prosecution could be attempted. The following year, Older worked overtime to create the conditions necessary for a graft investigation. He made a trip to Washington to elicit the aid of President Roosevelt, and was assured that Heney would be relieved from his governmental duties if the prosecution became a reality. Subsequently, he brought Heney together with Rudolph Spreckels and James D. Phelan, with the result that the two wealthy men guaranteed to supply the necessary funds if they could not be otherwise raised. And so by June of 1906 William J. Burns, the nationally famous detective, was at work making an unofficial investigation of all municipal corruption in San Francisco.[9]

The quirk of fate that aided in the downfall of Ruef was the election in 1905 on the Union Labor ticket of a district attorney who, ironically, was an honest man. When Fremont Older disclosed the extent of undercover activities to William H. Langdon, the district attorney promised immediate coöperation in the crusade against the boodlers. As a first step, the district attorney promised to call a grand jury when the reformers felt they had accumulated conclusive evidence. He also agreed to appoint Francis J. Heney as special prosecutor even though he personally favored another young attorney, Hiram Johnson by name.

The fall of 1906 was a most happy time for launching the

antigraft movement. The machine appeared to be cracking up; so did all civic law and order. After the great fire, the San Francisco police apparently had neither the inclination nor the power to quell the hoodlum elements in the city. A rebuilt Barbary Coast shone with more evil luster than before. Looting, mugging, rape, and murder were almost daily occurrences, not only in the lower depths of the city but almost everywhere. Among respectable people there was serious talk of the need to revive vigilante action. And almost spontaneously a huge civic meeting was organized on October 10 to discuss ways and means of freeing the city from the looters and making it safe again for law-abiding citizens. But this pro-law-and-order meeting came to a dismal end. With rare impudence Ruef and his henchmen addressed the crowd and so completely took over the activities that nothing was accomplished.

Just a week after the abortive reform meeting, District Attorney Langdon announced the calling of a grand jury and the appointment of Heney as a special graft prosecutor. But even then prosecution of the culprits was not assured. With both the mayor and the district attorney out of town, Abraham Ruef played a desperate card. To a startled city the acting mayor announced that Langdon was suspended from office and that Ruef was the new acting district attorney. This incredibly insolent action, however, served to awaken even the most somnolent citizen to the true state of affairs. Before a tense and threatening crowd, a municipal judge issued a restraining order against this burglary of office, and upon Langdon's return, the honest selection of a new grand jury was started. With the call for the convening of the Oliver Grand Jury on November 7, 1906, the graft prosecution officially got under way.[10]

Few more tempestuous trials ever have been held in San Francisco than the graft trials starting in late 1906 and destined to continue for the next five years. The Ruef-Schmitz forces, and later the gentlemen of wealth under indictment, were ready to use any means that came to hand to stop the affair. The prosecution, in turn, admittedly was ready to fight fire with fire. As a result, during the course of the trials, witnesses were suborned, jurors bribed, prosecution documents stolen, and private offices and safes rifled for possible incriminating evidence. Fremont Older, editor of the *Bulletin,* was kidnapped, the house of a supervisor who had turned state's evidence was bombed, and the chief prosecutor himself, Francis J. Heney, was shot in the open courtroom, his assailant later either committing suicide or being murdered in his jail cell.

Through all this stark drama and violence Heney stalked the center of the stage until he was forced to retire by his near-fatal wounds. Born of immigrant parents of German and Irish extraction, Heney had been brought up in San Francisco. After being expelled from the state university for fighting, he had tried his hand at mining and later at running an Indian trading post in Arizona. There he read law, and being admitted to the bar, engaged in local Arizona politics as a Democrat. This two-fisted, hard-drinking young lawyer, true to the traditions of the old West, had killed a man in gunplay on the streets of an Arizona town. Possibly that was why Theodore Roosevelt became interested in him. At any rate, he was appointed a special United States prosecutor, in which position he acquired a limited national reputation by successfully prosecuting the wealthy and powerful Oregon timber thieves. There was no question but that the fighting attorney, once started on the graft prosecution, would unmercifully seek to convict anyone connected with the corruption of San Francisco. And if his past was to be any criterion, the bigger and more powerful the opposition, the more it would be to his liking.[11]

On presentation of the evidence uncovered by Heney and Burns, the grand jury indicted Ruef and the absent Schmitz with dispatch for extorting money from the city's notorious "French restaurants." A short time later three supervisors were caught redhanded in outright bribery. After a promise of immunity, eighteen supervisors and even the president of the Parkside Realty Company confessed either to the taking or the giving of bribes. And then, with a promise of at least partial immunity, Abraham Ruef confessed in May, 1907, implicating William F. Herrin of the Southern Pacific, Patrick Calhoun, president of the United Railroads, and many other potent San Francisco financial and industrial names. From the testimony of the confessed sinners it became evident that not only the city's tenderloin, but a great part of the business and commercial community, was tarred with the dirty brush of corruption. Almost immediately one other thing became clear—that the prosecution was more interested in convicting the great corporate bribe-givers and their agents than they were the bribe-takers. This Rudolph Spreckels expressed in court when he said: "I would be willing to grant immunity to any man who would bring to bar a man of great wealth . . . who would use his wealth to corrupt individuals and tempt men of no means to commit a crime in order that he might make more money." [12] In fact, according to Fremont Older, Spreckels had agreed to finance the antigraft movement only if the investigations included William F. Herrin and the Southern Pacific in their scope. The prosecution, then, was to be pointed not only at the graft-takers, but at the unseen corporate sources who often through the power of money ruled the city and the state. Toward this end the grand jury, at the behest of Heney, soon indicted some of the leading officials of the Pacific Gas and Electric Company, the Parkside Realty Company, the United Railroads, the Home Telephone Company, and the Pacific States Telephone and Telegraph. And thus the graft prosecution jumped from the city hall to the Pacific Union Club.

The indictment of the "men in broadcloth" resulted in a split in the support behind the graft trials. Previously, almost the entire business community had stood solidly behind the prosecution. The most conservative antilabor papers throughout the state had been loudest in their cries for justice, and ignoring the fact that the official state labor journal as well as the San Francisco Labor Council had also attacked the grafters, the conservative press used the trials to denounce the entire labor movement.[13] Now that Older's *Bulletin* could refer to the "corrupt alliance between massed wealth on the one side and political machines and organized vice on the other," the shoe was on the other foot. The conservative anti-labor groups rapidly changed their position and opposed the prosecution. Hastening this movement of sentiment was the trial of Patrick Calhoun, president of the United Railroads, and the violent streetcar strike of the summer of 1907.

In May, 1907, many labor contracts ran out in San Francisco. With labor asking for raises, with money and credit scarce, and with many employers still busy rebuilding facilities destroyed in the fire, strikes were inevitable. Labor talked of a general strike. But because of Governor Gillett's threat to order out the troops if there was violence, and hostile public opinion built up during the trials, the teamsters and other vital unions were not called out. Instead, the union leaders concentrated their forces on the United Railroads and its president, Patrick Calhoun, who was then under indictment for bribery in the acquisition of the overhead trolley franchise. Calhoun, grandson of the great John C., was a tough-minded corporation lawyer and organizer of railroad combinations. While managing the legal work for the House of Morgan in the organization of what was to be the Southern Railroad, he had fought one of the last duels staged in the Old South. A capitalist of ante-bellum views, he believed that the state should keep its hands completely off business and that labor had no rights except to work where, when, and at the price dictated by property owners.[14] Within eight days after the calling of the strike, he imported 1,200 strikebreakers from the East, and housed them in fortified carbarns in San Francisco. His continued decisive action broke the strike and made Calhoun a hero to the antilabor groups all over California. From that time on the capital-labor issue was inextricably intertwined in the graft prosecution. The dominant conservative sentiment of the state and city was reflected in the remark of a San Francisco businessman with reference to the Calhoun bribery trial: "I believe him guilty and I would vote to acquit him . . . simply on account of his heroic stand on the street-car strike."

With many of their own members directly threatened by the graft prosecution, and with the labor issue clearly involved, the wealthy conservative population of San Francisco became incredibly class conscious. From that time on there was no middle ground. One was either for or against this "attack upon property and men of large interests." Wherever business classes met, the men who continued to support the prosecution were cut socially. Rudolph Spreckels especially was ostracized, and a movement was begun to drop him from the Pacific Union Club. Led by the great conservative journals and the subsidized press, an extensive state-wide campaign was started to discredit the prosecution and its leaders. The prosecution was attacked for harming business and for aiding the unions. Spreckels' and Phelan's only interest, it was charged, was in persecuting and ruining "their business rivals and personal enemies." Much was made of the fact that the streetcar company supported by these two men had been defeated in its fight for a franchise immediately before they had started the graft prosecution. Personal quarrels between members of the Spreckels family were dug up and plastered over newspaper pages.[15]

Most of the personal venom poured out in these months, however, was reserved for Francis J. Heney. Heney was easy to attack. The fiery prosecutor fought with no holds barred. Never delicate, he used the same scathing language on Calhoun and other indicted men of substantial property that he had used on Ruef. Moreover, he and his operator Burns unquestionably winked at the law in order to get evidence. Even his friends admitted, "He has bluffed and has blown . . . offended against good taste and shocked the proprieties." The campaign against Heney was relentless, "a systematic course of poison," as Hiram Johnson later wrote, "daily instilled by rotten publications." [16] William H. Crocker, the San Francisco banker, who had first backed the prosecution and then offered bail for Calhoun, but mildly expressed the opinions of his class when he spoke of Heney's "passionate, revengeful, and criminal methods." [17] When Heney was shot in the open courtroom, Montgomery Street could scarce forebear a cheer.

After the Heney shooting, Hiram W. Johnson and Matt I. Sullivan agreed to carry on the prosecution. Ruef was convicted and sentenced to fourteen years in the penitentiary, but Calhoun escaped conviction by a divided jury in the fall of 1908, and was altogether acquitted in 1912. By that time the prosecution was under heavy attack not only in the courtroom but also from the political rostrum. As early as 1907 a nonpartisan Good Government League had been organized in San Francisco, ostensibly to support the antigraft campaign. In the fall elections of that year all the League's candidates, including District Attorney Langdon, won easily over a Union Labor ticket. But well before the elections of 1909, most of the business elements in the city were convinced opponents of the trials and opposed to their continuation. Headed by I. W. Hellman, a so-called Citizens' Committee of seventy businessmen met before the primaries to select a ticket that would be safe not only on the issue of the trials but also on labor and the equally burning question of municipal ownership of public utilities. Their candidates won easily in the Republican primaries despite opposition by a ticket endorsing the graft prosecution. With Heney running for district attorney on the Democratic ticket, the final election became a clear fight between the friends and enemies of the trials.

Heney entered the campaign with the ostensible blessing of the Democratic organization, but his real support came from a group of nonpartisan friends of municipal reform headed by Phelan, Spreckels, Hiram Johnson, Matt I. Sullivan, and Charles S. Wheeler. In the bitter fight that followed, Heney was badly defeated by Charles Fickert, the nominee of both the Republican and the Union Labor parties. The Union Laborites also elected a mayor and eleven of the eighteen supervisors. No more crushing blow could have been dealt the graft prosecution forces. Within a few months after he had entered office, the new mayor announced that he would make the city "the Paris of America," and the new district attorney set about to call quits to further prosecution.

On the basis of legal results, the achievements of the graft prosecution appeared to be microscopic. Not one of the wealthy bribe-givers was convicted. Of the three or four hundred indictments made, conviction was secured in only four cases, and three of those were set aside by higher courts. Ruef alone went to the penitentiary, and even he would have escaped had the will of a clear majority of the California Supreme Court not been obstructed by a legal technicality. The meager results were enough to make men of good will heartsick and agreed that:

Plate sin with gold, and the strong lance of justice hurtless breaks;
Arm it in rags, a pygmy's straw does pierce it.

But even though the graft prosecution failed in its immediate ends, it had been an important step in the struggle to break the stranglehold of the Southern Pacific and its allied corporations. This movement could not possibly have been successful without strong support in San Francisco, then the state's major city.

The carefree city by the Bay had apparently been unaware of the extent of the ramifications of vice, graft, and politics until Heney and his associates had made unmistakably clear its connection with the giant corporations that dominated San Francisco and the state. More to the point, until 1906 there had been no organized group in the city around which to build a reform movement. Ruef and Herrin had seen to that. But out of the three years of good government and nonpartisan support for the graft prosecution, a small, powerful group of leaders arose. Significantly, the nonpartisan group that stood by Heney in the elections of 1909 were even then the northern leaders of a state-wide rebellion. Spreckels, Phelan,

Johnson, Sullivan, Wheeler, and Weinstock were already co-operating with a similar group in southern California, where the progressive state-wide revolt had originated.

If San Francisco was one of America's most amoral cities at the turn of the century, Los Angeles, some four hundred miles to the south, more than compensated for its erring sister by its air of middle-class Christian respectability. Hollywood had not yet veiled the town with its glamour and suggestion of sin; oil and the great real estate and tourist booms were just beginning to pour their corrosive wealth into the city. The pulse of its people was certainly beginning to quicken after the long hard times of the 'nineties, but its leading citizens were still largely sober sons of the Puritans, not far removed from their Eastern and Middle Western forebears. The breath of their spirit could be caught in the city's bustling eagerness to expand and make dollars for its residents. Their morality was also implicit in the closing of the gambling houses in 1896 and of the saloons on Sundays a few years later. By 1906 Los Angeles boasted that it had more churches for its size than any other city in America.

In 1900 Angeleño virtue and industry were apparent everywhere but in its politics. For the hand of the Southern Pacific lay, if anything, more heavily on this town than it did on San Francisco. In this garden of open shops there was no great labor movement or labor machine that had to be cultivated for support in the city council and at the ballot box. To a greater extent possibly than Herrin controlled the north, his lieutenant, Walter Parker, ruled the south. Heavy of mustache and jowl, a caricature of the bartender of the gay 'nineties, Parker knew his politics. He was intelligent, generous, and indifferent to harmless criticism. In Los Angeles he had built up a pervasive municipal machine that regularly took care of its friends and the interest of the railroad. Most of the time the Christian businessmen of the city supported it and received its gratuities. After a long struggle the machine was beaten on the harbor fight, but its power elsewhere remained unbroken on matters both small and large. For example, it still selected the surgeons at Los Angeles hospitals to testify in settling disputes with persons injured on its trains. And as it had done many times before, it was able to push a franchise for additional trackage through the council even though the coöperative councilmen were threatened with the recall.[18]

For many years repeated attempts to smash the power of the railroad had been made in Los Angeles, as in San Francisco. In 1887 a nonpartisan movement led by a group of ministers failed, as did the Citizens' League six years later, in its attempt to get a new city charter. In 1895 a Direct Legislation League was organized to transfer the power from boss government into the hands of the people. Mainly the child of Dr. John Randolph Haynes of Los Angeles, the League saw its ideas partly adopted by San Francisco in 1899 and then fully accepted in the new Los Angeles charter of 1903. During the following year Los Angeles became the first city in the United States to recall an elected official. But even with the initiative, referendum, and recall, the government of Los Angeles was still a tool of the Southern Pacific in the early part of 1906.

The complete subservience of the city was clearly indicated in March of that year. With the mayor away from town, the "solid six" on the council voted to give a free franchise to a Mr. E. W. Gilmore for a railroad right of way into the city over the dry Los Angeles River bed. When the grant, said to be worth more than a million dollars by President Ripley of the Santa Fe, was attacked, Gilmore and the council announced that the gift had really been made to the Western Pacific, then being constructed as a competitor to the Southern Pacific in the north. Only after the Western Pacific president denied the story point blank was it revealed that the franchise had gone to the Pacific Electric, controlled by Henry E. Huntington and the Southern Pacific. Fortunately, the city clerk refused to sign the grant even though, as he subsequently testified, Walter Parker had offered him a thousand dollars for his signature. When the mayor returned, the franchise was killed by a direct veto.[19]

Meanwhile, whipped up by the news stories and editorials of the Los Angeles *Express* and the *Record,* a few citizens were growing indignant at the crass maneuverings of the Southern Pacific machine. Both the *Record* and the *Express* in March, 1906, called upon the people to organize against the affront to civic decency. But only Edward A. Dickson, the young man who was writing the editorials for the *Express,* and a few of his friends, did much more than talk. Dickson, born in Wisconsin and a graduate of the University of California, had entered newspaper work on the San Francisco *Chronicle* after a short time teaching in Japan. Early in 1906, Dickson, then working in northern California, was offered the position of associate editor with the Los Angeles *Express.* When he came to Los Angeles for an interview with the publisher of the paper, Edwin T. Earl, he asked that he be allowed to launch an editorial attack upon the Southern Pacific machine. He had in mind, Dickson recalled later, state as well as local politics. Earl refused Dickson's request because he felt that the project was doomed, and would only result in harm to the paper. Disappointed, Dickson walked out of the office, intending to go back north. But in a matter of minutes the publisher called him back and promised him support for at least a local reform campaign against the railroad. Dickson's hand was already apparent in March when the *Express* castigated the city council as being tools of the machine.[20]

As a start toward making the young editor's campaign more than a verbal attack, Earl introduced Dickson to Russ Avery, a young attorney who had already gained some reform reputation as president of the Los Angeles Voters' League. Agreeing on the immediate objectives, the two men cast about for recruits. Avery had talked casually about the possibility of reform with Meyer Lissner before Dickson came to town, so Lissner was brought into the group as well as Marshall Stimson, a young Harvard Law School graduate who had already tilted with the machine in an uptown ward. For a time Homer Lea was included in the conversations. But finding his ideas of reform at variance with the rest of the group,

Lea went his own way to find fame in the Orient and through his writings. Thereafter the newspaperman and the three lawyers met regularly for lunch at the University Club, where they planned the movement that was to overthrow the Southern Pacific machine in Los Angeles.[21]

William F. Herrin, a nominal Democrat, was consistently bipartisan where affairs of the Southern Pacific were concerned. Aware of this proclivity of the railroad to play no favorites in politics, the young reformers decided that their movement too had to be nonpartisan. They also realized the vital necessity for choosing the organizing nucleus of a nonpartisan group with extreme care. It was long and occasionally heartbreaking work. Only after weeks of effort were they able to obtain the consent of enough well-known business and professional men to form the Non-Partisan Committee of One Hundred. With the group finally organized and a public meeting announced, the whole life of the movement was threatened by the resignation of the man selected for the chairmanship. A high public official, he had succumbed to pressure from the machine. A happy thought then occurred to the four youthful organizers: to get for their chairman the attorney for the Los Angeles *Times,* probably the most conservative paper in the area and certainly the one most devoted to Republican party regularity. After W. J. Hunsaker had agreed to serve, a public meeting was held Monday, July 2, 1906, at the Los Angeles Chamber of Commerce assembly hall. There the purpose of the group was first publicly announced by Meyer Lissner, the temporary secretary. It was their intent, Lissner said, "to bring together the businessmen who are interested in good government." Another interpretation of the movement came from the banker, M. N. Avery. "It is unquestionably a movement," he wrote, "in behalf of the businessman, the taxpayer, and decent government." [22]

Because of the agreement that none of the founders of the nonpartisan movement should run for office, good candidates for all the city positions were difficult to find. And yet time was short if the nonpartisans were to carry through their intention of selecting a complete city ticket before either of the old major parties had announced its candidates. Finally, after six weeks of painful labor, a slate of twenty-three candidates, headed by Lee C. Gates for mayor, was formed. Gates had previously declined the nomination, but was finally persuaded to accept by Edward A. Dickson when both were attending the Republican state convention at Santa Cruz.[23]

Possibly because of expediency, Gates in his campaign did not attack the Southern Pacific by name, but inveighed against the local machine and its tie-up with the liquor and vice interests. Quoting Theodore Roosevelt and James W. Folk of Missouri, Gates attacked the concept that national party issues had relevance in municipal affairs. His supporters, however, including the Democratic *Herald* and the Republican *Express*, attacked the Southern Pacific outright.[24]

Opposition to the reform movement came from both old parties and from organized labor. Suspicious of the Chamber of Commerce flavor surrounding the reformers, the labor press attacked them as supporters of the antiunion Citizens' Alliance. Moreover, the laborites pointed out that the chairman of the nonpartisan group, W. J. Hunsaker, was the attorney for Harrison Gray Otis, the tough, old, labor-baiting owner of the Los Angeles *Times*.[25] But however close their other connections, Otis was attacking and not supporting the movement headed by Hunsaker. In part, perhaps, that was because of his long personal feud with E. T. Earl, owner of the *Express*. Next door neighbors, the two men had for many years carried on a personal quarrel that bordered on an aberration. At any rate, the *Times* unceasingly assailed the city nonpartisan movement for disrupting the Republican party and endangering the business interests of the city.

One of the more sensational incidents of the campaign was the *Express'* charge that the *Times* had descended to forgery to discredit the nonpartisan movement. The *Express* had been conducting a preëlection poll in its columns, and its officials had been disconcerted by the large number of returned ballots marked against the reform ticket. A sharp-eyed employee of the paper then noticed a slight difference in the printing of more than 4,000 of the adverse ballots from those carried daily in the *Express*. After an investigation the *Express* publicly charged Harry Chandler, Otis' son-in-law, with printing and marking wholesale quantities of forged ballots and published affidavits of the workman from the independent printing shop which had printed the fraudulent ballots.[26]

As the December election neared, the Southern Pacific machine became aware that their own candidate, the Republican Lindley, had little chance against the nonpartisan Gates. Consequently, just four days before the election they changed their support to the Democratic nominee, with the result that Harper was elected by a scant plurality. Nevertheless, by electing seventeen of their twenty-three candidates, the nonpartisan group had made an excellent start in destroying machine rule. Moreover, the nominees of the Republican party, in which the Southern Pacific was most influential, came out a poor third in the results. All in all, the four young men who had started the reform movement had done extremely well in their first attack upon the great railroad corporation, a fact given national publicity by both Theodore Roosevelt and Robert LaFollette.

The four made a happy combination. Dickson, with his enthusiasm for reform, organizing ability, influence as the associate editor of the oldest Republican paper in Los Angeles, and close connection with its wealthy owner, Earl, was an invaluable asset. Meyer Lissner was "the card index man of the movement." Born in Oakland, Lissner made a success of a small jewelry and pawnshop as an orphan at the age of fifteen. Moving to Los Angeles, he studied law, and after seeing his brothers educated, acquired a comfortable fortune from law and real estate. Efficient, cold-blooded, and at times unpopular, Lissner brought strength to the cause through his amazing passion for detailed organization and his unselfish devotion to the principles he was to serve for the next twenty years. Affable and tolerant Marshall Stimson, together with Russ Avery, were the speechmakers of the four. A young

Harvard graduate of somewhat dandified taste in clothes, Stimson carried to California as a boy all the courage and moral earnestness of his Puritan fathers in Massachusetts. They made an able and determined group, and not the least of their strength lay in the agreement, kept for many years, that no one of them should accept an important office.[27]

With the elections out of the way, the four set about to construct a permanent organization with which to combat the machine. Soon Lissner, Stimson, Dickson, and Avery had organized a Good Government group and a City Club modeled after the Boston organization, but devoted almost entirely to reform. So successful were both of these organizations that by 1909 they constituted a permanent and powerful political group. These two organizations plus the city's Chamber of Commerce were largely instrumental in securing the passage of amendments to the city charter abolishing the old ward system and making the municipal elections nonpartisan. But nothing short of complete nonpartisan control of the city government would satisfy the four. Their opportunity came early in 1909.

Arthur C. Harper, elected mayor in 1907 ostensibly through the support of Parker and the Southern Pacific machine, appeared to be a man of complete integrity. A member of an old and wealthy Los Angeles family, his connections with a large mercantile establishment entitled him to be described by his friends as "a practical businessman." Soon after his election, however, it became apparent to the knowing that Harper was engaging in "practical politics" as well as business. The mayor's misdeeds first came to light when a reforming assistant prosecuting attorney, Thomas L. Woolwine, started a law enforcement campaign in Los Angeles against the stock-jobbing, liquor, and vice traffic. Refusing to cease his activities in spite of repeated warnings from the mayor and powerful businessmen, he discovered a trail of graft and corruption that led straight to the mayor's desk as well as to many so-called respectable businessmen in the city. Before he could finish his investigations, Woolwine found himself dismissed from office. Meanwhile, several newspapers, led by the Los Angeles *Herald,* had started investigations of their own. In January the *Herald* began a long series of front-page articles revealing in red ink the true connections of the mayor with the underworld of the city. Harper and some business friends, leaving the petty cash to underlings, had organized several extremely questionable joint-stock companies. Thereafter thousands of dollars had been regularly extorted from underworld establishments by forcing them to buy the bogus stock as "certificates of protection." The system was neither as extensive nor as perfected as it had been in San Francisco, but it was well on its way.[28]

Aroused by the exposures, the Municipal League, the Chamber of Commerce, and the City Club called a meeting of five hundred of the "best citizens of Los Angeles" to initiate recall proceedings against the mayor and select a Good Government candidate. Once again at the meeting the Southern Pacific Railroad was roundly denounced as the fountainhead of graft and as the ubiquitous link between vice and politics. And once again the reform campaign was carried on in the name of respectable business. At the meeting and in the subsequent campaign the workingmen's vote was appealed to, but the voice of labor was carefully excluded from any participation. Lissner explained that the group felt they had to "draw the line somewhere," and that if labor were invited the meeting would be packed. Not even Francis Heney's advice that labor should.be consulted, since he knew from experience that business government was not good government, swayed the reformers. Consequently, all the reformers' efforts to obtain the support of Edward W. Scripps' Los Angeles *Record* were in vain. As for the labor unions, they were unreservedly opposed to the reform candidates.[29]

The persistent exclusion of labor almost lost the election for the Good Government people. Under heavy fire Mayor Harper resigned, declaring that he did so only because Walter Parker and the Southern Pacific had deserted him. This left as the two contending candidates the old and undistinguished

George Alexander, supported by the reformers, and a Socialist candidate, Fred Wheeler. A perceptible shiver of fear swept through the business community when the Socialist, practically unknown and without funds, came within 1,600 votes of defeating the so-called respectables.

From the spring of 1909 on, in fact, the fear of a Socialist government was almost a constant bogey to the business classes of Los Angeles. This fear dominated both the regular Republican organization and the Good Government faction and helped to explain the bitterness existing between these rival organizations, even though at times they were to cooperate in staving off the challenge of the left. Certainly, Harrison Gray Otis' increasing rancor toward the Good Government reformers can be laid in part to his antiunion mania and his morbid dread of socialism.

By 1909 Otis saw the Good Government reformers as a serious threat to continued business control of the city. As early as 1908 the *Times* was preaching through news stories, editorials, and cartoons, that the "goo-goos," by splitting away from the grand old party machine, were opening the way for government by the "labor thugs." The strong Socialist vote in the spring of 1909 simply confirmed all of Otis' dreams of terror. When the Good Government organization, in the fall of 1909, endorsed Mayor Alexander instead of George A. Smith, the regular Republican candidate for mayor, Otis was beside himself with rage. During that campaign the *Times* sank to a level of journalism that was low even for that master of the dirty smear. Denouncing "Our Set Reform Bosses" as the "most selfish and the most partisan" group that had ever existed in Los Angeles, the *Times* baldly accused them of seeking power to insure themselves real-estate profits through the convenient erection of public buildings near their personal holdings. Far worse was the attack upon "Boss Lissner." Spelling the name "Lissnerski," the *Times* referred to his "jewelry-shop past," and lest anyone mistake the implications of that remark, Lissner was cartooned as a dirty, ill-kept pawnbroker rubbing his hands in greed and muttering "chent by chent."

The newspapers supporting the Good Government group answered with an indictment against the Southern Pacific as "the Beast," together with its allies—booze, vice, and the "vulture press, led by the 'tricky *Times*.'" [30]

Neither Otis' fears nor hopes were realized in the December election. The labor vote diminished, but the regular Republican candidate was beaten easily by Mayor Alexander, supported by the Good Government organization. However, in the following years Otis' Socialist-labor nightmares almost became a reality. Class war broke out in the factories and in the streets of the city, and before that bloody struggle was finished the relations between capital and labor in Los Angeles had become a subject of national concern.

If one man's influence was responsible for Los Angeles labor policy from 1880 to 1917 that man was Harrison Gray Otis. Born in Marietta, Ohio, the grandson of the noted Revolutionary soldier, Otis acquired an early liking for barefisted struggle. After gallantly serving in the Civil War, Otis came to Los Angeles in the early 'eighties and purchased the *Times*. He built the newspaper into one of the most lucrative journalistic enterprises in the state and further enhanced his wealth by speculation in California and Mexican real estate. Robert G. Cleland is probably right in saying that the city owed more to Otis and the *Times* for its development in the early part of the twentieth century "than to any other comparable influence." Utterly fearless of the power of an opponent, Otis had led the fight against the Southern Pacific for a free harbor. To him must go a great deal of the credit for much of the city's physical expansion. In addition to bringing to the city the precious Owens Valley water that made expansion possible, he made available huge private fortunes to the promoters of San Fernando real estate, among whom he was a leading spirit.

White-haired in his older days, with a shaggy mustache and goatee, Otis still had all the predatory spirit and something of the nature of the Sierra grizzly. Equally violent in his likes and dislikes, he was true to his limited number of loyalties

47

and profanely and vitriolically opposed to his boundless hates. A true son of the Civil War generation, one of his gods was the conservative Republican party. He had little use for reformers, Republican though they might be. Perhaps he was most devoted to the ethics of capitalism, as that institution was understood by American capitalists in the 'eighties and the 'nineties. It is possible that no man in all the United States hated organized labor more, and it is certain that few did more to obstruct its advance.[31]

Otis first fought labor in California in 1890 when the *Times*' printers struck for preservation of their wage scale and the institution of a closed shop. After a long, bitter struggle, Otis crushed the union, and from then on began a lifelong crusade against these "industrial vampires" as he called them. Otis' antiunion aberration did not spring from economic reasons alone. Also involved was the question of social power and of respect for the great owners of property. Testifying before a Senate committee in 1914, the stout old reactionary spoke at length in terms of "the respect due" to the employers of labor from "the men under them." Otis did not run an open shop; his was a closed shop, closed against any man bearing a union card, he testified before the committee.[32] Moreover, due in large part to his personal and editorial proselytizing, practically all Los Angeles employers practiced the same industrial principles. Laboriously over the years, central labor bureaus had been set up for each industry, in which a secretary and staff kept a record of each employee's activities. This constituted a black list, as the president of the Founders and Employers' Association disclosed, and was regularly used in hiring and firing men in the individually owned plants. Repeatedly Los Angeles employers testified before the Senate committee that they operated a "closed" antiunion shop.[33]

Arching over the entire Los Angeles antiunion structure was the Merchants and Manufacturers' Association. Largely an Otis creation, the association organized the antiunion campaign on a city-wide basis, supplying funds, strikebreakers, and special police to members confronted with labor difficulties. The association was also a quasi-political organization charged with the purpose of seeing that the Los Angeles city government was at all times "friendly" to its ideals. Its effectiveness in the realm of practical politics can be judged from the statements of F. J. Zeehandelaar, long-time secretary of the association. Referring to the period from 1905 to 1914, Zeehandelaar testified that when difficulties arose protection was "always granted" by the police and mayor, and that during labor disputes these city officials regularly permitted men paid by the association to be sworn in as special deputies. To that extent at least, the Merchants and Manufacturers' Association, under either the regular party machines or the Good Government people, was a functioning part of the Los Angeles city government.

By 1910 it was apparent that Los Angeles was far outstripping San Francisco in the rate of industrial advance. And the Angeleño capitalists, who could scarcely overlook the startling differential in wage rates between the two cities, were convinced that freedom from unions was an important element in this development. Four years later the open shop was described as the basic factor contributing to the prosperity of the southern city. Moreover, by 1910 most Los Angeles employers, although they admitted that a ceaseless vigilance against unions was needed, believed that the fight had been won. Otis, for example, was so hopeful that he wrote an article describing how the victory had been achieved.[34] That this confidence was premature was indicated by the rise of the Socialist vote in 1909 and by the events of 1910.

In that year, undoubtedly prompted and aided from the outside, a general strike committee was organized in Los Angeles for the purpose of smashing the antiunion shop. National unions aided, intent upon breaking the Los Angeles employers' monopoly of power. But most of the outside help came from San Francisco labor, spurred by the threat from their own employers that unless Los Angeles was unionized, an open-shop campaign would be started at once in San Francisco to equalize the costs between the two towns. By the first of May most of the workers in the metal shops and the leather and brewery trades had left their jobs.[35] During the ensuing battle, the Good Government–dominated Los Angeles city council unanimously passed an antipicketing ordinance prepared by the Secretary of the Merchants and Manufacturers' Association. One of the most stringent laws of its type in the nation, the ordinance completely forbade picketing of any kind "quiet" or otherwise. And there was no doubt after four or five hundred arrests had been made that the Los Angeles reform government was just as intent upon breaking the strikes as was the employers' association.[36]

With the pickets receiving sentences of "fifty dollars or fifty days," labor was bitter indeed. In the light of what they received from the hands of the reformers, the old Southern Pacific–dominated government looked like a benevolent institution. Then right in the midst of these taut times three representatives of national unions struck back at capital with a terrible weapon. On October 1, 1910, the McNamara brothers and Ortie McManigal dynamited the Los Angeles *Times* building, killing twenty-one innocent employees and injuring scores more. As angry citizens massed to identify the killers and bring them to justice, the public attitude toward labor became menacing. In Los Angeles, and in fact almost everywhere in the country, conservatives and a large part of the middle-class liberal element indicted the whole labor movement for the terror, even before a shred of justification for the wholesale indictment was produced. One of the few public voices in Los Angeles urging caution in prejudging the labor movement was the Los Angeles *Express*.

The frightful bombing of the *Times* and the subsequent trials of the dynamiters set the stage for the Los Angeles municipal election of 1911. It was the most crucial one the Good Government forces were to face. On one side they were assailed by the more conservative forces charging that the labor terror had been released on the city by "goo-goo" activity. Assaulting them from the other side were the workers, bitterly remembering the strikes of 1910 and the part the reform government had played in them. As the *Times* demanded an end to "Earlism" and its encouragement to labor, the Socialists depicted the Good Government forces as just another, but more hypocritical, variety of labor baiter. The results of that three-cornered primary threw the whole city into an uproar: Job Harriman, the Socialist candidate, polled a plurality of votes! The fact that Alexander had beaten the regular Republican candidate, and thus would stand against Harriman at a final election, was only a meager source of satisfaction to the Good Government organization.

When the implications of Harriman's victory became clearer, a panic swept through the business elements of the city. Almost immediately regulars and reformers joined forces to down this threat of "the lawless elements," as Earl of the *Express* called them. Otis and the *Times*, momentarily forgetting their quarrel with the "goo-goos," announced that "the time for difference between the good people of Los Angeles has passed," and pledged their support to the Good Government candidate. The *Examiner* and practically every paper in Los Angeles, save the labor sheets, soon followed. These in turn were joined by practically every nonlabor political and quasi-political organization in the city. According to the Fresno progressive, Chester Rowell, "Churches and saloons, partisans and nonpartisans, Republicans, Democrats, and Independents, reformers and performers, Otis and Earl, Parker and Lissner, men who hate and distrust each other [were] united against the menace of class rule." [37]

Money in amount never before seen by the Good Government organization poured into Alexander's headquarters; men who had never bothered with active politics before offered their personal services. This was the church militant of middle-class capitalism drawn up against "the forces of evil." As the election neared, confidence among the combined forces of the right waned, and an extreme case of political nerves afflicted everyone from the mayor down. Fearful of the results, the aged Alexander kept muttering to Lissner and Stimson, "We can't lose, we just can't lose." Finally distrusting the ability of the reformers to win, the most conservative, open-shop businessmen of the city demanded that the direction of the campaign be turned over to them, a demand to which the Good Government forces supinely submitted. And thus the Los Angeles elections of 1911 became a clear-cut struggle between capital and labor, while the issue of "reform" was temporarily forgotten.

Even with this strange change in leadership, victory was not certain. As late as two weeks before the election, a Good Government official speaking at the Los Angeles Union League Club predicted: "Nothing short of a miracle can save us from the impending political cataclysm." But events were kind to the harassed businessmen politicians. A man-made bargain struck off just a few days before the contest, and not divine interposition, turned the course of the election.[38]

Occurring simultaneously with this heated campaign were the sensational trials of the McNamara brothers and Ortie McManigal for the dynamiting of the *Times*. After months of nation-wide work, William J. Burns and his detectives had accumulated a mass of incriminating evidence against the three men and their collaborators, including a full confession from McManigal. But Burns' actions in abducting the two brothers from an eastern state without waiting for legal extradition had raised a storm of protest among national union leaders, who charged that the brothers were being illegally railroaded toward conviction with the real aim of indicting labor. Rallying behind the brothers' plea of not guilty, labor employed a brilliant staff of defense attorneys, headed by the formidable Clarence Darrow and including the Socialist candidate for mayor, Job Harriman. Leading the prosecution in the murder trial of J. B. McNamara, was John D. Fredericks, district attorney of Los Angeles County. Through most of October and November the contesting legal staffs wrangled without agreeing on a jury. With the contending charges of jury fixing, subornation, and bribery, and with an inflamed public opinion neatly divided along class lines, it appeared that the trials might go on for months. Then, as startling as

52

lightning from a clear sky, on December 1 the McNamaras confessed. To an astonished public and heartsick labor it was announced that a bargain had been made between the defense and the prosecution; this with the all-important elections just four days away.

The events behind the McNamara confession started over the weekend of November 19, at the Scripps ranch where Lincoln Steffens, reporting the trials for the press, and Clarence Darrow were resting from their labors. Assured that Darrow desired a compromise of the case, Steffens went the next day to Meyer Lissner to see whether a settlement could be obtained. Lissner was "extremely sympathetic" to the proposal and the two men soon talked with Thomas E. Gibbons and Harry Chandler, the son-in-law of Harrison Gray Otis. There followed a series of secret meetings which resulted in the calling of a conference of "about twenty important businessmen" including Lissner, Earl, Otis, Chandler, and former Senator Flint. The exact details of those meetings have never been revealed. But both sides were ready to make concessions for what they considered good and substantial reasons. The defense apparently asked for complete freedom for the McNamaras in return for their full confession of guilt. Otis, Chandler, and the other hard-chinned businessmen, according to Steffens, were willing to agree to this generous settlement. But the politically ambitious prosecuting attorney, Fredericks, demanded some punishment. Eventually a compromise was worked out, the exact terms of which are still in doubt. Steffens wrote that they included a life sentence for J. B. McNamara, a much shorter term for his brother, no further prosecutions, and an agreement to hold a labor-management conference in the city after the trials, where all the points of conflict between capital and labor could be openly examined and perhaps settled "in the spirit of the golden rule." As a matter of fact, more than fifty additional union men were later indicted, and the conference upon which Steffens had set so much hope was never held.[39]

From several aspects the ending of the dynamite trial made

it one of the most curious in American legal history. In view of the gravity of the offense it was certainly extraordinary for the state to strike a bargain with the indicted. Even more unprecedented was the way in which that bargain was arranged, for essentially the understanding was worked out by a group of powerful industrialists and merchants and was in a very real sense a bargain between capital and labor, not between the state and alleged criminals.

The question of why the Good Government reformers initiated the action and why Otis and his conservative colleagues agreed to the compromise has often been raised and has never been definitely settled. It is probable that had the business group been certain of a complete conviction, they would not have bargained. Considering the state of public opinion and Darrow's skill as a lawyer, a conviction was not an absolute certainty. And even if they were convicted, the possibility of the accused becoming martyrs might have been an important consideration to the business group. Certainly a confession of guilt would destroy any chance of that. But probably most important was the consideration of the effect of a confession upon the election to be held in a few days. No development in public life could have been more obnoxious either to the Los Angeles reformers or to the conservatives than a Socialist victory. In addition to the extremely important matter of group prestige, there was the fate of the open shop. A Socialist city government would certainly repeal the antipicketing law, and the hitherto "fine coöperation" shown the industrialists by the city police would be at an end.

According to Lincoln Steffens, the business group accepted the compromise largely because he won them over by his idealistic preaching that the labor-capital struggle in Los Angeles could be solved only in "the Spirit of Christ." If the businessmen were to forget and forgive the McNamaras, Steffens argued, and a labor conference were held, then he was sure truth and justice would prevail. Not once during the conferences, he wrote immediately after the affair ended, were political considerations mentioned, although he did admit later that such motives might have existed. With all due respect for the potency of ideals, it is doubtful that without the election a settlement would have been offered or accepted. Four facts are relevant to that argument. The outcome of the election was in grave doubt. Otis and his colleagues would have done almost anything to win, as evidenced by the support they gave to the Good Government candidate. Steffens himself wrote that the compromise had to be "hurried" at a time when it seemed as if the trials might go on for months. For reasons of politics, of course, time was essential. Finally everyone agreed, when the deed was done, that the Socialist cause was hopeless. So unanimously was that opinion held that not one word of the negotiations had been whispered to Job Harriman, attorney for the defense and Socialist candidate for mayor. As Steffens said, no one had the heart to tell him.[40]

On December 5, with 140,000 of the 180,000 registered voters in Los Angeles casting their ballots, Alexander defeated Harriman for mayor by a comfortable margin. The Good Government organization had beaten the Socialists as it had already beaten the old machine crowd, even though the latter victory had been largely engineered by elements previously opposed to the reformers. But since both the new mayor and the new council were Good Government men, the 1911 victory, however achieved, was a triumph for the new politics.

The rise of the reform spirit in both Los Angeles and San Francisco was remarkably similar. In point of time the movements were almost identical, both starting early in 1906. Both movements were pointed against a pervasive and corrupt political machine tied in locally with the public service corporations and with organized vice, and at the state level with the Southern Pacific Railroad and its allied corporations. Both movements had been led by journalists, attorneys, and independent businessmen, and both movements had attacked politically organized labor as well as politically organized capital. At least in Los Angeles, the new reformers had even fought labor's nonpolitical aspirations, for the antipicketing ordinance passed by a Good Government–dominated council went far to insure the continuance of an open-shop city.

Throughout the first decade of the twentieth century, anti-machine movements had existed in other cities in California. As early as 1900 the brothers E. A. and J. O. Hayes had formed a Good Government League in San Jose, which in 1902 captured control of the Republican party in Santa Clara County. In Fresno and Palo Alto, groups in both Republican and Democratic parties had revolted with some success. And in San Diego Judge W. A. Sloan organized the Roosevelt Republican Club in 1906 in an unsuccessful attempt to wrest control of the party from the bosses and the plug-uglies who ruled it.[41] Some of these rebellious local groups were to coöperate and lend strength to state-wide reform when once this movement had started. But without power in San Francisco and Los Angeles any such state movement was doomed to defeat. These two cities had almost 40 per cent of the state's population and most of the great influential daily journals. Support there was vital for success. In particular, the city of Los Angeles was a critical factor. It was there that the Republican railroad machine, through its large majorities, was able to control the state party, and, since California was a Republican state in the early twentieth century, state politics as well.

When Dickson, Lissner, Stimson, and Avery organized the Los Angeles nonpartisan movement and won the municipal election of December, 1906, they struck the first substantial blow for the redemption of the commonwealth from the Southern Pacific. Heartened by the 1906 Los Angeles success, Dickson in particular was now ready to carry the battle to the state.

CHAPTER III

And Then, the State

*

At first glance the years 1906 and 1907 seemed to be most unpropitious for state-wide reform in California. Never, in fact, had the Southern Pacific machine appeared more powerful. Ruef's difficulties with the reformers in San Francisco delighted Herrin. The Curly Boss had been too presumptuous in his demands of late. To be sure the reformers in Los Angeles were stirring up local trouble. Governor George C. Pardee was not all that Herrin could wish for in a chief executive, and Pardee was intent upon being renominated. But these were only scattered and insignificant clouds on the Southern Pacific horizon. The nonpartisans in Los Angeles could be left safely to Walter Parker. As for Governor Pardee, 1906 was an election year, and Pardee was doomed to serious trouble in the state Republican nominating convention.

As former mayor of Oakland, Pardee had not proved to be a pliant tool of the machine. True, the machine had nominated and elected him in 1902, and he had returned the favor two years later by his steady support of the Southern Pacific candidate for United States Senator Frank P. Flint, against the extremely conservative but independently minded incumbent, Thomas R. Bard. But on other important matters Pardee had been a wayward son. He had consistently opposed the interests of the railroad in the Oakland waterfront fight and again on the conservation issue. But perhaps his greatest sin lay in aiding the construction of the Western Pacific Railroad as a competitor to the Southern Pacific in northern California. At least Pardee thought that his encouragement to the Western Pacific was the determining factor in the machine's decision to oppose his renomination.[1]

Independent Republicans felt that Pardee was not a happy choice for governor in 1906. By helping to defeat Bard he had antagonized many of the "respectable independent" elements in the Republican party. Moreover, the would-be reform group was never completely sure of him. They admitted that he was in some ways antimachine but they disliked his penchant for compromise and procrastination. As Chester Rowell noted, Pardee could be counted upon "to do the right thing just too late." But in the spring of 1906 the independents and reformers could not be too particular. Already it was apparent that the Southern Pacific had tapped the shoulder of Congressman James Norris Gillett of Humboldt County as its heir apparent. And the only man with a conceivable chance of beating Gillett was this ten o'clock scholar at reform, the incumbent, George C. Pardee.[2]

In choosing Gillett as its candidate for governor, the machine had acted with characteristic consistency. Never once in Congress had Gillett wandered away from the Southern Pacific reservation. The reward for such exemplary behavior came in June, 1906, at a dinner in Washington, D.C. When a toast was proposed to the congressman as the next governor of California, E. H. Harriman, president of the Southern Pacific, smiled graciously and drank. Gillett returned the amenities the following month by agreeing with Mr. Herrin that he, Gillett, was the logical candidate for the governorship.[3]

But even with machine help Gillett's nomination was not a certainty in the summer of 1906. Wherever primaries were held in California the incumbent Pardee consistently won. Placed upon the American Federation of Labor's black list, Gillett was assailed by the building trades in San Francisco as a foe of organized labor. Moreover, no one knew how earnest Abraham Ruef was in his support of J. O. Hayes of San Jose, least of all Herrin, who had opposed Ruef in the San Francisco elections the year before. Ruef's sizable bloc of amenable delegates might be the deciding force in selecting the nominee. The organization, therefore, worked hard. The nonpartisans in Los Angeles County were defeated, offices were dangled before Pardee delegates, and important conferences were held with the Curly Boss. It was rumored, after one meeting between Gillett and Ruef that a deal was consummated: Gillett was to be nominated; Ruef was to get the local city patronage; and Herrin was to appoint all judges, railroad commissioners, and members of the board of equalization. The rumor was false. But at the opening of the state Republican convention at Santa Cruz in the first week in September, the machine was obviously confident of victory.

Never in the history of California had the Southern Pacific been so brazen in dominating a state convention as it was at Santa Cruz. The master mind, William F. Herrin, was not there, but his lieutenants, Walter Parker and George Hatton, were everywhere, threatening the wavering and providing for the faithful. In the drive to nominate Gillett, even the higher judicial positions were traded like commodities. When Appellate Court Justice W. A. Grey refused to support Gillett, his name was ruthlessly struck from the machine slate for renomination. On the other hand, the Union Labor leaders from San Francisco were heartily welcomed. Schmitz was cheeringly escorted to the platform while Ruef and Walter Parker held hour-long conferences during the first day of the meeting. The San Francisco boss apparently wanted too much for his support, because Parker appealed to the Pardee forces to beat Ruef by supporting Gillett. When this was refused, Parker went back to Ruef and a bargain was sealed. As Ruef later testified, he agreed to support the Humboldt congressman for a consideration of $14,000. After that the show was over. The machine nominated its man for governor on the first ballot by a vote of 591 to Pardee's 233, hand-picked nearly every minor office, and wrote the platform as it had done four years before. The platform was not illiberal. It recognized labor unions as "the true and only way in which the rights of labor can be safeguarded," favored the passage of a direct primary law, and "sympathized" with labor's attempt to obtain an eight-hour day on all government work.[4]

Jubilant over their complete success, the masters of the convention gathered to celebrate at a dinner later to become notorious in every corner of the state. Attending the banquet given by Frank McLauglin, one-time chairman of the Republican State Central Committee, were Gillett, Walter Parker, Abe Ruef, Justice F. W. Henshaw of the California Supreme Court, George Hatton, and Congressman J. R. Knowland, among others. Fortunately for the cause of reform in the state, a picture of the celebrant group was taken and inadvisedly published in the San Francisco *Call*. Squarely in the middle of the photograph was Abraham Ruef; directly behind with his arm on Ruef's shoulder was the nominee, James N. Gillett. Later known as "the Shame of California," the picture was reproduced in practically every reform paper in the state and even in national magazines. It was to become a heavy burden for Gillett and the Southern Pacific to carry.[5]

Even before the Santa Cruz convention adjourned a flame of resentment against it and its servile members ran through the state. Hitherto staunch Republican papers denounced the railroad and its apparent ownership of the party. As the attack continued, even party regulars felt they must apologize for the convention methods. The political friends of Pardee were particularly wrathful at the treatment they had received and practically every party member, save the agents of the Southern Pacific, deplored the "dragging of the candidates for judicial positions through the mire of the political barnyard." [6] Edward A. Dickson, covering the convention for the Los Angeles *Express,* was so disgusted that he came home determined not to support the Republican nominee. In his editorials Dickson had charged that the regular Republican organization was merely a pseudonym for the Southern Pacific political bureau. Now he was ready for outright attack. But with his publisher, E. T. Earl, demanding caution, Dickson went to the Democratic gathering at Sacramento without agreement on pledging the support of the *Express* to an acceptable Democratic nominee.[7]

For the first time in years the Democratic party was meeting

in 1906 without the usual blessing of William Randolph
Hearst. Having formed the Independence League, Hearst had
already nominated District Attorney Langdon of San Francisco as his personal candidate for governor and was interested
only in getting an endorsement of his protégé. But if the usual
Hearst influence was lacking, the Southern Pacific's was not.
Herrin, a nominal Democrat, was too adept at the game of
real politics to place the railroad's confidence entirely in one
party. At Sacramento as at Santa Cruz, the railroad was in
ubiquitous attendance and word went along the convention
aisles that Marshall Diggs was to be the nominee. The slender
hopes of the antirailroad men were further diminished by
James D. Phelan's refusal to become a candidate. Then one
of those curious currents that sometimes arise in political
conventions took hold of the delegates. Led by Anthony Caminetti, a back country Democrat who had been fighting the
Southern Pacific for years in the legislature, a movement
started for the nomination of Theodore A. Bell, a young,
progressive Napa lawyer. Bell's cause undoubtedly was aided
by the report that he could count on the support of the oldest
Republican paper in Los Angeles, the *Express*. After meeting
with Caminetti, Dickson wired and received Earl's consent
to promise support if Bell were selected. Bell was chosen by
acclamation, William Randolph Hearst was read from the
party, and a thoroughly liberal and anti–Southern Pacific
platform was adopted. In a fighting speech of acceptance the
nominee emphasized his antipathy for both Hearst and
Herrin. Rarely had the Southern Pacific been so roughly han-
dled by a candidate for the governorship.[8]

Throughout the following three-cornered campaign Bell
consistently talked the language of advanced progressivism.
In complete support of the party's platform, he spoke for
the direct primary, the popular election of United States
senators, public ownership of utilities, legislation for the limitation of labor injunctions, and control of monopolies even
to the price-fixing of their goods. But the greater part of his
time was spent in assaulting the railroad and its control of the

state. True to its promise, the *Express* gave him loyal support, as did organized labor, except for the Ruef-Schmitz machine. In particular, the pro-Bell journals emphasized the connection between Gillett, Herrin, and Ruef by printing and reprinting the picture taken after the Santa Cruz convention. Much was also made of the fact that President Theodore Roosevelt failed to endorse the Republican candidate at the same time that he was supporting Charles Evans Hughes in New York. Had Bell received either the Democratic votes given to Hearst's candidate, Langdon, or the support of the antimachine Republicans, he would have won. But except for the Los Angeles *Express,* none of the Republican papers, so wrathful at the Santa Cruz convention, came to his aid. Most of the powerful newspaper editors, who were shortly to join in the formation of the Lincoln-Roosevelt Republican League, like Chester Rowell of Fresno, Irving Martin of Stockton, and A. J. Pillsbury of Sacramento, swallowed their opposition and loyally supported the organization. In self-justification, Rowell's paper lamely editorialized that the railroad had not been pro-Gillett at Santa Cruz, but had been anti-Pardee, and that the state had Gillett's word that the winning votes "had come to him without any 'deal' on his part, or any promises to the railroad bosses." Even with the support of these antirailroad Republicans, Gillett did not receive a majority and only defeated Bell by some eight thousand votes. The Democratic candidate had not only waged the first straight-out fight of the twentieth century with the Southern Pacific; he had also made it clear that opposition to the railroad was no longer a political liability in California.[9]

Whatever interpretation the Southern Pacific political machine put upon the election of 1906 did not affect its actions during the legislative session of the following January. Whether or not this was the worst legislature in the state's history, as some editors thought, is open to dispute. But certainly its sins were given the widest publicity. From the moment the body convened to the last roll call, the entire state was informed of the daily doings of Walter Parker and George

Hatton in the House and of Jere Burke in the Senate. According to the daily journals and antirailroad legislators, no important action was taken in either house without the sanction of these three top members of the Southern Pacific's legislative directorate. Thus a loyal Republican member of the Senate wrote after the session: "Scarcely a vote was cast in either house that did not show some aspect of Southern Pacific ownership, petty vengeance, or legislative blackmail." [10]

Despite continuing criticism, the three bosses made no attempt to conceal their presence. With complete freedom of the floors of both houses, they were clearly in evidence at almost every session. So was their work. With painful frankness one senator, pleading for an extension of the right of eminent domain, frankly stated that his bill had the complete approval of the Southern Pacific. Another as indiscreet withdrew a bill after Jere Burke had whispered to him that it would be harmful to the railroad.[11]

But if the railroad received, it also had to allow its faithful legislators pap and patronage at the expense of the state treasury. Under the existing rules of the body each member was permitted a daily allowance for personal employees and other services. In the first two sessions the maximum patronage allowable to members of the majority party was raised to twenty-five dollars a day in the Senate and thirteen in the House. Then, following Grove Johnson's adjuration: "Open the doors of the treasury, it is better to put money in circulation than to keep it locked up," the two houses went on a "drunken hiring spree." By January 10 the House had on its pay roll thirty-six sergeants at arms, ten doorkeepers for four doors, eighteen watchmen, the same number of porters, seven postmistresses, twenty-seven engrossing and enrolling clerks, thirty-one "straight clerks," and forty other people. Later investigations showed that a newspaperman drawing full pay from his paper was also in the pay of both houses, that a high school student drew a full salary, and that persons who never left Los Angeles for the term of the session received regular checks from the state. When Governor Gillett signed the patronage bills, he was bluntly charged by one Republican newspaper with delivering "to the thieves in the Assembly the key to the State Treasury." Another paper inquired what the Southern Pacific was asking from the legislature. "If price is any index," it concluded, "it should be something important." [12]

But the railroad was more interested in stopping than in forcing action in this California legislature. During previous years of power it had been well taken care of on the statute books and in the regulatory commissions. Now it wished to be left to enjoy its privileges. During the 1907 session it was content with stopping any direct attack upon its preserves, aiding its friends a little here and there, and quietly forgetting about troublesome reform. The platform of the party was for the most part conveniently passed over, and the legislature addressed itself to the direct primary alone. But instead of passing an amendment to the constitution providing for primary machinery, the final bill simply empowered the legislature to put the primary into effect at some future date, provided the people of the state ratified the action. Other measures, like Grove Johnson's five antirailroad bills and John M. Eshleman's proposal to outlaw racing and gambling at Emeryville, were killed outright. For years a Southern Pacific stalwart, Johnson was then in temporary rebellion against the railroad, primarily perhaps to increase his nuisance value.

Eshleman was a man of different salt. After the death of his father, he had worked his way through high school and the University of California as a common laborer on a section gang. Soon after his graduation at the head of his class, he became a deputy to the district attorney of Alameda County. When a university official was convicted of embezzling funds to gamble at the Emeryville track, Eshleman and his friend Edward Dickson were indignant at the close connection between university employees and a gambling ring. At the suggestion of Dickson, Eshleman became a candidate for the legislature on an anti–race track platform. Elected by the reform element of Berkeley, he came to the legislature with a concept of public morality strikingly different from the prevailing code of that body. Both his political education and his indignation were sharpened as he watched the Southern Pacific machine ruthlessly cut down his bill. Not only Eshleman but a good part of the state fervently agreed with a chaplain who, in an opening prayer on the day following the defeat of the Eshleman bill, characterized most of the legislators as men "who draw pay, draw corks, and draw poker." [13]

Walter Parker, George Hatton, and Jere Burke were in effect "the people of California" during the session of 1907, but unlike the three tailors of Tooley Street, they proved it. As they defeated the reform bills of their enemies they passed the not-so-enlightened measures of their friends. The state press responded with uproar when it became known that a group of Berkeley real-estate agents were sponsoring a resolution to remove the state capital from Sacramento to Berkeley. In the very teeth of state-wide opposition, as Burke and Hatton openly lobbied for it, the resolution passed both houses.[14] A short time later the governor gave complete proof of his loyalty to the real rulers of the state by declaring that the adjourning legislature would be judged "one of the best that ever met in the state capital."

A different judgment on the session came from the state. There the verdict from almost every newspaper, including the Los Angeles *Times,* agreed with Chester Rowell's bitter valedictory editorial entitled "Adjourned, Thank God." The editor of the Fresno *Republican* declared that in "shameless servility, blatant indecency, and total unfitness, this legislature stands at the very bottom of the long list of boss-ridden legislatures that have disgraced California." The state had lost, Rowell continued, the things for which the Revolutionary and Civil wars were fought. Unless California arose and overthrew corrupt corporation government as Wisconsin had done, then its peoples were not fit for self-government. "If we are fit to govern ourselves," the impassioned editor concluded, "this is the last time we will submit to be governed by the hired bosses of the Southern Pacific Railroad Company." [15]

Rowell's editorial was more than a general invocation to the state for revolt; it was a statement of aims for a specific movement already organizing against the Southern Pacific. Even before the Santa Cruz convention and the legislature of 1907, a number of men had talked about reform. During March and April of 1906 a group led by Arthur J. Pillsbury, then secretary of the State Board of Control, and Chester Rowell urged Governor Pardee to campaign for reëlection on a straight anti–Southern Pacific platform. Pillsbury submitted a manifesto of freedom from the railroad to the governor who, according to Rowell's memory, agreed after long consideration to issue it on April 18, 1906. But in the confusion that followed the great earthquake of that morning, the manifesto was forgotten. And when Pardee again turned his attention to politics he felt the time for the document had passed.[16]

Chester Rowell may have inherited some of his distaste for railroad politics from his father, Jonathan Rowell, a United States congressman from Illinois for twenty years. Growing up in Washington, he had watched his father battle the land-grant roads of his native state and later dabbled in politics himself, eventually becoming the clerk of the House Committee on Elections. After a combined American and European education, Rowell turned to journalism as a profession and in 1898 became the editor of his uncle's paper, the Fresno *Morning Republican*. There again he watched the railroad machine operate as it twice defeated his uncle and later Senator Bard, for whom Rowell had been a Washington secretary. Always tolerant of man's foibles, Rowell was a complacent conservative in those early days. As he grew older he became more and more indignant at the existing control of state politics. In 1903 he wrote an editorial asking the newspapers of the state to band together against the railroad, but threw it in the wastebasket "knowing it wouldn't do any good." From that time on, however, while still supporting the regular organization, he looked for an opportunity to strike at the Southern Pacific. Annually covering the legislature for his paper, he became one of the state's most intelligent and able journalists.[17]

Simultaneously with the Pardee episode, powerful newspapers were calling for a revolt against the railroad. Leading these voices were Dickson's Los Angeles *Express* and Older's San Francisco *Bulletin.* After the incredibly corrupt Santa Cruz convention, A. J. Pillsbury, A. B. Nye, and Irving Martin, all backers of Governor Pardee, discussed the possibilities of organizing a reform wing of the Republican party. Pardee himself echoed their sentiments by calling for "the decent forces" in the state to organize just as the bosses had organized.

The following month the editor of a small southern California paper, ignorant of other plans afoot to organize the state, wrote confidentially to three fellow publishers proposing that the independent editors of the state meet to launch an "unflinching crusade" against the railroad. Thus by the time the legislature met in January, 1907, rebellious sentiment was scattered all over the state. But what was lacking for a determined move against the railroad domination of the state was strong and competent leadership to ignite and organize the rebellion and then to shape its course. That leadership was to be supplied by Edward Dickson and Chester Rowell, who by great good fortune, occupied adjoining desks in the press row of the 1907 legislature. These two men share the honor for starting and organizing the successful movement to free the Republican party and the state from the Southern Pacific Railroad.[18]

After supporting Theodore Bell in his campaign against Gillett and the railroad in the autumn of 1906, Dickson had made a trip to Sacramento and told State Controller A. B. Nye and Robert A. Waring of a plan to launch a state-wide movement within the Republican party against the Southern Pacific. Both men wished him luck. On his return to Los Angeles Dickson informed Stimson, Avery, Brundige, Lissner, and his publisher, Earl, of his talk with Nye and Waring. The Los Angeles group expressed some interest, but only Stimson and Avery were really enthusiastic, the remaining three men feeling that the plan was too ambitious for success.[19]

Not discouraged by this halfhearted reception, Dickson went north again in January, 1907, this time to cover the legislature for his paper. There he met Chester Rowell. Dickson and Rowell were not acquainted when they sat down in their adjoining seats at the opening of the legislature. But both were ardently opposed to machine politics and both had come to the session hoping that they could find support for a state-wide reform movement. Soon, as they observed the Southern Pacific circus below them, they began to talk politics. Finding Rowell sympathetic, Dickson told him of his scheme for an organized state rebellion against the Southern Pacific. And both men agreed that because of its recent municipal victory the nonpartisan group in Los Angeles would be an ideal nucleus around which a reform organization could be started.

Rowell promised that if Dickson called an anti–Southern Pacific conference in Los Angeles during the late spring, he would be responsible for the attendance of several northern California editors. They grew more optimistic about the project after they had carefully sounded out a few more journalists in the capital. Among others, G. B. Daniels, Colonel E. A. Forbes, A. J. Pillsbury, Robert Waring, and former governor Pardee indicated a strong interest in the plan. By early February Dickson wrote Stimson and Lissner about his talks with Rowell. Giving an account of his progress at Sacramento, he concluded that in his opinion the state reform movement "would find instant support." Rowell, meanwhile, had gone back to Fresno, where he obtained the consent of his uncle to swing the Fresno *Morning Republican* behind the plan. On February 20, the *Republican* called for a state-wide organized reform movement in the Republican party. Three weeks later the paper announced that the first practical steps had already been taken to free the state from the hold of the Southern Pacific.[20]

By the time the legislature adjourned, tentative plans for

calling a meeting of reform leaders in Los Angeles had been made. A proposal also had been drawn up to start a progressive magazine, a publication that later became known as the *California Weekly*. But most of these brave plans were still hopes and by no means realities. Dickson had still to win approval for the project from some of his reluctant confederates in Los Angeles and, most important, from E. T. Earl, the owner of the *Express*. Then too, the promises of support from other parts of the state had merely been promises. No one knew how many of these good intentions would evaporate when the time came to stand up and be counted openly against the powerful Republican organization. When Dickson returned home in early March he discussed with the Los Angeles group the proposed conference that he and Rowell had planned. Stimson and Avery approved, but Lissner, Brundige, and Earl were again reluctant to commit themselves. Finally, as a compromise, it was agreed that if Dickson were to issue the call for the meeting under his own name, and if he could assemble a sizable and influential group, all would attend.

Armed only with this conditional promise, Dickson worked throughout April to enlist support for the new movement. By the first week in May he was writing to a score of prominent reform-minded Californians, announcing that May 21 had been set as the tentative date for a conference and asking them to attend and join in this movement to secure "political and economic independence." For a while the future of the meeting looked bleak; Rowell wrote that he had not been able to get in touch with the northern group of men as he had promised. But working through Robert Waring and State Controller A. B. Nye, Dickson secured promises from enough northerners to warrant holding the conference. Eventually all but one of those approached, promised either to attend the meeting or to give their strong support.[21]

On May 21, at Levy's café in downtown Los Angeles, fifteen or more determined men, including eight publishers and four attorneys, met in response to Dickson's invitation. This small group adopted Dickson's suggestion of Lincoln-Republicans as a provisional name for the organization and elected S. C. Graham, a Los Angeles oil man, chairman, and A. J. Pillsbury secretary. Opposition to the railroad headed their agenda, but they also gave their attention to a long list of social and humanitarian reforms. Among these were proposals for the direct primary, the initiative, referendum, and recall, the regulation of utility rates, conservation of forests, the outlawing of race-track gambling, a workmen's compensation law, woman suffrage, a blue-sky law, and a minimum-wage law for women. But by far the most important action taken that night was the agreement to issue an "emancipation proclamation" and a call for a state-wide organization meeting to be held in Oakland during the summer.

In their first statement of aims incorporated in the "emancipation proclamation," these Lincoln-Republicans unqualifiedly struck at the Southern Pacific and identified themselves with the national progressive movement. Among the provisions agreed to at Los Angeles were:

(1) The emancipation of the Republican Party in California from domination by the Political Bureau of the Southern Pacific Railroad Company and allied interests, and the reorganization of the State Committee to that end.

(2) The selection of delegates to the next Republican National Convention pledged to the nomination of Theodore Roosevelt, or if that were impossible, to vote for a candidate known to be truly committed to and identified with his policies, and to oppose the nomination of any reactionary styled "safe and sane" by the great corporate interests.

(3) The pledging of all delegates to the next state convention against "trading."

(4) The enactment of a state law giving the voters an "advisory voice in the election of senators until an amendment to the national constitution could be passed." [22]

70

With minor modifications this statement of basic purposes became and remained the program of the rebel group until their victory in 1910.

At the May 21 meeting in Los Angeles Dickson had been made chairman of the committee for organizing the coming Oakland conference. To assist him in obtaining prospective delegates, Lissner, Stimson, and Avery promised to cover the south while Nye, Waring, Martin, and Pillsbury undertook the same work in the north. Unfortunately, Rowell was so busy with his affairs in Fresno that he neither attended the many meetings of the organizing group nor joined in the work of obtaining delegates. Since there had been no San Francisco representatives at the original meeting at Levy's, Dickson and Lissner made a trip north to meet Older and Heney. Soon after the visit Dickson wrote Rowell that Older would support them in the *Bulletin* and that Heney had promised to stump the state for the movement. This was cheering news, for it meant not only an important step into San Francisco's tangled politics, but also perhaps the powerful financial support of Rudolph Spreckels.[23]

The August 1 meeting at the Hotel Metropole in Oakland was not so large as its sponsors had hoped—less than fifty people attended. But with a good part of the metropolitan and the small-town press either represented or pledged to support, the group went ahead to organize on a permanent basis. After a good deal of discussion, the organization was officially named the League of Lincoln-Roosevelt Republican Clubs. Francis Heney wanted the name changed to the Roosevelt League, but Dickson insisted on keeping Lincoln in the title, and a friendly compromise resulted. Officers of the new venture included Frank R. Devlin of Vallejo as president, Daniel Ryan of San Francisco, Harold T. Powers of Auburn, and Lee Gates of Los Angeles as vice-presidents, and Chester Rowell, who was absent from the meeting, as secretary. On the executive committee were D. E. Collins, T. J. Nolton, E. A. Forbes, A. H. Breed, Ralph Hathorn, Duncan McPherson, Marshall Stimson, and John Eshleman.[24]

The first sharp division in the movement occurred over the platform. The statement of aims adopted at Levy's café in May was agreed to almost unanimously, except for the sections endorsing the renomination of Roosevelt and the provision for direct election of senators. With 25 per cent of the delegates opposed to the third-term movement, the wording of the resolution was so changed that the endorsement was dropped. The platform, however, still pledged the League to a candidate "truly committed" to the President's policies and against a "safe and sane" candidate. Since there was much less opposition to a direct primary, that remained. But many people who were ready to join the League in attacking the railroad were against any further "political excursions." They agreed with former Senator Bard that while the influence of the Southern Pacific should be eliminated from the political life of the state, the Republican party should "not be made a revolutionary party" in the process. Obviously this fundamental difference between the two factions spelled trouble for the future.[25]

The public organization of the Lincoln-Roosevelt League placed many of the state's active Republican politicians in the embarrassing position of having to choose between the old and the new politics. A few who had been defeated by the machine the previous year were quick to join. But the great majority, doubting the permanence of the new movement and its ability to challenge the Southern Pacific successfully, refused to associate with it. On the other hand, the League's already strong journalistic flavor was increased by the numerous daily journals which came to its support after the Oakland meeting. By September, 1907, thirty-odd newspapers, including at least one major sheet in every important city in the state, had pledged their editorial columns to the League's purposes. Thus the reform organization was not only originated but also nourished by the publishers and editors of the state.[26]

But even with a major part of the state press insisting that the California Republican party could not remain "half Harriman and half Roosevelt," much more had to be done before the infant organization became more than a collection of state officers and a paper plan. If the League were to be the influential force that its sponsors hoped, its enemies had to be answered, its funds built up, and most important—it had to be organized on a local level in every corner of the state. And since the most promising way of keeping a political organization together is to provide jobs for the faithful, local elections had to be fought and won. For all of these varied tasks the Oakland meeting raised an organizing fund of five hundred dollars. Small wonder that the professional politician viewed the League askance.

Throughout southern California the work of organizing local units of the League was not very difficult. All that was needed was the transformation and extension of the already functioning reform organizations in the city and county of Los Angeles. This Meyer Lissner and Marshall Stimson were able to do as a part-time activity. But elsewhere in the state, north of the Tehachapi, no unified nucleus for the reform movement existed, and the organization had to be built up town by town, city by city.

Fortunately for the future of the League, the Oakland meeting had provided for the opening of a permanent headquarters in San Francisco. And for the next two years the guiding spirits in that headquarters were Chester Rowell, the secretary of the youthful organization, and Edward Dickson. In the beginning, both men were able to devote most of their time to League affairs by arrangements with their papers. Later, they continued to share the onerous tasks of this important grassroots work. When Rowell was occasionally unable to carry his full share of the work because of his editorial responsibilities in Fresno, Dickson cheerfully assumed the burdens and kept the movement alive and growing. During the important 1908 campaign, for example, Rowell found that his editorial duties prevented him from assuming any sort of executive responsibilities in San Francisco for a month. He would continue to make speeches, he wrote to Dickson, but could do nothing more. "I can be a pack horse within limits," he wrote, "but not a driver." [27]

With Los Angeles and the south fairly well taken care of, the League leaders agreed that the most important areas to be won in the north were Oakland, Sacramento, and San Francisco. Each of these cities was a major population center, and each had been for a long time a Southern Pacific stronghold. A victory in any of the three cities would enormously encourage the reform forces throughout the state. Consequently, Rowell and Dickson divided the work, with Rowell attending to San Francisco and Dickson turning his attention first to Sacramento, where a municipal election was to be held in November, 1907. Journeying to the capital, Dickson soon had a local League group organized which persuaded Clinton L. White, a prominent attorney, to run for mayor against the machine candidate. Throughout the following short but hectic campaign Dickson and his League friends devised most of the strategy, which included cornering the white bone collar-button supply in the city, the buttons being used as campaign insignia for the followers of the reform candidate. On election day, much to the surprise of professional politicians, the railroad machine was badly beaten. The League had won its first straight-out victory over the Southern Pacific, and in doing so gave a great impetus to the reform movement throughout the state.

Because of its late start, the League was handicapped in the scattered local elections of 1907. The stakes were to be much higher in 1908, a presidential year. In addition to the delegates to the national convention, a new legislature, all the state's congressmen, and a United States senator were to be chosen. Of even more importance to the reform forces was the Republican state convention scheduled for August, when control of the state party machinery would be determined. To prepare for these vital contests the League's executive committee, meeting in January, again threw most of the burden of organizing local communities on Dickson and Rowell. And since Rowell again was unable to leave his

Fresno paper for any long period, most of the field work fell upon Dickson. Concentrating on Oakland and Alameda County, Dickson arranged for organizing meetings in practically every community center in the country. Largely because of this thorough groundwork and Rowell's compelling speeches, Alameda was won. In the county convention held in late summer the League mustered a commanding majority, and the second great railroad center in the north fell to the reformers. Designating the results in Alameda as a personal triumph for Dickson, Rowell congratulated his colleague for having accomplished the "biggest thing that has been done in California politics." [28]

One of the most immediate difficulties that had to be overcome was the constant lack of money. E. T. Earl had already contributed and promised a substantial sum for the summer's campaign. In the north Rudolph Spreckels was equally generous. But in those early days angels with sizable fortunes and an inclination to contribute were rare. As a result, the League's resources were thin, and both Rowell and Dickson worked without compensation. From the viewpoint of the two journalists even some of the available money did not come as an unmixed blessing, for almost from the start, there was a fundamental clash in personality and opinion between Rowell and Rudolph Spreckels.

A wealthy banker, sugar baron, and fancier of thoroughbred horses in 1900, Spreckels was to spend the rest of his life supporting reform movements of one kind or another. Foregoing the opportunity of a college education, Spreckels at the age of seventeen chose to enter his father's sugar factory. From that time on his business career was punctuated by one sharp struggle after another. After waging a victorious fight against the eastern sugar trust, he had a violent quarrel with his father and later one with his brother, after which he set out on his own and did as brilliantly for a time as he had done in the family firm. Untainted by formal learning or culture, he was extremely opinionated, and according to his contemporaries, sought to dominate every movement in which he engaged. In his earlier days he was also exceedingly thin-skinned and could not brook opposition. Rowell commented that you needed to disagree with Spreckels only once, and then he was through with you for-ever. Nevertheless, this autocratic reformer for more than thirty years made his purse and his energies available to practically every liberal cause that needed help. In 1906 he started his public career by opposing Ruef and supporting the progressive revolt. Thirty years later he was still doing business at the same old stand by proposing a low national ceiling on individual incomes and by supporting Franklin D. Roosevelt.[29]

One major issue on which Rowell and Spreckels differed concerned the way in which the organization should be con-structed and controlled. Devoted to the democratic method, the newspaperman saw the League movement built on active local organizations and controlled from below; the wealthy businessman and banker, distrusting popular control, insisted, according to Rowell, that any efficient organization must have central authority "with summary veto power on the actions of local bodies." [30] In this fundamental argument Spreckels was undoubtedly reflecting not only the ideas of his economic class but also his experience with the San Francisco graft trials, where democracy had neither started nor pursued the prosecution. Spreckels' disposition to take action without in-forming other League leaders added to the friction between the two men, and Rowell was greatly disturbed when he first learned in the daily journals that Spreckels was financing the People's Lobby as a journalistic reform organization to pub-licize the misdeeds of the next legislature. But perhaps Spreckels' most irritating habit was to demand that the men working with his generous funds "take orders." At one time Rowell was on the point of placing Spreckels on the state executive committee, but he finally concluded that the cost was not worth the candle. "We have to sacrifice something for the privilege of dealing with each other as free men," he wrote to Heney, "and he [Spreckels] is not willing to make that sacrifice." Rowell was finally willing to see Spreckels "go it alone with an organization consisting of himself and his employees." This parting of the ways was not publicized at the time nor did it mark the end of Spreckels' financial contributions to the League. But the incident was to have considerable influence on the later history of the progressive movement in the state.[31]

Intimately connected with the problem of Spreckels was that of the organization of San Francisco for the League. The difficulties in the bay city were complex. At least four so-called reform organizations had developed there during the graft trials, and when Rowell first came to the city each was highly suspicious of the other's good intentions. To complicate matters further, Rowell found in San Francisco a resentment of outside leadership or even of suggestions "so intense as to amount almost to a mania." It became necessary to organize the League in a dual fashion, with one group responsible for the south and another for the north. To the end of its days the League was in reality almost two organizations, with each group maintaining its own directing committees and raising its own funds.

But the immediate problem at hand was to select the leadership for the local organization. Finding no one whom all the local reform organizations would trust, Rowell finally placed the confidence of the League in the hands of Daniel Ryan, a vice-president of the state League and also leader of the San Francisco Regular Republican League. That was a mistake. Ryan grew ambitious, almost immediately announced his candidacy for mayor, and won the nomination on the Republican ticket. Opposed to him was not only the Union Labor candidate but the Democrat, Taylor, who was being supported by Heney, the graft prosecution, and the San Francisco Good Government League. For a short time the Lincoln-Roosevelters were placed in the position of opposing Heney and the graft trials.

As Rowell grimly remarked, without Heney and with the reform forces divided, there was small hope of capturing San

77

Francisco for the League. And without San Francisco, the Fresno journalist continued, the League had only a "discouraging fighting chance" of carrying the state. There was no choice but to repudiate the Ryan organization that had been built up so laboriously, and after the League executive committee formally called upon Ryan to renounce his candidacy, Rowell had to start anew to construct the San Francisco reform forces. It was hard and discouraging work. In the dark swirling currents of San Francisco politics one could not be sure of any man or organization. After the Ryan fiasco one had be be twice cautious—of the claims of "too ambitious reformers" as well as of "Maestretti's steam beer boys." Eventually Rowell obtained through Spreckels the resources of the Burns detective agency, to inquire into the past habits of every potential League leader from the top of the city organization down to the precincts. A biography of each man was gathered, including his voting record in state and local politics, church membership, business activities, and even snatches of private conversations he had held with friends. After ten days of combing through these "personal files" Rowell selected and met with only four trusted men. A week later sixteen more were chosen, and within a month a city organization had again been painfully constructed around thirty-eight carefully certified individuals.[32]

Meanwhile, League affairs outside of San Francisco were running more smoothly. By the first of April, Rowell and Dickson had completed the skeleton organization in virtually every population center in the state. Immediately following that achievement, the League set at the work of controlling the state convention for the selection of delegates to the national Republican nominating convention. All through April and May the League's oratorical talent, including Rowell, Pardee, Heney, Hiram Johnson, W. R. Davis, Charles S. Wheeler, Lee Gates, and Mayor White of Sacramento, appealed to all Republicans to down the machine by voting for righteousness. With something of the air of a revival meeting, Californians were told that the day "of their deliverance was at hand" if they would but accept it.[33]

Committed to a Roosevelt man by its Oakland program, the League supported Taft for the nomination as soon as the President indicated his choice of a successor. In January, when the California State Executive Committee refused to endorse Taft it appeared as if a straight fight would develop between the regular Republicans and the Lincoln-Roosevelt League. When, after some delay, the standpatters also endorsed Taft, the issue between the two groups was simply who should go to Chicago. It was surprising that, handicapped by this lack of a sharply drawn issue, the League nevertheless came within forty votes of controlling the May convention. Of even more significance for the future were the facts that the Lincoln-Roosevelt League had won a decided majority of all delegates elected by a primary and had also carried San Francisco, "the Gibraltar of the organization." [34]

Of far more interest than the presidential contests to both Leaguers and regulars were the August primaries and county conventions where nominations for the state legislature and elections to the state Republican convention would be made. Success there meant control of the state during 1909 and perhaps in 1910 when a governor was to be elected. After the League announced a complete slate of anti–Southern Pacific candidates for both primaries and conventions, the regular organization attacked with fury. The regular press promptly depicted these "Lincoln-Roosters" as a "sorehead Pardee organization" based upon hate and hope—hate for the men who had defeated them at the Santa Cruz convention and hope for future office. At other times the League was described as a vast blackmailing scheme organized to "traduce honest Republicans who built the state." Nor were its leaders treated less gently. "Earl the rebater" and "Lissner of the three ball sign" were described as men who had sold out decent Republicanism in 1906; Rudolph Spreckels was referred to as a "race-track gambling sport," and Heney as a "swaggering and vulgar fraud." With the League journals tossing dead cat for dead cat, the whole state enjoyed a back alley brawl.[35]

The results of this intraparty warfare were not too encouraging to the reform forces. Possibly reflecting the changing attitude toward the graft trials, the League lost thirteen of the eighteen assembly districts in San Francisco by an extremely close vote. Combined with their victory in Los Angeles, this result enabled the regular machine to control the state convention and thus the party machinery. Elsewhere in the state the League prospects were better. Thanks to victories at Long Beach, Fresno, and in many county conventions including Humboldt, the home of Governor Gillett, the reformers had elected a sizable number of state legislators and local officials. If the Southern Pacific's hold on the state had not been broken, it had at least been shaken. With that mollifying thought, the League announced that it would not oppose any Republican nominations and that its work was through for the year. A short time later Rowell's Fresno *Republican* advised the voters that "the easiest way to vote is to vote a straight [Republican] ticket." [36]

At first glance, the legislature which convened in January, 1909, appeared to be just another meeting of the old machine crowd. In charge of the campaign to reëlect Senator George C. Perkins was George Hatton, who regularly "took care" of the Assembly for the Southern Pacific. After both houses were organized to the satisfaction of the machine, Perkins, who, in the opinion of the reformers, had regularly "merchandised" his patronage "to rivet the chains of Southern Pacific domination on California," was duly elected. But before many days had passed both Governor Gillett and the legislature were reflecting the rising reform pressure in the state. In part, that was due to the considerable minority group of legislators pledged to the program of the Lincoln-Roosevelt Republican League, in part to the constant stream of publicity poured out of Sacramento by the People's Lobby and duly published by a great part of the state press. Financed by Rudolph Spreckels, E. T. Earl, and Dr. John R. Haynes, the lobby covered the daily doings of the legislature and prepared a reform-slanted account of its activities that was offered free to any newspaper in the state. In his opening address to the legislature, Governor Gillett surprised both his friends and enemies by calling for strict regulation of railroads. Bending just as far before the wind as the governor, the legislature barred all lobbyists from the floor of the two houses while they were in session. For the first time in the memory of living men, paid agents of the Southern Pacific were not in evidence during the actual debates. Since Jere Burke still had an office directly across the hall from the Speaker, the "third house" of the legislature had not been abolished, but its prerogatives had certainly been substantially curtailed.[37]

Trying desperately to look respectable, the legislature actually went on to consider railroad regulation seriously. In the course of the debate the effective Stetson bill, giving the state railroad commission power to set absolute rates, to base such rates on physical evaluation of the roads, and to prohibit any and all discrimination against individual shippers, was defeated and the more innocuous Wright Bill passed. True enough, nothing had been done to change the complexion of the California Railroad Commission, or the "Southern Pacific Literary Bureau," as it was variously designated. But the Wright Bill, not entirely without teeth, was the first significant antirailroad measure that the California legislature had passed for many years.

Reform prospects continued to look up as both houses passed an antiracing and gambling bill which Eshleman had tried to get approved two years before. But perhaps the greatest battle of the session revolved around a direct primary measure. The bill as introduced did not incorporate a completely free primary in the selection of state officers, and was only advisory in the selection of United States senators. Unsatisfactory to the more advanced reformers in the state, it was entirely too much reform for the machine. With Jere Burke of the Southern Pacific rounding up every possible opposition vote, there was intense pressure on individual legislators to vote against the bill. "Threats, persuasions, and promises" were offered to legislators to change their votes, and it was made clear that their support of the bill would hurt them "in a business way at home." [38] Instead of submitting to this pressure in the traditional fashion, fifteen anti-machine Republicans and a small number of like-minded Democrats left their parties' caucuses and held a bipartisan reform meeting of their own. The machine's old technique of divide and rule was losing its effectiveness.

After amendments in both houses and in a free conference committee, the primary bill which finally emerged was so emasculated that many antimachine men felt the necessity of explaining their votes for the measure on the grounds that it was this bill or nothing. Notwithstanding the fact that a few Lincoln-Roosevelters like Rudolph Spreckels, who "was tired of being fooled," were opposed to its passage, the bill was not an inconsiderable step forward in the fight against the railroad machine. Without it the Lincoln-Roosevelt Republican League could not have appealed directly to the people of the state in support of their candidate for governor in 1910.

For the remainder of the session the reform forces were clearly outnumbered. All the sixty-five Commonwealth Club bills to amend legal procedure in the state were voted down or delayed until their passage was impossible. Led by Grove Johnson, described by a prejudiced source as having "controlled more California legislatures than any other man unless it be Mr. Herrin," the machine rallied to defeat these proposals to remove the legal loopholes brought to light during the San Francisco graft trials. A local option bill, a provision to extend the initiative, and numerous railroad regulatory measures met similar fates. But measured by the past, the legislature of 1909 was a relatively successful, enlightened, and uncontrolled body. As Chester Rowell commented, it had laid "a foundation of superficial reform" upon which real reform would soon be constructed. Rowell was referring to the Lincoln-Roosevelt Republican League's announced intention to dominate the state after the 1910 elections. Even in 1909, however, the effect of the League upon state politics was already apparent. The striking contrast between the legislative sessions of 1907 and 1909 was eloquent evidence of that.[39]

For the remainder of 1909, the Lincoln-Roosevelt Republican League was so silent that the regular press, giving thought to their wishes, declared that the organization had quietly if not decently died. In a November meeting at Oakland, however, seventy delegates gathered again by invitation to perfect plans for the following campaign year.

After that conference Chester Rowell, the newly elected president, announced that an entire antirailroad ticket from the governor down would be presented to the people of California at the next election. As far as principles were concerned, the League still stood behind the Oakland resolutions of the previous year. But in the coming campaign, Rowell declared, there was to be just one major aim: to kick the Southern Pacific out of California politics. "No other reform," he wrote, "is even within practical consideration until that is accomplished." [40]

If the November, 1909, statements of the League indicated a momentary drift to the right, other developments clearly showed an increasing and more comprehensive spirit of "liberalism" among its membership. The very name of the League and its support of Roosevelt's policies in its program indicated an awareness of the conjunction between national and state politics. From the day of its origins, the majority of its leaders were fervid supporters of Theodore Roosevelt, and no one needed to be very acute to see that the machine men to whom they were opposed in California were also opposed to Roosevelt policies when they got to Washington. Thus the Leaguers were early supporters of a third term for T. R., and barring that, for a man committed to his policies. Some of them also debated whether they should try to defeat the incumbent congressmen who were supporters of the machine at home and dedicated to standpat politics in Washington. It was only after concluding that the League had neither the organization, the time, nor the money to defeat Congressmen McKinley, Englebright, and McLachlan, that they decided to wait until 1910 before entering the broader field of national politics.[41]

With Taft's easy election in November, 1908, the Lincoln-Roosevelt Leaguers felt they had a friend in the White House. They continued to feel that way during the turbulent tariff session of Congress in the early part of 1909. Devoted to high protection for their many competitive products, the California reformers were not disturbed by the Payne-Aldrich Tariff Act as were the Midwestern progressive senators and representatives. "The tariff as now revised," the Fresno *Republican* stated, "is as good a bill as a good President could impose on a good Congress." [42] But Taft's apparent defense of Speaker Cannon's standpat rule in the House of Representatives and his growing friendship with Nelson W. Aldrich, boss of the Senate and representative extraordinary of big business, were other matters. League papers, while still apologizing for the President, were beginning to be a bit uneasy about the man at 1700 Pennsylvania Avenue. Then in the autumn of 1909 came the startling struggle between Gifford Pinchot and Secretary of the Interior Ballinger over conservation of the nation's resources, and the President's defense of his cabinet member. Leaguers were still reticent about the big jolly man in the White House, but they did not spare Ballinger in their open defense of Pinchot.[43]

Speaking in support of Taylor's campaign for mayor of San Francisco on the Democratic ticket in September 1909, Hiram Johnson, now a vice-president of the Lincoln-Roosevelt League, defended Heney, attacked Ballinger, and predicted the election of Theodore Roosevelt as President in 1912. At a subsequent meeting Johnson explained that although he was supporting Taylor locally, he was still a Republican. But, he continued significantly, "I do not take my politics from Aldrich, Cannon, or Herrin, or Tim Sullivan." [44] At the same time, Johnson was outspokenly connecting the fight in California with a much greater struggle throughout the nation, and Chester Rowell was editorializing for the organization of a national "progressive or radical party" around the group of insurgents who were then fighting the regular Republican organization in Congress. Two months later the Fresno *Republican* announced that "Progressive Republicans" from all over California were to hold a meeting at Oakland under the auspices of the Lincoln-Roosevelt Republican League.[45] This was the first time, apparently, that the president of the League had publicly used the word "progressive" in connection with that organization. To Chester Rowell and his close friends, hyphenated Republicanism in California had come to mean something more than state reform and war against the Southern Pacific. For by the use of the term "progressive," Rowell had connected the Lincoln-Roosevelt Republican League with a national movement dedicated to changing the Republican party from its traditional standpat, big business bias, to a party of reform.

CHAPTER IV

What Manner of Men: The Progressive Mind

During his controversy with Rudolph Spreckels over the organization of the League, Chester Rowell had argued for a democratic body to be controlled by numerous and flourishing local chapters. Despite his aspirations, the state organizer of the League never achieved his goal. Public apathy and perhaps the disinclination of local leaders to share their power kept the organization extremely small. At the opening of the 1910 campaign no more than a hundred men in the state were really active in League affairs. Rowell had to admit that it was impossible to attain a popular basis and popular control of the League. Except in the city of Berkeley, where Dickson had organized a well-knit group, a lack of interest made democracy impossible. If any action were to be achieved of necessity it "had to be autocratic." [1] From the time of its origin to its disintegration, the progressive movement in California was really inspired, kept alive, and directed by an extremely small group of men. This was particularly true before November, 1910, when the League had neither money, jobs, nor honors to pass out among its followers.

Just what was a California progressive before he took office in 1910, and before power and the exigencies of politics altered his beliefs? What were the springs of his action, his personal aspirations, his concepts of what constituted the good society? Fortunately for the purpose of answering these important questions, the men who organized the California progressive movement were both literate and historically minded. The solid collections of personal manuscripts they so considerately left behind them, the diaries, documents, and innumerable published articles afford the historian an unrivaled opportunity in recent American history to inquire into the origins and the mentality of a grassroots movement. Moreover, the progressive group was small. Fewer than a hundred men attended the two state-wide progressive conferences held in Oakland in 1907 and 1909 before victory swelled the number of the organization's would-be leaders. Of this number the author has been able to track down biographical data on forty-seven men, data which produces a striking picture of similarity in background, economic base, and social attitudes, and which furthermore suggests the strongly selective process inherent in such movements.

Compositely, the California progressive leader was a young man, often less than forty years old.[2] He had probably been born in the Middle West, in Indiana, Illinois, Wisconsin, or Iowa. If not, then he was native to the state.[3] He carried a north-European name, and unless he was one of the two notable exceptions, came of old American stock. These statistics of national origin are even more striking when cast upon the total character of California's polyglot and immigrant population in 1910.

The long religious hand of New England rested heavily upon California progressivism, as it has on so many American movements. Of the twenty-two progressives whose biographies indicate a religious affiliation, seven were Congregationalists, two were Unitarians, and four were Christian Scientists.[4] The educational history of the League's leaders lends additional testimony to their social stratification. In a day when higher education was almost monopolized by the upper middle classes, three of every four had had a college education, and three of the group had studied in European universities. Occupationally, the California progressive held a significant niche in the American economic structure. In the sample obtained, there were seventeen attorneys, fourteen journalists, eleven independent businessmen and real-estate operators, three doctors, and three bankers. At least one-half of the journalists owned their own papers or worked for a family enterprise, and the lawyers, with two exceptions, were not practicing politicians.[5] In the entire group, only two had any connection with a large industrial or financial corporation, save for the ownership of shares. This was a group of highly literate, independent free enterprisers and professional men.

While not wealthy, the average California progressive was, in the jargon of his day, "well fixed." He was more often than not a Mason, and almost invariably a member of his town's chamber of commerce. Finally, he apparently had been, at least until 1900, a conservative Republican, satisfied with McKinley and his Republican predecessors.[6]

Naturally, some fundamental questions arise about these fortunate sons of the upper middle class. Inheriting a secure place in society, earning a reasonably good living, and certainly not radical by temperament, what prompted their political revolt, and what did they want? The answers, of course, like those to most social questions, are extremely complex. They did not lie in California alone or even in the United States, for in its larger aspects the progressive movement was a western European phenomenon, its impulse being felt all over the Western world at the end of the nineteenth and beginning of the twentieth century. Wherever one found that characteristic ferment arising out of Western society's attempt to adjust its archaic agrarian social system to the new industrial and urban world, there one found the moral, humanitarian, and democratic strains of progressivism.

In the United States, what later came to be called the progressive movement started with the birth of the new century. Historically, it drew upon the farmer and labor protests of the preceding forty years, as well as upon the writings of the great nineteenth-century social critics. The Grangers and the Populists, Henry George, Edward Bellamy, and Henry Demarest Lloyd, along with the more strictly literary figures, all made their contributions to the national progressive mentality. But progressivism was not just a reformulation of an older radicalism. Late nineteenth-century tides of national-ism and social religion were also important in the evolution of its basic doctrines. On the whole, its leaders were drawn from a different class than were those of the Grangers and the Populists. In its origins it was an urban rather than a rural movement, and where it did touch the countryside it grew most spectacularly not in the Populist wheat, cotton, and mining regions, but rather in states with more diversified and wealthier economies.

In general, twentieth-century national progressivism was a protest by some peculiarly individualistic social and economic groups against the rapid concentration of twentieth-century American life and its attending ethical, economic, and po-litical manifestations. Since the newly arisen giant business corporation was both the most conspicuous example and agent of that concentrating force, the national progressive attack was launched first against the monopolistic corporation, with its economic and political power and vast corruption of public life. At the same time, whether the average progressive real-ized it or not, the movement was essentially a protest against the changing group and individual relationships growing out of the new industrial and urban social complex. Largely an upper middle-class movement, at least in its leadership, pro-gressivism was not opposed to private property but rather to the impersonal, concentrated, and supposedly privileged property represented by the behemoth corporation. Looking backward to an older America, it sought to recapture and reaffirm the older individualistic values in all the strata of political, economic, and social life.

This great wave of political activity, starting in the United States about 1900, soon left its mark upon literature, journal-ism, education, and the church. The governments of great cities like Toledo, Cleveland, St. Louis, and Minneapolis felt its touch. Its philosophy became the aim of state governments when Robert LaFollette was elected governor of Wisconsin in 1900 and Albert Cummins of Iowa in 1902. It invaded national politics when Theodore Roosevelt proclaimed it from the White House after 1901.

Since California progressivism developed relatively slowly, it was inspired and influenced by progressives and progressive achievements elsewhere. From 1906 to 1910, Robert La-Follette, Joseph W. Folk, Albert B. Cummins, Ray Stannard Baker, and Gifford Pinchot, all spoke in the state in behalf of the progressive cause. Throughout the early progressive campaigns in California, Folk's St. Louis and LaFollette's Wisconsin were cited repeatedly as a city and a state that had freed themselves from the old iniquitous politics. But of all the outside personal forces operating to inspire progressive rebellion in California, Theodore Roosevelt was by far the greatest. His name and his doctrines were grafted into the very origins of the movement, and his position in national affairs was repeatedly used by the Californians as an effective answer to the charges of party treason raised against them. But Theodore Roosevelt was not venerated simply for the advantage his position afforded them. To a great degree, the President's moral and political doctrines struck close to the California progressive ideal. He was a source of inspiration, a symbol of progressive virtues, and a protector at the highest court.

The California progressive did not need to search outside the state, however, for the crude social materials that resulted in the progressive mind. By 1900 California was essentially a microcosm generating all the conditions that led to the progressive ferment elsewhere. Many of the social forces necessary for the progressive revolt, in fact, were far more advanced inside the commonwealth than they were in the Middle Western states of its origin. Perhaps nowhere in the nation was the life of the state dominated to such a degree by one corporation as was California by the Southern Pacific Railroad. What the Standard Oil trust was to the United States in the 'eighties, the Southern Pacific was to California in 1900 —and more. Few other states were as urban as California where almost 50 per cent of its population lived in four metropolitan districts. That meant a large upper middle class of old American stock, composed of persons not too far removed from the attitudes of the individualistic Middle West. Labor, moreover, was organized in the San Francisco region as it was in few other places in the nation. There, as in open-shop Los Angeles, violent class conflict raged, expressing itself through the San Francisco Union Labor party, the bombing of the *Times* in Los Angeles, the state-wide rise of the Socialist party, the Southern Pacific's political machine, and the employers' organizations dedicated to destroying unionism.

When the younger representatives of the upper middle class in California became aware of these conflicting, organized class forces, progressivism was born. It is clear that the California progressive reacted politically when he felt himself hemmed in, and his place in society threatened by the monopolistic corporation on the one side, and by organized labor and socialism on the other. Proof for this general conclusion is not hard to find. The earliest manifestation of what later became progressivism in California is apparent in two local movements which started in 1906, one aimed against the Southern Pacific political machine in Los Angeles, and the other against the control of the Union Labor party in San Francisco. In the opening speech of the progressive crusade against the Southern Pacific in Los Angeles, Marshall Stimson voiced a fundamental principle. The three choices which confronted the voters of the city, he said, were between, "a government controlled by corporate interests, Socialism, or if we have the courage, unselfishness and determination, a government of individuals."

Although Rudolph Spreckels felt it necessary, in launching the graft investigation in San Francisco, to declare that this was not "a class question" between capital and labor but one "of dishonesty and justice," his very phraseology indicated that there was a third group interested in civic affairs with different public standards from those of either labor or capital. From that time until victory in 1910, progressive literature was critical both of politically organized capital and politically organized labor.[7]

The progressive revolt was not only, or perhaps even primarily, a matter of economics. A few progressives had been hurt economically by the railroad and other semimonopolistic corporations; certainly shippers and farmers had been. But the progressive leaders were mainly editors, attorneys, small businessmen, and real-estate operators. Instead of beggaring these men, the railroad occasionally subsidized them, as Fremont Older pointed out. Moreover, this was not a period of depression: mass immigration into the state and the resulting spiral in real-estate values, the great oil boom, the coming of the movies, and the expansion of fruit and vegetable farming produced a wave of prosperity in California which lasted until 1913. If the progressive leaders saw a real and immediate threat from the large corporation to their own economic stake in society, it is not apparent from their letters and their speeches. Nowhere did the California progressives suggest that the big corporation be abolished.

Not quite so much can be said of their attitude toward the labor union. Admitting in theory that the union was a necessary organization in the modern industrial world, the progressives' bias against labor was always greater than against the large corporation. Even the more radical progressives hoped that unions were only a "temporary expedient representing the necessity of one class standing against another" until the time the country got "beyond the questions of class and caste." [8] Most progressives felt that unions could do very little economically for the working man. "The law of supply and demand," Chester Rowell observed, "applies to wages as well as to other prices." In the long run there was "no escaping" that law. Even where unions had demonstrably raised wages for their members, the progressives were sure that the benefits applied only to the few and really hurt the many. Unionism was "but a war measure to provide relative justice to a few." Many progressives could not see why the skilled laborer needed the union for economic purposes, since they considered him the "American aristocrat," who "got the highest wages . . . fixed his own terms . . . and constituted our only leisure class." [9]

So long as organized labor was reasonably ineffective as an economic bargaining agent, the California progressives were inclined to view the movement more or less tolerantly. But as soon as labor aspired to a closed shop, Chester Rowell inveighed against this goal as "antisocial, dangerous, and intrinsically wrong." When the Johnson administration later considered a limitation to the issuance of labor injunctions, Meyer Lissner bitterly protested that if labor's legal status was changed the closed shop would soon be upon Los Angeles as it had been in San Francisco. Lissner was ready, he wrote to Governor Johnson, to let their entire reform movement go down the drain "rather than let Los Angeles be thrown under the sort of tyrannical domination of labor unionism that exists in San Francisco." [10]

The progressive's prejudice against organized labor is further indicated by the fact that not one progressive leader was recruited from the ranks of the unions. In the midst of an early fight against the Southern Pacific machine in Los Angeles, Meyer Lissner wrote that while it was all right "to work through the labor unions" and get their support, he was against any publicity of the tactics. "It may react," he added. Lissner's attitude in 1908 contrasts strongly with his willingness three years later to coöperate with anyone, including the remnants of the old Southern Pacific machine in the city, to stop the challenge of the Socialist party, supported by organized labor.[11]

Despite the attitudes of the Los Angeles group, the progressive opposition to labor on economic grounds should not be overestimated. In the north, Fremont Older, Rudolph Spreckels, Francis Heney, William Kent, and Hiram Johnson were all supporters of labor unions even though they did attack the corrupt Union Labor party. Johnson had acted as counsel for several San Francisco unions, and for years

Older's paper had been frankly prolabor. Both Kent and Heney felt that a large part of their political support came from the laboring ranks, and Heney remarked that it was wiser to trust the labor vote "to stand for what is right and decent in government" than it was to trust the businessmen. Returning from a vacation, Rudolph Spreckels found that the directors of his bank had voted to give $20,000 to the open-shop fund of the San Francisco Chamber of Commerce. Spreckels risked his presidency to fight the action and succeeded only after two antilabor directors had resigned. With Chester Rowell and Irving Martin, editor of the Stockton *Record,* he went to labor's defense repeatedly when industry organized to break the unions and create an open-shop economy.[12]

If there is some evidence to suggest that the progressive orientation against labor was partly economic in origin, what explains the progressive opposition to the Southern Pacific Railroad and its associated corporations? Disgruntlement with insufficient political rewards may have activated some of the older progressive leaders, who, according to Senator Works, had previously worn "the collar of the railroad without seeming irritation."[13] And undoubtedly some of the younger men who later became progressives were incensed when their youthful and independent political efforts were defeated by the machine. But to ascribe the later reform zeal of this minor group to these early defeats begs the larger question. Why did so many young progressives originally engage in independent politics and why, when once spanked, did they not learn their lesson as so many generations of young men had before them, and either quit the game or make their peace with the machine? The answer does not lie entirely in the realm of immediate self-interest but in the broader reaches of human intellect, emotion, and group psychology. Squarely to the point is the fact of the opposition of many progressives, including some of the very rich, not only to the privileged corporations but also to great wealth, particularly if it had been accumulated by means they considered unsocial. As most of them later distinguished between "good" and "bad" trusts, so did they distinguish between "good" and "bad" wealth. Like a repentant sinner, William Kent opened his congressional campaign in 1910 with an apology for his wealth accumulated by land speculation and with a promise to use his fortune to wipe out the system by which he had accumulated it.[14] Few, if any, progressives would have agreed with the novelist Boyensen that all efforts to achieve great wealth were a denial of beauty. But many of them did believe with Goldsmith that:

> Ill fares the land to hastening ills a prey
> Where wealth accumulates and men decay.

"Modern politics," Henry Adams wrote in *The Education of Henry Adams*, "is a struggle not of men but of forces. The men become every year more and more creatures of force massed about central power houses." With the struggle for power between capital and labor penetrating almost every level of California life, and with the individual more and more ignored, the California progressive was increasingly sensitive to that drift and increasingly determined to stop it if possible. This was obvious in his obsession with the nightmare of class consciousness and class rule. "Class government is always bad government," the progressive Los Angeles *Express* vehemently declared, and added that unions "have no more right to usurp the management of public affairs than have the public service corporations." [15] Chester Rowell, probably the most literate of the California progressives, went on to gloss that statement. "Class prejudice among the businessmen," he wrote, "excuses bribery and sanctifies lawlessness and disorder among labor. When the spectre of class rule is raised, then all questions of truth, right, and policy disappear, and the contest is no longer over what shall be the government but wholly who shall be it." This class spirit on both sides, the editor of the Fresno *Republican* lamented, "is destroying American liberty." When it became predominant, he predicted, American institutions would have to be changed.

"For upon that evil day reform ends and nothing but revolution is possible." [16]

Clearly what troubled the independent progressive about both organized capital and labor was not only economics, but questions of high politics, group prestige, group morality, and group power. Involved also was the rising threat to an old American way of life which he represented and which he considered good.

The progressive was a member of an old group in America. As businessman, successful farmer, professional man or politician, he had engaged in extremely individualistic pursuits and had, since the decline of the colonial aristocracy, supplied most of the nation's intellectual, moral, and political leadership. Still confident that he possessed most of society's virtues, the California progressive was acutely aware in 1905 that many of society's rewards and badges of merit were going elsewhere. Before the days of the Rotarians and kindred organizations, he was excluded from or did not care to join the Union League Club or the union labor hall. Although well-educated, he was all but excluded from politics unless he accepted either corporate or labor domination, a thing he was exceedingly loath to do. His church, his personal morality, and his concept of law, he felt, were demeaned by the crude power struggle between capital and labor.

On the defensive for the first time since the disappearance of the old aristocracy, this class of supreme individualists developed a group consciousness themselves. Although generally overlooked by the historian, this consciousness had already developed in some farming elements in the Populist period. Nothing else can be concluded from the words of the official organ of the Michigan State Farmers' Alliance. "It has been truly said," remarked that paper, "that the People's Party is the logical and only nucleus for every element of the American population that stands for social stability and constitutional rights. It is the bulwark against anarchy of the upper and lower scum of society." [17]

Now in the twentieth century, flanked by organized labor

on one side and organized capital on the other, the urban California progressives took up that song. Their letters, journals, and speeches are full of the phrases, "our crowd," "the better element," and "the good people of the state." Even their political enemies recognized their separateness as indicated by the names they conferred upon them. The phrases "goo-goo" and "Our Set" dripped with ridicule. But they also indicated awareness of the progressives' claim to ethical and political superiority. A clear expression of the progressive's self-confidence in his own moral elevation and his contempt for other classes can be found in an editorial of the progressive organ, the *California Weekly*. "Nearly all the problems which vex society," this illuminating item ran, "have their sources above or below the middle-class man. From above come the problems of predatory wealth. . . . From below come the problems of poverty and of pigheaded and brutish criminality." [18] Notwithstanding the average progressive's extreme individualism, this statement was unmistakably an expression of a social group on the march.

The California progressive, then, was militantly opposed to class control and class consciousness when it emanated either from below or above him. This was his point of opposition. What was his positive creed? In the first place this "rank individualist," as he gladly styled himself, was in most cases an extremely religious man. His mind was freighted with problems of morality, his talk shot through with biblical allusions. He often thought of the political movement he had started as a part of the "Religion Forward Movement." [19] As early as 1903, A. J. Pillsbury, who was later to become a leading progressive, praised Theodore Roosevelt for coming nearer "to exemplifying the New England conscience in government than any other president in recent times." [20]

But if the religion of the California progressive was old American in its form, much of its content was a product of his recent past. Gone was the stern God of the Puritan, the abiding sense of tragedy and the inherent evilness of man. As William Allen White later wrote, the cult of the hour was

97

"to believe in the essential nobility of man and the wisdom of God." [21] With an Emersonian optimism, the California progressive believed that evil perished and good would triumph. Sin may have been original, but it did not necessarily have to be transmittable. There was "no natural compulsion," William Kent wrote, "including the lust for blood, the savage passion for reproduction, and the cruder forms of theft that ought not to be overcome by education and public opinion." [22] Under the influence of Darwinism, the rising social sciences, and a seemingly benign world, the progressive had traded some of his old mystical religion for a new social faith.[23] He was aware that evil still existed, but he believed it a man-made thing and upon earth. What man created he could also destroy, and his present sinful state was the result of his conditioning. An editorial in Fremont Older's San Francisco *Bulletin* expressed this reasoning: "The basic idea behind this age of liberalism is the simple one that all men, prisoners and free, rich and poor, are basically alike in spirit. The difference usually lies in what happens to them." [24] And from that one could conclude that when men were given justice, they would return justice to society. The progressive, then, not only wanted to abolish a supernatural hell; he was intent upon secularizing heaven.

There were, of course, individual variations from these generalized patterns. Chester Rowell, for one, while agreeing that men should not be treated as free moral agents, protested against considering them as "mere creatures of environment." "If we try to cure the trouble by curing the environment," Rowell argued, "we shall never go far enough, for however much we protect men from temptation there will be some left and men will fall to that. . . . Dealing with society the task is to amend the system. But dealing with the individual man the task is to reiterate forever, 'thou shall not steal' and tolerate no exceptions. . . ." [25] But Rowell was more of a child of his age than even he realized. Despite his strictures on the sinfulness of man, one found him writing later that Taft's peace treaties made international war impossible because "the moral influence on nations [for peace] would be tantamount to compulsion."[26]

"The way to have a golden age," one progressive novelist wrote, "is to elect it by an Australian ballot." This was an extreme affirmation of democracy, but it followed logically from the progressive belief in the fundamental goodness of the individual. To a surprising degree, this fervent belief in the "rightness" of the democratic process separated the progressive from the conservative politician who usually insisted upon a "representative government" and held that "pure democracy" was a dangerous thing. A few progressives, like Rudolph Spreckels, Chester Rowell, and Senator Works had serious doubts about the efficacy of absolute democracy. For most of them, however, democracy was a thing to venerate.[27]

According to progressive thought, behind every political question was a moral question whose answer "could safely be sought in the moral law."[28] Since most men were ethical agents, public opinion was the final distillate of moral law. It was a jury that "could not be fixed," observed Lincoln Steffens, and to some progressives, it was "God moving among men."[29] For this reason C. D. Willard objected to Theodore Roosevelt's characterization of democracy as just a means to an end. To Willard, democracy was a positive moral force in operation, a good in itself. "It is," he wrote, "a soul-satisfying thing."[30]

Back in the 1890's, Senator Ingalls of Kansas had remarked, "The purification of politics is an iridescent dream." Dream or not, that was one of the major goals of the California progressive a decade later. There was but one law for him—that of the church-going middle class—and he was convinced that it should be applied equally to the home, to government, and occasionally even to business. It was in this spirit that Hiram Johnson admonished his followers to forget how to make men richer and concentrate on how to make them better.[31] This attitude helps to explain much of the progressive interest in sumptuary legislation. Individualism was a sacred thing as long as it was moral individualism; otherwise it needed to be corrected. Thus the progressive proposals for the abolition of prize fighting ("a form of social debauchery"), gambling, slang ("since it is a coverup for profanity"), prostitution, and the liquor traffic. And thus his demands for the censorship of literature, the drama, and social dancing.

In protest against these "holier-than-thou-people" among his fellow progressives, C. K. McClatchey, owner of the Sacramento *Bee*, wrote that he was his "brother's keeper only in so far as I should set him a good example. . . ." [32] And though the progressive, on the whole, vehemently denied the full import of this statement when applied to morality, generally he was not in complete disagreement with McClatchey's views when they were applied to economics. Good Christian that he was, and on the whole benevolent, the California progressive did not quarrel with the doctrine of wardship, provided it was not pushed too far. He stood ready in 1910 to protect obviously handicapped individuals and he was ready and even eager to eradicate what he called "special privilege," which to his mind fundamentally limited opportunity for the man on the bottom to make his way economically upward. A few individuals on the left of the movement, like Congressman William Kent, felt that the progressive and socialist movements were "only different phases of the same tendency" and that soon property rights were going "to tumble about the heads of the men" who had built themselves "pyramids of money in a desert of want and suffering." And Fremont Older raised the disturbing question of why men should be paid fortunes who were lucky enough to have been born with brains or in fortunate environments. One might as well go back to the feudal system, Older answered himself, because there was no more personal merit "in having talent than in having a noble lineage." [33]

But for the most part, the progressive was content with the basic concepts of the economic system under which 1910 capitalism awarded its profits and its pains. He firmly believed in private property, profits, and especially the competitive system and even acknowledged that the corporation and the labor union were necessary instruments of modern business. What the progressive did object to in the year of his triumph was not 1910 capitalism as such, but rather the ideological, economic, moral, and political manifestations which had arisen from that system. He was confident, at least in 1910, that no inevitable causal relation existed between that system and its social results. Moreover, he felt sure that the nexus between the great corporations and the government, on the one hand, and organized labor and government, on the other, could be broken. Once those links were destroyed, he was certain that most of the political corruption would vanish; once "special privilege" was removed, the system would right itself and the individual again would be supreme in economics as well as in politics.

"I would not be a dredger Congressman, or a farm Congressman, or a fresh egg Congressman, or a dairy Congressman," William Kent assured the voters of his district in which all those pursuits flourished. "I would like to be an American Congressman, recognizing the union and the nation." [34] This denial of economic representation and the emphasis upon the general welfare is a perfect example of what the progressive politico saw in himself. Subjectively, he pictured himself as a complete individual wholly divorced from particular economic as well as class interests. Ready to do justice in the name of morality and the common good, he was, in his own estimation, something akin to Plato's guardians, above and beyond the reach of corrupting material forces.

California progressivism was an expression of an older America objecting to the ideological and social drifts of the twentieth century. Representing a particular strain of middle-class individualism, the progressive became militant when he felt himself hemmed in between the battening corporation and the rising labor unions. Considering himself the solid moral element in America, he became exceedingly group conscious even though his group was a collection of supreme in-

101

dividualists. His was a psychological group as well as an economic one, and his rising sensitivity was due as much to social, moral, and political causes as it was to the economic factor. If one can generalize on admittedly shaky grounds, his opposition to the corporation was more political and psychological in nature than it was economic, while perhaps the reverse was true of his attitude toward organized labor. The progressive end—a classless state—was also one of the ends of the Marxists; the difference lay in the kind of classlessness. Whereas the communist, after a violent political and economic revolution, would have frozen his state on the proletariat level, the progressive thought it possible to achieve and perpetuate a middle-class, capitalist level through the peaceful political instrument of democracy. Unlike the Marxists, the California progressive believed it possible to stop the rise of class loyalties without removing existing economic inequalities or destroying existing economic groups. Since he thought primarily in political terms, his main concern was to remove class consciousness from politics. "Progressivism," Chester Rowell wrote in 1912, "believes in nationalism, in individual citizenship, and in the whole people, not in any class as a unit of government. It opposes class government by either the business, the laboring, or any other class, and resists the formation of class parties. It is, in other words, the twentieth-century evolution of democracy." [35]

The California progressive, then, wanted to preserve the fundamental patterns of twentieth-century industrial society at the same time that he sought to blot out, not only the rising clash of economic groups but the groups themselves, as conscious economic and political entities. But he sought to do all this, at least before he had actually taken power, without profound economic reform. "The people," Rowell observed sometime after the progressive victory in 1910, "elected Governor Johnson to get moral and political reform." The word "economic" was significantly absent from the statement. From today's vantage point, the progressive's aim of a capitalist commonwealth:

102

Where none were for a class and all were for the state,
Where the rich man helped the poor and the poor man loved the
    great,[36]

may seem incredibly naïve. His stress on individualism in a
maturing industrial economy was perhaps basically archaic.
His refusal or inability to see the connection between economic institutions and the rising class consciousness indicated
a severe case of social myopia. His hope to avert class strife
by political and moral reform alone were scarcely realistic.
And paradoxical in the extreme was the coexistence of his own
intense group loyalties with his strong antipathy to the class
consciousness of organized capital and organized labor.

When the California progressive confidently took control
of the state in 1910, the road ahead was uncertain indeed.
What, for example, would happen to the fundamental beliefs
of this group if they found their ends could not be achieved
without substantial economic reform; if in spite of their efforts, labor threatened their economic and political estate; if
many of them became economically and psychologically ab-
sorbed in the advancing corporate system; if in a less prosperous age than 1910, the clash between economic groups for
a livelihood created intense social friction? Would their moral
calculus, their spirit of benevolence, their faith in men, their
reverence for democracy still persist?

The fate of progressivism and perhaps the fate of democracy in the twentieth century were wrapped up in the answers
to those questions. For between militantly organized and
class-conscious capital and equally militant class-conscious
labor, the progressive represented for California a makeweight
for compromise, a pivot on which the democratic process
could swing. California urgently needed that makeweight in
1910, until the state and the nation could reconcile the contending ambitions of capital and labor on a better basis than
dynamite and the general strike, and company police and the
lockout. Time was needed to relax the taut emotions of men,
time and just enough action to lull the social pangs of the

economic groups below, and not frighten the wealthy groups above.

Whether or not the progressive could fulfill this role of skillful broker depended not only on his intelligence but also on his heart and ethical sense. Whether he realized it or not, he was himself a capitalist and belonged to one of society's more fortunate groups. In trying to modify the struggle between organized capital and labor, he would be faced in the long run with the necessity of giving up some of his own social perquisites as well as some of the social power of his class. William Kent, for one, believed that it could be done. During the 1910 campaign he wrote an open letter to the working people of his congressional district maintaining, "While the inspiration has always come from below in the advance of human rights . . ." the final accomplishments had come from "the disinterested work of men who, having abundant means, have ranged themselves on the side of those most needing help." A year later he went on to gloss that statement. "I don't believe in the class struggle," he said, "because while the impulse must come from the underdog, every great reform has been taken up and worked out by those who are not selfishly interested. I believe altruism is a bigger force in the world than selfishness." [37] In the largest sense, the rock of progressivism was to rest upon this faith. Whether it was true, and to what degree, only the years following the progressive victory could tell.

CHAPTER V

Rebellion Becomes Revolution

*

A governor of California was to be elected in 1910, and in January of that year the first and most important business of the Lincoln-Roosevelt League was to select a candidate. Since League strength was weaker and more divided in the north, the executive committee in its November meeting decided that the candidate should be a northerner. But little agreement was obtained then or afterward on who the man should be. During 1908 both Chester Rowell and Edward Dickson had proposed Francis J. Heney in their papers, and as late as October, 1909, Heney was still their choice. Heney had other powerful support. William Kent, Fremont Older, and a good share of the Los Angeles group were for him. Compared with other proposed candidates, William R. Davis, Mayor Mott of Oakland, Charles M. Belshaw of Antioch, Harris Weinstock of Sacramento, and Hiram Johnson of San Francisco, Heney seemed far and away the most logical man. By his courageous stand in the San Francisco graft trials, Heney had placed himself in the ranks of any serious state reform movement. He was probably the best known man in the League and perhaps its most effective speaker. He was a friend of Theodore Roosevelt and he was supported locally by a group of powerful men, men to whom the League owed its very existence.[1]

Heney's name was proposed in the first informal gathering the League leaders held to talk over possible candidates. The San Francisco contingent and the more conservative elements in the group raised immediate and strenuous objections to his personal qualities and his political convictions. They pointed out that his conduct during the graft trials had been

105

unbecoming to a candidate for the governorship. More to the point, they protested against his violent attacks upon the wealthy men of San Francisco, as well as his alleged fondness for labor. Conservatives had not forgotten Heney's public remark during the trials that he had more faith in the laboring class vote to secure decent government than in the business vote. His former Democratic affiliations and his close attachment to Theodore Roosevelt alienated him further from the more politically cautious. Heney was given up, Rowell wrote, as an "impolitic choice because of his radicalism." In his stead, the conservative faction proposed the names of state legislator Charles M. Belshaw and Frank K. Mott, then thrice mayor of Oakland. Most of the League leaders were inclined to consider the Oakland mayor seriously but they were adamant against Belshaw.

Of all the prospective candidates, Belshaw alone had been making an active campaign. Early in May of 1909 he had written to Dickson in an obvious attempt to enlist the Los Angeles man's support. But Dickson, remembering Belshaw's refusal to commit himself to the League, and his insistence that he did not want to be a candidate of any "political faction" but rather of the entire party, was not enthusiastic, and said so to his League comrades. Rowell, for his part, was prepared to be "very stubborn and ugly" about Belshaw, and Older threatened that he would not support the Contra Costa man in his paper even if he were selected by the League.[2]

Rowell and many other northern Californians would probably have been satisfied with Mott as a compromise candidate. But Older again interposed strong objections to the proposal. Writing that he had fought Mott in his last Oakland campaign, Older flatly stated that his *Bulletin* would not support either Mott or Belshaw in the coming primary campaign. And when Mott failed to secure the support of the southern California group, his cause seemed lost.

By the first of January, 1910, it was apparent that only three men of all the possible candidates, namely Johnson, Davis, and Weinstock, would satisfy the great majority of the League directorate. Of the three, Johnson, who by this time had the fervid support of Rowell, Dickson, Lissner, Stimson, and Older, was by far the most popular. But despite great pressure, Johnson steadfastly refused to run. And to intensify the predicament, neither Davis nor Weinstock wanted the honor.

With the future of the League at stake, Rowell, Dickson, Stimson, and Lissner twice held informal, unsuccessful conferences with other members of the organization's executive committee. Rowell feared that Belshaw, who had already threatened to run independently if Heney were selected, might make capital out of the conflicting sentiments. And so once again strenuous efforts were made to persuade either Johnson or Davis to accept the honor. Both, according to Rowell, were preëminently qualified because of their reputation as "conservative reformers." [3]

Since a majority of the League obviously preferred Johnson to Davis, and Davis again insisted that he would not run, a concerted campaign was started to persuade him to change his mind. An unsigned article written by Rowell in the *California Weekly* of January 21, praising Hiram Johnson as the coming man of the League, indicated the drift of the wind. A few days after its appearance, a meeting which Rowell felt would be the "most important conference of the campaign," was held at Johnson's house in San Francisco. With an executive committee meeting a week away, Rowell, his uncle, Dickson, and Stimson gathered for a Sunday dinner at which they tried to persuade Johnson to become a candidate. Gloomily, the four returned home after Johnson told them "with absolute positiveness" that he would not even consider the candidacy. Gloomily, Rowell wrote to Davis asking him to reconsider his refusal "as something less than absolute." At that hour, Rowell pointed out, Mott and Heney seemed to be the only two alternatives to Belshaw, and he realized that Davis was opposed to the selection of either. Therefore, Davis and Johnson were "the only two paths at once safe and creditable. . . ." [4]

When Davis again unqualifiedly refused, Rowell once more turned to Johnson. Among the reasons that Hiram Johnson had given for his decision were the financial loss he would incur by leaving his law practice, his wife's opposition to his entrance into politics, her dislike of Sacramento as a place to live, and his own aversion to being placed in a position where he would have to repudiate everything his father had stood for politically. But another potent, if unspoken, factor in Johnson's refusal was his attitude toward Francis J. Heney, whose place he had taken in the graft trials after Heney was shot. The relations between the two men were already sensitive, and the search for a League candidate increased the tension. Johnson was aware that Heney wanted to be "coaxed" into accepting the candidacy. The only thing left to do, Rowell wrote to Heney's closest friend in the League, Fremont Older, was to get Johnson's consent to run and Heney's promise not to. But he feared that neither could be had and, in the case of Heney, he did "not have the heart to try to obtain it." Fortunately, Older took the hint, and a certain Mr. Kuhl left the *Bulletin* office the next day for Oregon, where he sought Heney's support for the concerted attempt to get Johnson's acceptance. This campaign was to start publicly as soon as "Older pulled the first trigger." [5]

These intricate plans, however, were almost destroyed by a dispatch in the San Francisco *Examiner* that Heney had announced his candidacy. Following a telegram from Rowell, Heney repudiated the dispatch as "a willful misrepresentation" and denied his candidacy. With the proper effusion of regret for the "widespread disappointment at this decision," Rowell printed Heney's statement the next day in the Fresno *Republican*, accepting it as only "provisionally final." [6] He added the heartfelt wish that "if some strong and positive candidate—Hiram Johnson for instance—could be induced to stand for the nomination, it would solve the whole problem of fairness to everybody." In reply to Heney, Rowell wrote that he realized Heney "was itching to get into the fight," but that the situation within the League made the choice of Johnson "imperative," a fact of which Older was also convinced. If Johnson did not run, the alternative was to transform the best of the League into a "personal Heney organization with a big Belshaw split and a general breakup." But Rowell and Older, in order to stop Belshaw and Mott, were now placing all their bets on Johnson. The first formal vote was taken on the proposed candidates at the League executive committee meeting on February 7, with the result that Johnson was an overwhelming choice. As against four first place votes for Belshaw and one apiece for Mott and Heney, Johnson obtained sixteen.[7] The only obstacle now in the way of a united League was Hiram Johnson's consent to be the candidate.

Approached immediately after the vote, Johnson still declined, even though he thoroughly understood the dangerous situation that existed within the League. Then the effects of the concerted, persuasive campaign began to tell. When Heney disclaimed any interest in the candidacy and generously announced his support of Johnson, at least one of the latter's "absolute conditions" had been complied with. But even a greater deterrent to the Johnson candidacy was Mrs. Johnson's attitude. When Rowell first approached her she remarked that she "would rather die than have her husband run for the governorship." She disliked the demands of official life, objected to living in Sacramento, thought that her husband would thoroughly detest the job, and was sure that he would be defeated. If her husband went into politics at all, she preferred that he run for the United States Senate instead of for governor. Extended conversations with Rowell, Stimson, Dickson, and Lissner, about which her husband apparently knew nothing until much later, began to change Mrs. Johnson's mind. Perhaps what contributed to her reversal of opinion was Stimson's assurance that the governorship was a perfect springboard for the Senate, and his specific promise that he would support Johnson for the Senate if he first tried for the state office. After two long talks with Rowell over the long distance telephone, Mrs. Johnson urged her husband to accept the League offer. Ill and confined to his bed, Hiram Johnson was still reluctant. According to Rowell, it was only after the persuasive Heney talked to him that he agreed to become a candidate, provided a state convention of the League were called and he were nominated by such a body.

Meanwhile, the southern California group was apparently unaware of Johnson's change of heart. They had gone home assured that Johnson would not run, and with that in mind, Dickson had proposed that they consider Harris Weinstock, president of the Weinstock-Lubin Company of San Francisco and Sacramento and a man who had supported the League idea from the days of its infancy. The suggestion was accepted by the Los Angeles contingent, except for a few people, in particular Marshall Stimson, who insisted that one more effort be made to persuade Johnson to accept. On February 19 when the executive committee met in San Francisco to take final action, it appeared that Weinstock might be the one chosen. After the third ballot, Weinstock, with eighteen of the twenty-eight votes cast, was formally selected. But although he agreed to accept the nomination if necessary, the San Francisco merchant also insisted that one last effort be made to persuade Johnson to accept the nomination. The suggestion was accepted and Marshall Stimson was appointed chairman of a committee to approach the reluctant favorite. Johnson yielded, and the executive committee, by a vote of twenty-one to six, named Johnson the official candidate of the Lincoln-Roosevelt League. On the same day the new-found candidate issued the prosaic statement, "I go to bat." [8]

On the morning of February 20, League papers jubilantly announced that Hiram Johnson had been selected to "redeem the state" in the name of decency and democracy. In the midst of such moral elation it was perhaps discourteous for the opposition press to point out wryly that this champion of democracy had been selected in a most undemocratic fashion, by twenty-eight men at best and probably by a good many less. This embarrassing question of boss rule had even more point than the foes of the League knew.

A majority of the League executive committee had voted

three times in January, 1910, to assemble a "full representative assembly" to select a candidate. But each time, according to Rowell, the southern California delegates, accustomed to choosing their candidates in Los Angeles by the "cabinet method," refused to accept the majority will. Rowell, the president of the League, protested vigorously, and as late as the first of February wrote that he was for Johnson but, "The committee will not take the final responsibility of committing the League to him or to anyone if I can help it." In the face of the stubborn resistance from southern California, however, principle retreated before expediency and Johnson was selected by the few. As the opposition pointed out, the League reformers had used the same "star-chamber caucus methods" as the machine. An identical pattern was to be followed in naming the other League candidates in 1910 and thereafter. Even when the Progressive party was founded as an ostensible protest against boss rule, the same procedures, except on one notable occasion, prevailed. Thus the organizational ideas of Rudolph Spreckels partly triumphed. The League, unquestionably striving for democratic reforms in the state, was either unable or disinclined to adopt democratic methods in the selection of its own candidates.[9]

However undemocratic the League's process of selection, its candidate, measured by the typical California politician, was undoubtedly a most unusual man. In 1866 Hiram Johnson had been born into a politically conscious family. His father, Grover Johnson, had moved to California from the East. Making an early alliance with the railroad machine, Grove Johnson quickly ascended the political escalator until he became a member of the United States Congress in the 'nineties. Defeated because of his support of the Southern Pacific in the refunding struggle, he still remained a power in the state legislature and regularly led the forces of the standpat machine. Even his enemies admitted his intelligence and political ability. In an attack on the notorious legislative session of 1907, Older's San Francisco *Bulletin* called it the creature of the Southern Pacific and Grove Johnson. "In fact," the *Bulletin* concluded, "at most sessions, as in the present session, Johnson is the whole assembly." [10]

Young Hiram was educated in the Sacramento public schools and at the University of California. He left the University in the middle of his junior year to marry and soon entered the law firm of his father and elder brother, the brilliant but erratic Albert M. Johnson. For a time, relations between the three men were outwardly peaceful, and the two sons managed their father's first campaign for Congress. But both sons advised him against a try for reëlection on the grounds that his lack of faith with the people of California and his support of the Southern Pacific made his defeat inevitable. When they refused to take part in the second campaign, father and sons were estranged for many years. The two brothers themselves first ventured into politics by supporting a reform campaign to clean up wide-open Sacramento. As a reward for his support, Hiram was appointed city attorney by the reform mayor, George H. Clark, from which office the young crusader declared open war on the vice and gambling interests battening on the town. During Clark's reëlection campaign, Sacramento was regaled by the unusual scene of a father bitterly attacking his sons from a political rostrum. As the two brothers toured the town speaking in Clark's defense, the father replied for the machine. One night, at the height of the campaign, when the tent meetings of Johnson and his sons were within a block of each other, old Grove referred to his "two chief enemies down the street, one Hiram, full of egotism, and the other Albert, full of booze." [11]

Shortly after the successful reëlection of Mayor Clark, the two brothers moved to San Francisco, where they established a joint law firm. They drifted apart; Hiram became one of the best trial lawyers of the city, and Albert went on his way to an alcoholic's death. Because of his courtroom reputation and his reform record, Hiram Johnson was appointed as Heney's successor in the San Francisco graft trials. As the chief graft prosecutor he first attracted the attention of the state reform element. He further enhanced his antimachine reputation by his forceful speeches in support of the Lincoln-Roosevelt Republican League, speeches in which he repeatedly called himself a progressive Republican and a follower of Theodore Roosevelt. Such talk was music to the reformers, and Johnson was soon placed on the city executive committee. His selection as the League's candidate for the governorship followed.[12]

Hiram Johnson was a rather short and stocky man. His round and somewhat florid face set upon a high celluloid collar was rarely caught smiling. Almost invariably, his public photographs depicted him in a fighting mood, his body tense and a clenched fist held out in front of him. When not on public view his manner was pleasant rather than urbane. He despised formality, whether in public or private life, and he was direct and simple with all of his associates. Johnson could not be called a cultured man. He rarely read anything not connected with law or politics, and the extremely rare allusions in his speeches were drawn from those fields. His favorite evening recreation was attending moving picture shows.[13]

Even on political or legislative matters Johnson, according to his colleagues, was not a profound student. Instead of digging for facts he preferred to analyze a situation in conversation with his advisors. He was not quick to act and was often extremely cautious. He preferred the advice of "practical men" and tended to distrust too much intelligence. Aside from the moralities that peppered his speeches, Johnson rarely indulged in speculative thought. On the stump, as before a jury, he relied almost entirely on emotional appeal.

Considering his family history, it is little wonder that Hiram Johnson was a sensitive and thin-skinned rebel. Emotionally, he was a lifelong member of the opposition, and his greatest talents lay in tilting with existing forces which he considered evil and not in constructive statesmanship. A fighter in every ounce of his body, Johnson greatly admired men "of fighting guts." His own attack upon a problem was never subtle or diplomatic. He met the enemy head on and rarely varied his thrust. This was in part what Chester Rowell meant when he told Johnson that he reminded him of a local doctor who knew a great deal about curing fits. If a patient had fits he quickly cured him, but if he did not exhibit the customary signs, the doctor promptly gave him fits and then promptly cured him. Johnson, who was then governor, did not appreciate the comparison.[14]

Hiram Johnson had a curious mental tenacity. Once he adopted a position he held to it with all his strength, often irrespective of later evidence. It is doubtful whether he ever really forgave what he considered a personal slight, whether real or fancied. Viewed most kindly, Hiram Johnson's inflexibility, if not downright narrow stubbornness, might be considered consistency and fixedness of purpose. Completely partisan in any struggle he entered, Johnson also had the Roosevelt characteristic of seeming righteously cocksure. In a struggle, his outward attitude belied all doubt. He stood for the forces of light, and the opposition was obviously allied with the devil. Carrying his courtroom habits into politics, he could and did impugn the motives and good intentions of the most honest and intelligent of men who happened to oppose him. Senator Borah's later statement, "When a man opposes Johnson, he hates him," may have been true, at least in the heat of a struggle.[15]

Perhaps these traits came from a more basic one of a feeling of insecurity. For Hiram Johnson was a nervous, moody, and insecure person. On a night before a big speech he was rarely able to sleep for fear that his effort would not come off well. Inclined to overestimate the strength of his opposition, he was invariably pessimistic about the results of a campaign. Even in the most one-sided elections he was certain that defeat lay ahead. As he magnified his troubles, he often became certain that he was being persecuted by friends and foes alike. At such times he was a hard man to live with. But then his spirit might change with the speed of the wind for reasons his close confidants could never discern. Rowell realized that

Johnson's occasional irascibility might give way to a contrary feeling "whenever the moon changes or whatever is the phenomena which shifts his moods." [16]

Johnson was described by some of his contemporaries as a profoundly self-centered man, egotistical in the extreme, enormously ambitious, and without a shred of loyalty to his friends and supporters. Certainly facets of his character bordered on all of these qualities, perhaps to a greater extent than those found in the average ambitious politician. One of his close colleagues was probably right in accusing Johnson of having such an intensely jealous nature that he hated to see other leaders emerge "who would not place their hands in his and express their undying loyalty." Probably not in jocularity and friendship alone did Johnson as governor sometimes sign his letters to political subordinates, "The Boss." Unquestionably, Johnson disliked Francis J. Heney because he saw him as a possible rival for acclaim and votes. If not enviable, that is a part of human nature not unknown in other men. But what explains Johnson's actions when he first walked into the Governor's office in Sacramento? Seeking to please him, some of his friends had hung a picture of George C. Pardee on the wall. While not strongly progressive, former Governor Pardee had acted independently of the Southern Pacific and had been defeated by the railroad machine for reëlection in 1906. In the campaign of 1910, moreover, Pardee had loyally supported the League and Johnson's candidacy. But when the governor-elect saw Pardee's picture, he brusquely ordered his staff to take it down, without comment or explanation. [17]

One historian of California has written that those of Johnson's friends who had sacrificed their own political ambitions, "later found that it was safer to trust a broken reed than to rely on Johnson's loyalty and good faith, for the man's self-interest was too highly developed to leave much room for gratitude." [18] Those are harsh words and probably somewhat unfair. They have been charged against most successful statesmen who have had to sacrifice friends and former supporters in the interest of self-survival and what they sincerely believe is the public good. Theodore Roosevelt and Woodrow Wilson are two cases in point from Johnson's own political generation. Public politics is a cruel game. As issues and events shift, today's supporters are tomorrow's opponents. Should a man be faithful to past friends, to his own concepts of statecraft, or to his constituents and his own self-interest? Sometimes an inexorable choice has to be made, and only the man who views his own beliefs and democracy with indifference can consistently place political friendship above conviction.

But if Hiram Johnson possessed human frailties, he also had many sterling virtues both as a man and as a candidate. He had a great desire to serve the public interest, and he was unquestionably incorruptible and courageous. Those qualities alone were striking indeed when measured by the usual pattern of California politicians. Moreover, he was not without native ability. It is interesting to note that while William Kent estimated him as only "adequate" in that regard, William Allen White, looking back from the vantage point of 1933, thought of him as the only Republican governor of the prewar years who was of "presidential size." [19] Johnson also possessed many valuable political assets in 1910. His long reform background and his eight-year connection with organized labor as an attorney for the teamsters were to serve him well, yet he had not antagonized the wealthier classes as Francis J. Heney had done. He had an enormous audience appeal for all strata of society. Although his speeches might not read well, his personal flair for exciting public interest and his vigorous delivery attracted huge crowds. Whether one agreed or disagreed with Hiram Johnson, there was no ignoring him on the stump. By 1918 Chester Rowell thought of him as "the most effective orator in America." While this statement was probably too inclusive, Johnson had little competition in California as a campaigner. The Lincoln-Roosevelt League had chosen its candidate wisely. Hiram Johnson's human shortcomings were not as apparent to the public as his many virtues. As an instrument of protest against the Southern Pacific Railroad and its heritage of machine and dishonest politics, this moody rebel, superb in invective and attack and dominated by a desire for public righteousness, was very nearly ideal.

With the main decision made, the League set about choosing the rest of its ticket by the same undemocratic methods used in selecting the candidate for governor. Since the lieutenant-governorship had been allotted to southern California, the Los Angeles leaders selected Albert J. Wallace for this second place. A self-made businessman, Wallace had proved his antimachine inclinations by serving on the Los Angeles reform city council. John M. Eshleman was selected to run for railroad commissioner, A. B. Nye for state controller, and William D. Stephens, former mayor of Los Angeles, for United States Congress. Except for William Kent and John D. Works, every important League candidate was hand-picked by the small inner group of League leaders. When Kent first proposed that he run for Congress as the League candidate in the Congressional district immediately north of San Francisco, Rowell and other members of the League directorate gave him no encouragement. They only agreed to his inclusion in their family of candidates when Kent threatened to support a Democrat or announce his own candidacy on an independent ticket. Since Rowell felt that League support of a Democrat for a partisan office would be "misinterpreted" throughout the state, they endorsed the Marin County man.[20]

Far more trouble and embarrassment for the League came over the selection of a candidate for the United States Senate. Since the incumbent senator was a northerner, Rowell, who had been mentioned for the position, was passed over. Lee C. Gates and Willis H. Booth were then offered the honor. They refused; Booth, according to a rumor, only after he had held a conference with William H. Herrin of the Southern Pacific. Meanwhile, John D. Works, a former Supreme Court Justice intimated that if he were not selected he would run as an independent. In the face of that threat to reform unity, and unable to agree on anyone else, the Los Angeles Leaguers

117

were finally and most reluctantly forced to accept Works. But almost as soon as the decision was final, serious efforts were made to remove him from the ticket, efforts that continued until Works was formally elected to the office by the state legislature. When the candidate, a few weeks after his selection, published an article critical of Theodore Roosevelt, a formal meeting of the Los Angeles leaders was held in the Hotel Alexandria to consider the possibility of withdrawing League support. At a League conference in San Francisco in December and again in the legislature of 1911, some of the southern leaders proposed that he be sacked. Perhaps this opposition arose from the suspicion that Works was a poor progressive at best, or perhaps as Rowell suggested, from the growing ambition of several Los Angeles Leaguers to try for the office themselves. At any rate, had it not been for the rigid opposition of both Rowell and Hiram Johnson, Works perhaps would have been repudiated. Johnson himself believed that what stilled the opposition was his declaration that no support would be forthcoming for any other candidate from southern California.[21]

Meanwhile, the old Southern Pacific machine had decided that Governor Gillett's record was too much of a burden to carry against the League threat; but the questions of whom to support and how to concentrate regular strength behind the chosen man were perplexing. The death of E. H. Harriman in the fall of 1909, the partial rout of the standpatters in the legislature, and above all, the passage of the new primary law had all dealt heavy blows to the machine. Where once power and unified command existed, there was now chaos. This was apparent when Secretary of State Charles F. Curry announced his candidacy in the fall of 1909 without the usual blessing by Herrin. Curry tried to obtain that support as a matter of course. But he also attempted to win over the independent Republicans in the state, and at one time even hoped to get an endorsement from the Lincoln-Roosevelt League. Twice in the autumn of 1909 Curry wrote to Dickson promising that he would be "no man's Governor" if elected. Dickson encouraged him to announce his candidacy at least twice. But Dickson was also craftily persuading other regular candidates to run so that the former consolidated regular strength would be splintered among several aspirants. And as Philip A. Stanton, former Speaker of the Assembly, Nathan Ellery, the state engineer, and Alden Anderson of Sacramento, all announced their candidacy as regular Republicans without consulting Herrin, the prospects of the League looked increasingly encouraging.

After a disastrous delay, the old machine made it known that Alden Anderson was the railroad's choice. But by then it was far too late to consolidate strength behind a single candidate, for the popular primary gave one man as good a chance as another. Curry, Stanton, and Ellery all refused to withdraw, and so in the spring of 1910 the old guard turned to face its new enemy with its prestige shattered, its ranks divided, and its spirits low.

Jubilant over the serious division in the opposition, League speakers, even though the primary was not scheduled until August, were already in the field by the end of March. Never before had a California campaign started so early, and rarely had the state seen such sustained activity. For the next four months Hiram Johnson practically lived on the road. Wearing out one automobile and switching to another, Johnson entered almost every county in the state and spoke in every sizable town and city. The drum and fife corps which regularly preceded him into a town and his "red devil" automobile became familiar sights to the average Californian. So did the energetic candidate waving his hands like Theodore Roosevelt and exclaiming, "Bully!" on every possible occasion.

For the next four months Hiram Johnson concentrated his attack upon the Southern Pacific Railroad. From his opening declaration of principles to his last speech in the Dreamland Rink in San Francisco, he cried to the four corners of the state, "The Southern Pacific must keep its dirty hands out of politics." It is not quite true that he made only one speech in the campaign—his first one. Here and there he elaborated the theme to denounce "the men in broadcloth," "the poison press," and the tenderloin, all allied against him in this campaign for righteousness. Johnson disclaimed "any attack upon property" but he continually referred to the corrupt alliance between big business and the criminal element. It was not the labor unions or "ye of common clay" who were the enemies of decency and honesty, but "your big banker, your big merchant, sinning respectability joining hands with the criminal and the thug." The League campaign had not touched only two elements in the state, the candidate explained in his home town: "One inhabits the hovels of Pacific Street, and the other populates the mansions of Pacific Avenue." [22]

The battle, Johnson maintained, was between "the great moral masses" and "the corrupt but powerful few." Quoting Carlyle in one of his rare literary allusions, he maintained that California stood in 1910 where the French common people had stood at the battle of Valmy when they triumphed over nobility. But in every speech Johnson returned to the railroad as Kearney had to the Chinese. This Beast, the Southern Pacific, which stalked the jungle of California politics, Johnson fairly shouted to his audiences, must be hunted out from its maze of organized wealth, vice, and corruption. [23]

Confining the primary campaign to a single issue was good politics, as an ironic Johnson supporter pointed out. It had the virtues "of relieving the candidate from the necessity of considering other issues and thereby subjecting himself to mental effort and also from being misunderstood." But such a campaign, whatever its merits, was scarcely designed to promote comprehensive progressive ideals throughout California. In fact, the only progressive candidate who attempted to fight the primary campaign on an avowed progressive platform was a Johnny-come-lately to the League ranks and one who had not been entirely welcomed. That was William Kent, who had left Chicago in 1908 and settled at Kentfield in Marin County.

A wealthy son of one of the founders of the lake city, young

Kent grew increasingly disturbed at the tremendous returns he was receiving from the Chicago traction stock inherited from his father. An inquiry acquainted him with the business and political practices of the Chicago traction magnate, Yerkes. Further investigation into municipal politics revealed the close and corrupt connection between some of the city's great corporations and the great vice interests. Indignant, Kent ran for the city council, was elected in 1895, and from that time until he left for California, he fought with a group of wealthy Chicago reformers in the interests of clean government against the Yerkes of LaSalle Street and the Bathhouse Coughlins of the famous first ward. Like many other members of this Chicago group, Kent began to interest himself in the more basic questions of American society. By the time he came to California he belonged to the left wing of the progressive movement and logically joined forces with the Fremont Older–Francis Heney group in the Lincoln-Roosevelt League. Characteristically, he refused to follow the lead of Hiram Johnson during the campaign of 1910 but chose instead to challenge his reactionary opponent, Congressman Duncan E. McKinley, with an advanced progressive platform. In reply to a shocked and protesting McKinley, Kent wrote, "An income tax will tend toward a levelling of property-holding, which is a desirable thing in a democracy. I also believe in the principle of an inheritance tax which will tend to dissipate great fortunes." [24] Among all the leading Lincoln-Roosevelt candidates, Kent alone in the primary did not confine himself to the railroad issue but supported an advanced progressive platform that included, in addition to progressive taxation, proposals for the freeing of organized labor from its legal disabilities and the complete control of large corporations in the public interest.

But if the great majority of League speakers refused to commit themselves to specific progressive measures locally, this was not their attitude toward national affairs. Every League candidate unqualifiedly aligned himself with the progressive Republican movement then taking shape in Washington and throughout the nation. Never once mentioning President Taft in his campaign, Johnson again and again reiterated that he was proud to be called an "insurgent Republican" and a follower of Theodore Roosevelt. "I am not a regular Republican," he exclaimed at Los Angeles just a few days before the primary election. And where Johnson led, William Kent, Albert J. Wallace, William D. Stephens, and even John D. Works followed. This was important for the future of national politics, because even then the Taft administration was engaged in a great battle to root out insurgency from the Republican party. In the Middle West everything possible was being done by President Taft, Nelson W. Aldrich, and Speaker Cannon to encompass the defeat of Senator LaFollette and his fellow progressives. Johnson was included in this purge, on the administration's admission. A victory for Johnson meant a defeat for Taft.[25]

With the administration against them, the Leaguers naturally sought encouragement from Theodore Roosevelt, then on his way home from his long visit in Africa and Europe. During his first speech in Los Angeles, Johnson paid a flowery tribute, "to him to whom we are holding out our hands and who is soon to come from Africa." But the former President was not in the mood for handholding with the Leaguers. On the contrary, one of the regular Republican candidates, Philip Stanton, boasted that he might obtain the Roosevelt endorsement. To stop such a frightful eventuality, Marshall Stimson was sent East to see the Colonel. There he, Heney, Mark Sullivan, and Gifford Pinchot devised a plan to make it appear that Roosevelt was extremely favorable to Johnson. Immediately after a conference with Roosevelt, Pinchot announced that he was leaving to speak for Johnson in California. The next day progressive papers announced that Pinchot's trip was a direct result of the conference and consequently could be interpreted as a Roosevelt endorsement. As such political tricks often do, the scheme boomeranged when Roosevelt publicly wired Stanton that he was not taking sides in the California struggle. The California progressives had to be content with a letter Roosevelt wrote to his son, which he was instructed to show them. "I am with the insurgents in this fight," the wily former President wrote, "but not for publication." [26]

Although the League was unsuccessful in getting Roosevelt's overt support, its affairs continued to look up. For the first time in its history the League found it relatively easy to obtain a goodly amount of money. With an important newspaper in every county of the state enrolled in its support, publicity was also easy.

By the time Johnson began to campaign, the organization started by Dickson and Rowell was state-wide. In every county and in practically every inhabited locality of the state, the League organization was at least equal in efficiency, if not superior, to the old Republican machine. For election purposes the state had characteristically been divided between north and south. The campaign organization was headed in the north by Rowell and Frank Devlin, in the south by Dickson. In Los Angeles, Lissner, Stimson, and Avery took the responsibility for running the campaign. Elsewhere throughout the state Edgar Luce, George Marsten, John Eshleman, H. L. Carnahan, former Senator Bard, Irving Martin, Robert Waring, George C. Pardee, A. B. Nye, Daniel Ryan, and A. E. Boynton, and a host of lesser figures contributed their time and energies to the struggle.

As the campaign wore on, almost everyone became more and more certain of the result, everyone that is, except the leading candidate. Characteristically, Hiram Johnson maintained his gloomy pessimism and grew touchier as each day of the campaign passed. In March he sulphurously expressed himself about campaigning with Albert J. Wallace, the League candidate for lieutenant governor, a bore on the stump, Johnson wrote, after whom it was impossible to speak effectively. When his automobile broke down the following month Johnson demanded that the League give him a new one. It proposed to lend him one instead, but he refused to accept and threatened to go on with his old one until it broke down completely and then stop his campaign. "God deliver me from the Lincoln-Roosevelt Republican League," was his acid conclusion. During May he felt that his whole two-week campaign in southern California had been a complete "frost." Even with red fire and bands, the local committees had not half filled the halls in either Riverside or San Bernardino. All through the campaign Johnson sourly objected to the entourage of newspapermen whom he claimed were living off him, and to the host of minor candidates who spoke before him and "tired the crowds" before he had a chance to get at them.[27]

Johnson's petulance was partly due to weariness from the most strenuous campaign California had ever witnessed and partly to his rising irritation at the tactics of the opposition press. Led by the Los Angeles *Times,* the San Francisco *Chronicle,* and the Hearst sheets, these regular journals spared neither their opponents' feelings nor their own dignity. It is hard to find a level to which they did not stoop. In that respect Harrison Gray Otis' *Times* led all the rest by a wide margin. In a way this was strange. Otis had fought the railroad in the *Times* years before the League had even been conceived. Strange also was the fact that Otis had never been invited to help organize either the Los Angeles nonpartisan municipal movement or the later Lincoln-Roosevelt League. The answer of course lay in the rivalry and personal bitterness between Otis and Edwin T. Earl, publisher of the Los Angeles *Express.* Since Earl was a leading spirit in the origin of both movements, Otis was never consulted. Realizing the powerful support that Otis could give the reformers, Lissner had tried as early as 1907 to interest Dickson in enlisting the aid of the *Times.* But the only answer he got, he reported, was silence.

Had not personal factors entered into the equation, Lissner and Stimson thought Otis might conceivably have supported both the nonpartisan group and the Lincoln-Roosevelt League, at least in its earliest days. Considering Otis' violent conservatism, it is doubtful whether he could long have supported the state organization when once it began to identify itself with national progressive politics. That would have been contrary to his deepest political instincts. But that contingency never arose. With some reason, Otis felt that the city of Los Angeles was peculiarly his preserve and his pointed exclusion from both local movements no doubt touched the old warrior's pride. The *Times* became the earliest and bitterest enemy of the reform movement and remained so consistently down through the spring of 1910.

At that time, however, Lissner, the practical politician, once again thought it possible and worthwhile to obtain the friendship of the powerful paper. With Stimson and a few others, he hatched the scheme to mollify the old man by nominating W. J. Hunsaker, Otis' own personal attorney and friend, for United States Congress on the League ticket. Since Lissner was definitely *persona non grata* at the *Times*, Stimson was sent to get Otis' reaction to the plan. Otis remained silent for a long time after Stimson made the peace proposal. Then he angrily jumped up from his chair, struck the desk with his fist, and in a masterful stream of profanity damned Earl and all his works. "That man, E. T. Earl," he shouted, "sent you here to bribe me by having my own attorney go to Congress. To hell with him. You never invited the *Times* to join the Lincoln-Roosevelt League." The *Times*, the old general continued, was fighting the Southern Pacific when Earl was still taking their rebates. Followed by a further burst of profanity, Stimson left the office.[28]

After that incident the *Times* fairly outdid itself inveighing against "Holy Hi," "Chattering Chet," "Mush Stimson," and "Three Ball Lissnerski." The latter, in *Times* invective, was acting "true to the traditions and the precepts of his race." All of which was bad enough. But for Johnson, worse was to follow. A little more than a week before he was to speak in Los Angeles, the *Times* started to attack him through his father. On July 27 a cartoon appeared entitled "Like Father, Like Son," in which both Grove and Hiram were depicted as hired tools of the railroad. Day by day thereafter the *Times*

125

charged that Hiram had left the pay of the Southern Pacific and his father Grove only when the grass was greener elsewhere. After the *Times* had opened this evil chorus Hiram Johnson was often slandered by an attack upon his father. Unquestionably reflecting his own family history, he was peculiarly sensitive to such charges. But never once in his life did he deign to answer his detractors by appealing for fair play or mentioning the subject of his family relations. He did not at Los Angeles. In the middle of his speech there, a voice from the rear asked him where he stood on Harrison Gray Otis. Johnson stopped his address and asked a colleague on the platform what the man had said. When the question, which may have been prearranged, was repeated to him, Johnson turned back to the crowd and proceeded to pour out the bile that he had stored in his soul against Harrison Gray Otis. Remarking that Otis had attacked him on the one subject which he could not discuss, he began one of the most searing excoriations heard in this country since the days of bitter old John Randolph of Roanoke.

"In our city," Johnson thundered, his eyes flashing hate, "we have drunk the dregs of the cup of infamy; we have been betrayed by public officials; we have been disgraced before the world by crimes unspeakable; but with all the criminals who have disgraced us, we have never had anything so degraded, so disreputable, and so vile as Harrison Gray Otis and the Los Angeles *Times*.

"The one blot on the fame of Southern California, and the bar sinister on the escutcheon of Los Angeles, is Harrison Gray Otis, a creature who is vile, infamous, degraded, and putrescent. Here he sits in senile dementia, with gangrened heart and rotting brain, grimacing at every reform and chattering in impotent rage against decency and morality, while he is going down to his grave in snarling infamy." [29]

Hiram Johnson was not a man to forget easily. Over a year later, while attending a military review, the adjutant general of the state approached him in company with Harrison Gray Otis. Otis had come to be presented to the state commander

in chief. But when General Forbes started to make the introduction, Governor Johnson put up his hand and shook his
head. In a moment of rare dignity the old fire-eating journalist
and soldier saluted and said, "Your privilege, Governor, your
privilege." For once, Otis had won an encounter with the
soft and graceful word.[30]

The attacks of the so-called regular Republicans were not
all personal; in many instances they raised issues that were
difficult for the Leaguers to answer. Among these was the
question whether the reformers, if they won the primary election, would support all the party's candidates including those
in the national administration. At a Republican state central
committee meeting in June a resolution endorsing Taft and
condemning the insurgent Republicans was passed over the
heads of the League members. Also approved was the draft
of a letter to be sent to each Republican in the primaries,
inquiring whether he would support the total Republican
ticket in the event he won the nomination. Johnson's reply
that he would support all Republicans who would "honestly
endeavor" to kick the Southern Pacific Company out of the
party, opened him and the League to the charge that they
were not Republicans and thus were not entitled to the party's
support.

Possibly a more influential charge with conservative voters
than that of party regularity was the claim of regular papers
that Johnson's election would open the way for an "unholy
and mysterious conspiracy" of organized labor to dominate
the state. Pointing to the Leaguers' attitude toward the unions,
the *Times* pontificated that Los Angeles would go the way of
San Francisco if the reformers won, and that "the twenty
years' struggle to maintain Los Angeles as a free city" would
be irrevocably lost. For those of the electorate who would
not read, a cartoon was published and circulated in Los
Angeles showing Meyer Lissner opening the gates of the city
to an obvious human snake bearing the title, "Union Thug." [31]
But of all the regular charges, the most embarrassing to the
League was the repeated assertion that the California re-

formers were low tariff men and were planning to attack the protection of California products. They were admitted insurgents, the argument ran, and the Middle Western insurgents had all voted against increases in the citrus rates and had helped reduce the schedules on other California products. "A vote for insurgency means uprooting your citrus trees," warned the Redlands *Daily Review*.[32]

In general, during the last two weeks of the primary campaign the reformers refused to answer the conservative charges on party regularity and labor. Contenting themselves with attack, they continued to blast at the railroad. Circulated all over the state was the picture taken after the Santa Cruz convention, now entitled "The Shame of California." Franklin Hichborn's book containing the roll-call votes in the 1909 California assembly was widely used to denounce the regular politicians, and the series of muckraking railroad articles by Charles E. Russell, then conveniently appearing in *Hampton's Magazine*, was extensively cited as proof of all of the reformers' anti–Southern Pacific charges. The Lincoln-Roosevelt Leaguers were forced to take the defensive only on the tariff issue. There was too much truth in this attack for them to remain silent. Every regular California congressman had loyally supported Aldrich and Cannon in their fight for higher rates in the special session of the Sixty-first Congress, whereas the Middle-Western insurgents had consistently voted against them even on items intimately affecting California produce.[33] Moreover, William Kent had spoken of himself as a low tariff man. These were damaging charges in the citrus belt, the very heart of progressive strength, and Johnson felt the necessity to deny them. In his last sweep of the southland, he repeatedly asserted that he stood with Theodore Roosevelt for adequate and scientific protection. But his most devastating answer to the conservative charge was that immediately after the lemon tariff had been raised in 1909 the Southern Pacific, in conjunction with twenty-five other western railroads, had raised their rates, more than wiping out the advantages granted in the Payne-Aldrich Customs Bill. Hiram Johnson had started his campaign with an attack upon this root of all evil, the Southern Pacific; there he ended.

On August 16, 1910, the voters of California attended their first and perhaps most important state-wide primary election in the state's history. It was a day of victory for the Lincoln-Roosevelt Republican League. Hiram Johnson, polling almost 50 per cent of the vote in a four-way election, carried every county in the state except five. The final tabulation of the vote gave Johnson 101,666, Curry 55,390, Anderson 38,295, Stanton 18,226, and Ellery 2,028. Save for one state office, the rest of the League ticket had also won by impressive margins. William Kent and William D. Stephens had been nominated for Congress. Only the advisory vote for United States senator was close. Although Works had a small popular majority, his leading opponent, A. G. Spalding, had won considerably more senatorial and assembly districts. Both houses of the state legislature were won by the reformers.

An analysis of the primary election returns indicates clearly that Johnson's main strength had been in the San Joaquin Valley and throughout all southern California. His vote was weakest in San Francisco and its surrounding counties except Alameda. Johnson had confidently expected to carry his home town, but there he ran second to Curry, and the combined votes of the opposition candidates almost doubled his. Receiving the returns on election night in his law office, he was filled with dismay at the results from San Francisco. But good news soon came from the valley, and soon after the results from Los Angeles indicated that Dickson's cheery prediction that the League ticket would sweep the county by a three-to-one margin was remarkably correct. During the campaign Johnson had insisted that the election would be settled in the south. And so it was. In a moment of unembarrassed candor the candidate wrote on election night to his friends in the south: "I can never get over the wonderful vote that you gave us in Los Angeles. I think it was marvelous and the men who conducted the fight I think are even more marvelous and wonderful."

Johnson was right, in the moment of victory, in ascribing much of the credit for his success to other people. The results clearly indicated that it was a League and not a one-man victory. With wild jubilation the reformers promised that never again would the state of California be scheduled on the Southern Pacific inventories as a piece of railroad property.

But even though the League had won easily in the primary, it was still confronted by a formidable opponent in the final November elections. Theodore Bell had been an easy victor in the Democratic lists and was now running against Johnson on an advanced reform platform, which included the assertion, "The emancipation of California from the Southern Pacific rule overshadows every public question. . . ." California had never been a certain Republican state, and the Democratic party had become increasingly stronger in the first decade of the century under the progressive leadership of men like Franklin K. Lane, James D. Phelan, and Theodore Bell. Lane had come within an eyelash of being elected governor in 1902, and Bell undoubtedly would have succeeded in 1906 had it not been for the opposition of the Hearst-supported Independence League. If one is to judge from the views of its candidates for governor, the Democratic and not the Republican party had been the more progressive up until 1910. In that year, led by Bell and supported by the Hearst papers, it was to be no mean protagonist, a fact of which Johnson and his followers were quite aware.

In addition to Bell's contesting the League's claim to reform representation in the state, Johnson's position was further weakened by the rather widespread defection of disgruntled Republican regulars who threatened either to take a walk to the Democratic side or go fishing on election day. Not a few regular papers refused to claim him as a Republican, and others announced that they felt themselves "relieved from all party obligations in so far as the governorship is concerned." The sentiments of many important standpat Republican leaders were summed up by George A. Knight, the national committeeman from the state and an attorney for the Southern Pacific Railroad. Refusing to attend a Johnson banquet, Knight publicly charged that Johnson's principles "are destructive to the vital interests of California and the Republican party." These outspoken opinions were only in part counteracted by a few regulars who, like Congressman McLachlan, admitted after the election that he was glad the Southern Pacific machine had been defeated.[34]

If anything else was needed to alienate the extreme conservative Republicans, the California Republican platform performed that function. Gathering at Sacramento on September 6, the League took over the party machinery by electing Chester Rowell temporary chairman of the meeting and Meyer Lissner chairman of the State Central Committee, and by substituting League officials en masse for any standpatters still in state party offices. The platform preamble pledged allegiance to "the Progressive Republican principles enunciated by President Roosevelt . . . and already in part enacted into law under the administration of President Taft." It further called upon the California representative in Congress "to join with the Progressive . . . in the elimination from control of the reactionary forces." Then, after defeating a resolution commending Taft in stronger terms, the Leaguers pounded out one of the most advanced reform programs of its day. Nationally, it called for the enactment of the income tax, the direct election of senators, the erection of a tariff commission, and vigorous enforcement of the antitrust law. For the state it prescribed a more democratic primary, direct legislation including initiative and referendum, and a nonpartisan judiciary, a state public service commission with power to fix rates on all public services, a limitation of labor injunctions, an employers' liability act, home rule for counties, a legal recognition of labor's right to organize, and the submission of an amendment enfranchising women.

Committed to reform, the progressives set out to win an election. Johnson, who apparently had little to do with making the platform, wanted to continue campaigning principally against the railroad. It was only by the strongest pressure that

131

his supporters persuaded him to discuss a few other specific issues. But even then the candidate could not be pushed too far. When urged to express himself on woman suffrage, for example, Johnson, who was emotionally opposed to women in politics, dodged by saying that he would speak neither for nor against the question. Most of his time on the stump was spent in belaboring the Southern Pacific and William Randolph Hearst, both of whom he said were in direct alliance with the Democratic candidate. Simultaneously, Johnson and his friends used every opportunity to win back the dissident Republican regulars. Very rarely now was it stressed that progressivism was opposed to regular Republicanism. Meyer Lissner announced that the League-dominated state committee would support all Republicans in the campaign irrespective of their views. In a further effort to placate the standpatters, Johnson and his campaign advisors attempted to keep Francis J. Heney out of the state until after the election was over. Heney, who had been in Massachusetts resting, had started West intending to campaign for the League ticket. But at Salt Lake City he received a letter from the new chairman of the state central committee, asking him to remain away from California until the campaign was over. The League forces, Lissner explained, already had the support of the ultrareformers, and Heney's presence would only antagonize the conservatives. A banquet to be held in San Francisco in honor of the former graft prosecutor was quietly postponed until December.

The plan to exclude Heney from the campaign on the grounds of political expediency backfired. As soon as news of it leaked out, a large group of Johnson supporters, including Chester Rowell, bitterly objected, and William Kent, who already had had a serious misunderstanding with Johnson over campaign tactics, spoiled the whole scheme by personally inviting Heney to speak in his district. His presence there, Heney was assured by Kent's campaign manager, would mean "hundreds of votes." The widespread criticism, plus the vision of Heney talking for Kent but not for the rest of the state ticket, finally forced Johnson's hand. A week before the election, the candidate for governor curtly wired Lissner that he wanted Heney to join in his campaign.[35]

Whatever Heney's presence in California might have meant to the final election results, one thing was clear—Johnson's eleventh-hour change of mind did little to remove the bitter feelings engendered by the incident. Heney was extremely hurt by this cavalier treatment. His friends, including William Kent and Fremont Older, were downright angry. They ascribed the move to Johnson and they felt, perhaps rightly so, that ungenerous personal motives, not only questions of political expediency, had dictated the scheme. At any rate, this feeling increased the tension in the already touchy relations between Johnson and Heney. Kent's eventual victory in a congressional district which Johnson lost certainly added combustibles to the existing animosity.[36]

Meanwhile the campaign was nearing its end. Between the two progressive candidates for governor there seemed to be remarkably little difference in political principles. Each attacked the other for his political associates, and each claimed to be the leading opponent of the railroad and corporation influence. Of the two, the Democratic candidate Bell discussed a much wider variety of reform issues. Chiding Johnson for his one-track speeches, Bell remarked that if elected he "would not tear up the railroad with his teeth." But in a very close election the electorate saw fit to choose Johnson by a vote of 177,000 to 155,000. The entire state Republican ticket, seven of eight congressmen, and great majorities in both houses of the state legislature were elected as well. Once again southern California proved its devotion to the ideals of the League. This time Johnson carried his home town of San Francisco by a small majority, but lost twenty-one of the forty-nine northern California counties to his democratic rival. In the south the League triumphed in all nine counties, and the majority given to Johnson in this less populous region was considerably more than the one he polled in the north.

Four years after its founding, the Lincoln-Roosevelt League

and its reform politics had swept to power. But election victories are one thing, legislative accomplishments another. Whether or not the defeat of the railroad and the regular machine meant a change in policies as well as in administrations, only the future and perhaps Hiram Johnson could tell.

CHAPTER VI

Harvest Time

*

During most of the campaign of 1910 Hiram Johnson was reasonably sure that he would be defeated. But one day, shortly before the election, he remarked to his traveling companion, Edward A. Dickson, that for the first time he felt he was going to win. Apparently, that was a sobering thought. For a long time he sat silent and looked at the road ahead. Then, obviously agitated, he turned to his companion again and asked, "What in the world are we going to do after we do get in?" His friend replied that they could institute a system of direct legislation, for one thing, so that when they were defeated at some inevitable date in the future, the old machine could never again have the power over the people of California it once enjoyed. Johnson was silent again for a period, and then, confessing that he did not know what direct legislation was, he asked Dickson to explain how the initiative, referendum, and recall worked. As Chester Rowell remarked afterward, the governor never seemed to realize throughout most of the campaign that if he were elected, he would actually have to outline and defend a long list of reform measures.[1]

Once sure of office, Johnson tried to make up for his previous lack of reform knowledge. He spent over a month in the East, where he talked to Theodore Roosevelt, Robert La-Follette, and Lincoln Steffens about the things that could be done in the state. With the benefit of these talks and a number of books recommended by Roosevelt, the new governor felt that he had a much better grasp of the meaning of the progressive movement. But his colleagues at home were still not confident of his abilities to devise a sound reform program.

135

Rowell, Lissner, Dickson, and Stimson were agreed that if a comprehensive reform program were planned, it would have to be conceived and worked out by the governor's friends and advisors. So sure of this was Meyer Lissner, the new chairman of the Republican State Central Committee, that without consulting the governor-elect, he appointed a series of committees to investigate all proposed reform measures. The committees were to report to a meeting of the progressive legislators at San Francisco a week before the legislature opened. There Lissner hoped that a comprehensive program of legislation would be agreed to, and made binding on the legislative members of the League. When Johnson returned and heard of the committees and the proposed "legislative conference," he was angry. In apology for his precipitate action, Lissner wrote that he thought he had spoken to the governor about the plan. But Johnson would not be mollified. At the conference he made an obvious point of refusing to sit beside Lissner, and for a long time thereafter he referred to the meeting with heavy irony as, "your famous San Francisco conference." [2]

After that, Lissner and his colleagues were more careful of the governor's *amour propre*. Nevertheless, the San Francisco conference, attended by practically all the progressive members of the legislature, served an extremely useful purpose. During its sessions every pledge in the platform was thoroughly discussed, and on the basis of the committee reports, measures were drafted which subsequently were presented as bills to the legislature. Without the committee work and the conference, the story of the famous reform legislature of 1911 might have been materially different.

If Johnson depended upon his advisors for a constructive legislative program, they were even more dependent upon him in a political sense. From the start Johnson made it evident that in this particular he was master in his own house. Not that he did not welcome advice. Time and time again, in the early days of his career, Rowell, Lissner, Dickson, Stimson, and Brundige were invited to Sacramento for political conferences. The last word, however, was always his, and a member of the conclave who disagreed with a Johnson decision was abruptly made aware that his intransigeance was regarded with disfavor. For instance, he had been informed, Johnson wrote to Lissner, that Lissner had been infected with a letter-writing germ and had been repudiating the conservation bill worked out by the famous San Francisco conference. The implications of the note, written in Johnson's own handwriting and without any softening phrases, were transparent.[3]

The governor also had two extremely definite ideas about patronage and its uses: first, that the state should receive the most efficient service; and secondly, that those best qualified to perform this service should naturally be chosen from the better side—Johnson's side. Consequently, opponents already holding state positions were given short shrift. When the governor found an official protected by law, like Alden Anderson, he persuaded the state legislature to repeal the law, forced a resignation, and then had the law passed again with some minor change. Any new appointments were made only after most careful examination of attitudes of the appointees. In answer to a proposed appointment to the state mining bureau, Johnson wrote Lissner that he was quite willing to approve the man in question, but he wanted Lissner to have a definite understanding in advance, that if he went into that bureau, he went as their representative. He had had too much trouble, he continued, with some of his appointees in the past after they were securely in office. If this particular man did not care to pledge his entire allegiance, the governor concluded, he would have to find employment elsewhere.[4]

Beyond swearing fealty to the governor's policies, all appointees were expected to support the administration in other ways. During the first balmy days of power, Lissner wrote that requests for campaign contributions from state employees would stop. Six years later, however, when Johnson was running for senator, Lissner asked the governor's secretary for a list of the "Union members" together with their salaries, so that they might be tapped immediately after payday.[5] Legislators were likewise expected to be amenable, if they wanted favors. Johnson frankly said that his office was keeping a record on every member of the two houses for later reference. This was effective reform politics. The main pressure that Johnson and his advisors maintained on the representatives was the threat of appealing to their constituents; the end objective was the passage of the platform on which they had been elected. After the first month Dickson wrote: "The legislature is in shape and taking programme nobly." The two exceptions to the statement were the Democrats and the San Francisco labor crowd. These "small time politicians," as Rowell called them, were just as frank. On labor issues they told Rowell they would vote the way Paul Scharrenburg, San Francisco labor leader, directed; on moral questions they would listen to the Royal Arch, the liquor dealers' association, but on all remaining items they were at the service of the administration.[6]

The Johnson administration was then and has since been criticized for building up as tight a political organization as ever existed in California, and rather invidious comparisons have been made between it and the "creaking" Southern Pacific organization that preceded it. As far as such comparisons go, they are usually correct. The Johnson organization was extensive, devoted to its own purposes, and sometimes ruthless with opponents. To a degree, its methods were the methods of any exceptionally efficient political organization. The three qualifying words are important. There was no discernible corruption in the Johnson administration, and certainly no bribery in the ordinary sense. As much cannot be said for most other political organizations in the history of the state to that time. And the comparison falls down entirely when one looks at the goals of the reformers. The Johnson group sought to serve what they called the people of the state. Perhaps their definition of the people was sometimes a little narrow, as most such definitions are. But by any measure, the group the progressives sought to serve was so much broader than the group served in the past that to press the point further is to belabor the obvious. If a few of these reformers were extremely ambitious and used their position for their own success, they were acting in an ancient and recognizable human pattern. But granted that one assumes a faith in democracy and in Christian ethics, a serious resemblance of the Johnson machine to the Southern Pacific political organization, either in their ends or means, becomes slightly fantastic.

"A successful and permanent government," Hiram Johnson observed in his first inaugural address, "must rest primarily upon the recognition of the rights of men and the absolute sovereignty of the people." The special interests of big business and the machine politician had prevented that in the past. Between "the political thug of the waterfront" and "the smugly respectable individual in broadcloth" who employed the processes of the state for his own private gain, he considered the latter much more dangerous to the common welfare. The governor proposed to wipe out vested privilege by making the people and their agents supreme. For that purpose, he recommended passage of the long list of reforms which the leaders of the Lincoln-Roosevelt League had written into the Republican platform. These included a railroad act empowering a commission to fix absolute rates on the basis of physical evaluation, the initiative, referendum, and recall (the last to include even judicial officers), an uncomplicated and direct primary, a short ballot, home rule for political subdivisions, and an employers' liability law. It was a good forthright reform speech; for the first time the governor talked about specific issues.

Three days later the chaplain opened the first session of the 1911 California legislature with an extraordinary plea: "Give us a square deal for Christ's sake." Within a short time the reform forces had the legislature organized and were proceeding to select a United States senator. Soon after the election of John D. Works, the governor sent his first message to the legislature asking for the passage of amendatory legislation incorporating the direct primary, the referendum, the initiative, and the recall as the first steps in democratizing the state constitution. On Johnson's request, Dr. John R. Haynes and Dickson had prepared the necessary amendments. That the governor was ready to use all the power of his office to obtain passage of these bills in the "must" class had already been indicated. When the resolution in favor of the direct election of senators had been referred to a committee of the House, it was removed the same day and passed on personal intercession of Johnson's executive secretary.

The proposal to enact the initiative, referendum, and recall brought forth the first long bitter clash of opinion in the body and throughout the state. The objections of the more conservative members to these "socialistic measures" were adequately summed up by Grove Johnson, who had resigned from the legislature after his son's victory. In this attempt to substitute an "Athenian democracy for a representative form of government," he foresaw all stability and moderation removed from government. "The voice of the people is not the voice of God," the tough old standpatter cried, "for the voice of the people sent Jesus to the cross." [7] But if the initiative and referendum were bitter medicine to conservatives, the recall including the judiciary was clearly iniquitous revolution.

Since the passage of the Fourteenth Amendment, the judiciary had increasingly endeared itself to the wealthier classes of the country by its consistent protection of private property against popularly supported regulatory laws. Its reputation was enhanced among these classes with the rise of organized labor. Through the injunction and other legal devices, it had shown throughout the previous forty years a strong antiunion bias. In California particularly the state judiciary had been responsive to the Southern Pacific Railroad and other large corporation influence. The Santa Cruz convention had made that clear. With progressive democracy on the march, the judiciary remained the most undemocratic element and the one farthest removed from the people in the state. Any attempt to democratize this mighty barrier to evolutionary politics was bound to produce an instant reaction among the propertied classes of the country. The recall of

140

judges, therefore, was branded as a "spewing of intoxicated radicalism" by "reckless and desperate revolutionary leaders." It was "a plan to tear down the prop upon which the integrity and security of society depend"; it was the scheme of "a convention of socialists to overthrow the Republic." "God save the commonwealth," shouted the choleric Los Angeles *Times*.[8]

Even in progressive ranks there was considerable opposition to the recall of the judiciary. The debate over the proposal had been so heated at the San Francisco conference that it had been tabled. Senator Works, Charles S. Wheeler, and William Denman were just a few of the many progressive leaders who were against this "reform run mad." Even the patron saint of the California Leaguers, Theodore Roosevelt, had "very grave doubts" about the recall of judges at this time, although he was soon to change his mind about it. Rowell and Lissner only supported the recall because Johnson wanted it. A few years earlier Rowell had referred to the measure as a "half-baked radical device." Among all the progressive leaders, the only real friends of the measure were Hiram Johnson, Francis J. Heney, Fremont Older, and William Kent. To Kent the problem of the American judiciary was much like Martin Luther's problem when he tried to remove "the intermediaries between the individual and his God." "The people," Kent remarked, "must get nearer the grub pile and nearer to their governmental agencies." [9]

At one time in the following legislative battle Governor Johnson felt that he would have to compromise and give up the recall of judicial officials. Then chance intervened, as it so often does in the affairs of men. Three years after his initial sentence Abraham Ruef, the San Francisco grafter, had managed to escape the penitentiary by appealing his case on technicalities to higher courts. Approximately a year before the recall fight the state Supreme Court, by a vote of four to three, had ordered the case remanded for a new trial. In all probability that decision would eventually have meant freedom for the unsavory politician. But the Johnson administration, when it came into office, undertook an investigation of the court proceedings. The fact was then brought out that Justice Henshaw of Santa Cruz banquet fame had cast his vote before the general decision of the court, and had then left upon an extended vacation outside the boundaries of the state. While Henshaw was out of the state three other justices signed the order. Johnson's attorney general took exception to the extraordinary procedure, and the court reviewing the protest sustained his point. Amid a general uproar in the state, Ruef finally went to San Quentin at the same time that the Assembly passed the recall bill in its original form by a vote of fifty-nine to twenty. Without the service of Ruef and Justice Henshaw it is extremely doubtful whether the recall measure could have passed the legislature.[10]

During the debate over the mechanics of democratic government, Governor Johnson sent the legislature his proposals for state utility regulation. Scoring the railroads for their "obvious extortions," Johnson asked for an extensive revamping of the decrepit and machine-controlled Railroad Commission. His message piled example upon example of prevailing injustice, not only in railroad rates but in express fees and city utility charges. He pointed out, for example, that Los Angeles was one hundred twenty miles away from its harbor at San Pedro when measured by existing comparative freight rates, instead of the actual distance of some twenty-three geographic miles. He ended the message by asking for a new commission with power to fix maximum rates on the basis of physical evaluations, classify all freight, and install a system of unified bookkeeping. When hearings were held on the bill prepared by John Eshleman, not one railroad representative appeared to protest its passage. What opposition did develop was focused on three accompanying resolutions which provided for constitutional amendments, the most important of which was a provision placing all public service corporations throughout the state, except for municipal owned utilities, under the regulatory power of the new commission. Loudest in objecting to the new regulatory measure were the southern California power companies. But so much hostility had been built up against uncontrolled monopolies over the years that the Eshleman bill, together with the three resolutions, was passed without a dissenting vote in either house.

No such unanimity of opinion, however, existed when the legislature turned from political reform and corporate regulation to the subject of labor. Since many of the proposed bills sought to alter somewhat the existing balance of power between labor and capital, sharp class divisions appeared. Although many progressives were eager to clip the wings of some of the great corporations, they had little intention of strengthening the power of organized labor. Representing farmers, small businessmen, and the professions, they might be benevolent to the underdog as an individual, but not as a competing social class. This was especially true of the southern California progressives, who reflected to some extent the economic views of the Los Angeles city reform government which had passed the stringent antipicketing law just the year before. Whether representatives of open-shop Los Angeles or of the southern California fruit growers, these legislators on the whole had a distinct antipathy for the pretensions of unionism, whatever their feelings might have been toward individual workers. Among northern progressives, except for a small group, a strong antiunion bias clearly existed. This was manifested even by Governor Johnson when he wrote that although the San Francisco union labor people had promised their support, their leaders who had the most influence were wholly corrupt.[11]

The fundamental antilabor bias of the southern Californians was sharpened at the start of the session, during the debates over the Weinstock arbitration bill. This measure, often erroneously called a compulsory arbitration bill, barred strikes or lockouts in any public utility until an investigation of the dispute had been made by an impartial board of inquiry appointed by the governor. After the board's report, either side was at liberty to use the customary pressure of a strike or a lockout to win its points. But it was hoped that the board's report, supported by public opinion, would go far to reduce work stoppages in vital public services. Calling the bill a step toward total compulsory arbitration, organized labor fought the measure with all its strength. In spite of the fact that every Los Angeles senator voted for it, this advanced labor measure, based upon the theory that the public had rights in a labor dispute as well as the two direct contestants, failed to pass. By way of explaining both the unanimous Los Angeles vote and the violent opposition of labor, it is interesting to note that the Los Angeles Merchants and Manufacturers' Association had for years been supporting a bill providing for state-wide compulsory arbitration of all labor disputes.[12]

With the same intensity that labor had opposed the arbitration measure, many progressive legislators objected to the bill limiting the working day for women to eight hours. Prior to 1911, California had regulated the maximum hours of work for children, druggists, and underground mine workers. But these were relatively small groups of employees compared to the thousands of women employed in the urban mercantile establishments and in the fruit and vegetable industry. The fruit growers and packers of southern California bitterly protested against the proposed legislation, and it was not even reported favorably from the committee until it had been amended to exclude farm labor and canning and packing workers. Even then Meyer Lissner, reflecting the opinion of Los Angeles merchants and hotel operators, appealed to the governor to defeat it. After the bill had passed both houses, E. T. Earl of the *Express* was still so violently opposed to it that he persuaded Theodore Roosevelt, who was his house guest at the time, to urge Governor Johnson to veto it. As the bill lay on Johnson's desk, the governor received a call from Rowell who, with Earl listening to the conversation, undertook to state Roosevelt's views on the matter. When Rowell finished, Johnson asked him to tell the former President that he was sorry but he had just signed the measure.

Sometime afterward Rowell learned that Johnson had signed the bill at the telephone during the conversation.[13]

A similar division in progressive ranks took place over the workingman's compensation measure, or employers' liability bill as it was known in California. The labor delegation from San Francisco, supported by the more radical progressives, asked for a compulsory measure and one that abrogated the "assumed risk," "fellow servant," and "contributory negligence" doctrines, doctrines of common law through which many employers in the past had escaped liability for industrial accidents. At the other pole, more conservative Leaguers, including E. T. Earl, objected both to the compulsory features and to the abrogation of any of the aforementioned legal concepts. Caught between the two forces, Governor Johnson devised and supported a compromise which preserved the doctrine of "contributory negligence" and stripped the bill of its compulsory features. Supported by labor and the moderate progressive, the measure finally passed in that form.[14]

By far the most serious clash among the progressive forces and one that was fraught with importance for the future of reform, came over a bill introduced to limit the granting of injunctions during the course of labor disputes. This measure stipulated that no court could issue a labor injunction unless there was positive proof of the threat of irreparable damage to property for which there was no adequate remedy at law. Moreover, the threatened property had to be described with particularity, and the bill defined customer patronage as not being property under the law. Still another provision of the measure prohibited employers from entering into an agreement with their employees not to join a labor union. The proposal thus recognized peaceful picketing and the primary and secondary boycott as legal. It prohibited the use of the yellow-dog contract and the black list. Had it been passed, the Los Angeles antipicketing act and many other measures used by the Los Angeles Merchants and Manufacturers' Association to maintain an open-shop town would indisputably have been contrary to law. The bill, as the Los Angeles *Times* said, threatened the "industrial independence of the South." [15]

Introduced by the Democrat Caminetti, the bill passed the senate after a stormy session of twenty continuous hours punctuated by a violent struggle over the rules of the body and the arrest of members to prevent them from escaping from the chamber. Of more significance was the fact that all five Los Angeles progressive senators voted unanimously against the act. With the blue chips down on the assembly vote, the conservative storm broke. The great reactionary journals were outraged and compared the Johnson administration to the cat who fell into the well and slipped back two steps for every one it climbed up so that it was "about half way to hell by this time." The bill threatened all private property in the state; it was conclusive proof of the revolution sponsored by the "laborite oligarchy," and the "cupidity" of the Johnson progressives who had been debauched and "rolled in the political filth of Tar Flat and the Barbary Coast" by the tyrannical San Francisco labor leaders; it manifested the real convictions of "Red Governor Johnson and Hooley Lissnerski." "Did not," the Los Angeles *Times* asked with malice, "the dynamiting and the assassination come full soon after one of his [Johnson's] speeches in Los Angeles?" [16]

These reactionary fulminations were not needed to defeat the anti-injunction measure. It was buried in the house of its supposed friends. Throughout the state the only large progressive paper which supported the measure was Older's San Francisco *Bulletin*. Other reform journals either actively opposed or damned the measure with faint praise and more criticism. Most of the progressive leaders were in accord and reflected the viewpoint of the Los Angeles Chamber of Commerce. Meyer Lissner appealed to Johnson to stop the bill at all costs, for its passage would wreck the progressive movement in Los Angeles. Lissner was convinced that no more "radical legislation" should be passed during the remainder of the session. The Los Angeles progressive made it clear that he and his colleagues would hold the governor responsible for "guiding"—that is, stopping—such legislation. On the same morning that Lissner made his appeal to Johnson, Rowell's Fresno *Republican* predicted the defeat of the bill in the assembly. It was soon apparent that the governor and other progressive leaders had decided that discretion was the better part of politics. Four days later only thirty-four of the fifty-four votes necessary to bring the bill to debate were cast. Forty votes were cast against it, and of these southern California supplied a large majority. The governor's office, like the tar baby, said nothing.[17]

The split in the progressive ranks first noticeable in labor legislation was also evident in the proposals for so-called moral reform. These measures, including a local-option bill for the control of intoxicants, an anti–race track bill, and one prohibiting slot machines, were consistently supported by the southern California and country delegations, and opposed by representatives from the bay cities, particularly San Francisco. A further division of the legislature on a geographical basis occurred on a reapportionment bill to provide more representation for rapidly growing southern California. Reapportionment failed to pass, as did the anti–race track measure. The progressive legislature wound up its first session with the passage of several conservation acts, the slot-machine measure, a bill to provide free textbooks for school districts, and a resolution looking toward the adoption of woman suffrage in the state.

As the legislators packed their bags to go home, they were saluted by the progressive press as the "most productive" and "intelligent" lawmakers ever assembled in California. Even labor, despite its defeat on the injunction bill, joined the chorus of approval. "There are more victories for labor measures to be chronicled as a result of this session," the official American Federation of Labor journal of northern California remarked in its best stilted fashion, "than in any other previous gathering of the solons."[18] Governor Johnson, and even Theodore Roosevelt, added to the general felicitations. The two houses, in eighty-five days of activity, had passed more than

147

800 bills and twenty-three amendments to the constitution. The latter, incorporating some of the more vital reforms, were to be submitted to the electorate in November, 1911. The people were to become the final judges of this harvest of reform.

During the autumn campaign of 1911 the conservative forces in the state attacked virtually every one of the proposed amendments to the constitution. The air was full of dire predictions that woman suffrage would "unsex society" and destroy the gallantry of men, that the adoption of direct government would prevent the more intelligent men from standing for office, and that the recall of judges would undermine all stable government and make it an instrument of the turbulent and radical few. President Taft's defense of the judiciary at Pocatello, Idaho, was quoted extensively by opponents of the recall. Attacking the critics of the courts, the President, an old judicial hand himself, had once remarked that American judges and courts were his "ideals on earth that typify what we shall meet afterward in heaven under a just God." Whether the new departures would lead to "autocratic despotism" or to "the anarchistic rule of the rabble" was never quite determined by conservative opinion. One thing at least was certain: nothing but evil could come from these dangerous innovations.[19]

Hiram Johnson and his friends chose to meet this attack head on. Virtually ignoring all other issues, the governor campaigned for almost two months in the interest of the public utilities amendments and the initiative, referendum, and recall. He defended the recall of judges in particular. If the recall was good for the legislator who made law, then it was good for the judge who equally made law by interpreting it, Johnson held. A court empowered to declare a law unconstitutional is a court empowered "to say anything it pleases with reference to that law. The power is there and it is nonsense to deny it." Moreover, Johnson emphasized, this was just another phase in the great fight between the corporation and vested wealth on the one hand and the people on the other. For the American judiciary was "the last great bulwark of privilege," the "last stand of corporate aggression." To the charge that the recall would force the judiciary to keep their ears to the ground Johnson answered, "We would rather that the judges keep their ears to the ground than to the railroad tracks in California." In one of his most effective speeches, the governor denounced the whole theory of checks and balances as a denial of popular government. In words reminiscent of the democracy of Andrew Jackson, he said: "No man is better able to govern than all others; no man is better in government than any other man." The initiative, the referendum, and the recall, he ended, were attempts to bring the government once more close to the people, "in the hope . . . that we may yet live in a free republic." [20]

Something of the low estate that the California judiciary occupied in the public esteem was revealed in the election results of 1911. Whereas the initiative just barely passed, the people approved the recall by over a three to one margin. Nearly all of the constitutional proposals were approved, including the three utility measures. Of the important measures at stake, woman suffrage came closest to defeat, largely because of the opposition of Catholic San Francisco.

In September, 1911, Governor Johnson called a special session of the California legislature to enact measures incorporating the powers granted by the recently adopted constitutional amendments. The resulting Sutherland-Burnett Bill was one of the most comprehensive statutes regulating public utilities that have been passed by an American state. Still operating today, the law empowered the reconstructed railroad commission to supervise the activities of all public utilities even to the issuance of securities. And the new commission, unlike its predecessor, rapidly gained the confidence of the state by its wise and careful administration. Like all laws, the public utility act was no better than its administrators. Under Governors Richardson, Rolph, and Merriam, the railroad commission was perhaps apathetic in its administration of the law; but during the Johnson and Stephens period, under the Young administration, and again more recently, the commission seems to have functioned as its creators had hoped it would—largely in the public interest.

Commenting on California's experience with direct legislation, a recent historian has remarked, "It neither fulfilled the hopes of its friends nor the dread of its enemies." Although it provided the people with potential control of the government, "its misuse has often done decided harm." [21] Such a judgment probably depends a great deal upon basic personal assumptions as to what constitutes "decided harm." By 1940 the people of California had voted on one hundred two initiative proposals, accepted twenty-eight, and rejected seventy-four. That indicates a high degree of selection. The state has also been more than moderate in recalling public officials. Surveying the history of direct politics by the people, another student of California government concludes that the people of the state have acted at least as wisely as their elected representatives. [22] During the most critical decade the state has survived, the tortuous 'thirties, the majority of the people, despite their suffering, invariably voted not only with a deep sense of their need but with intelligence and sincerity. Can as much be said for their representatives over the course of more placid and bountiful years? One is entitled to wonder, for example, what the state of California would now be like if the people, through their direct legislative powers, had ever governed in the spirit and with the objectives of the Southern Pacific machine before 1910.

At the end of the special session of the legislature in December, 1911, Chester Rowell wrote that the public utilities bill "completes" the reform program of the Lincoln-Roosevelt Republican League, a judgment with which Johnson concurred. [23] During the 1912 presidential year California progressive leaders were intensely interested in founding a new national party, and state reform was temporarily forgotten. Consequently, when the state legislature again met in January, 1913, there was no well-formulated legislative program as there had been in 1911. And although nominal progressives had swept both the Republican primaries and the final election of 1912, thus insuring a majority in both houses of the legislature, the group had lost much of the unity that characterized it in January of 1911.[24]

The split begun by the 1912 LaFollette-Roosevelt fight for delegates in California had been further accentuated by the founding of the national Progressive party. Many so-called progressive Republican legislators who supported Johnson in the state soon made it evident that they wanted no connection with the new party. In addition, not a few of the legislators felt that reform had gone far enough in the state with the completion of the 1911 program and opposed any further progressive measures. On the other hand, Governor Johnson had been nominated for vice-president by Theodore Roosevelt's new Progressive party in 1912, and most of his California friends had campaigned for that party nationally. Since the Progressive party espoused one of the most thoroughgoing programs of advanced reform in American history, Johnson and his friends were almost automatically committed to further action within California. To have rested upon their 1911 accomplishments would have been to deny their national birthright.

This complicated conflict between progressives who wanted to remain Republicans, and progressives who wanted to become Progressives, and between the tired reformers, and the ones still eager for the upward path, broke out even before the legislature met over the question of organizing the two houses. Some of the most ardent national Progressives, principally from southern California, wanted to establish a caucus on the basis of Theodore Roosevelt's new party. But so many reform supporters refused to enter any organization that did not bear the Republican name that the plan had to be discarded. A second scheme to organize the bodies on a simple "liberal-conservative" basis cutting through party lines, went by the boards when the resurgent Democrats, cheered by Wilson's victory, refused to give up their own party organization. With Johnson's confession that he was utterly "perplexed and confused," the reform leaders decided in the end to dispense with a caucus and permit the two houses to organize as they would.[25]

This seemed to be an admission of weakness, as did the governor's opening message to the legislature. Unlike his speech of 1911, Johnson asked only for two specific measures, one looking toward higher corporate taxes, and the other creating a state administrative board for the management of all state institutions.

But if Johnson was less public in his demands on the 1913 legislature, he was nonetheless even more insistent that a comprehensive reform program be passed than he had been two years before. Reflecting the national Progressive platform, the Governor evolved a "must" program of legislation, with the result that the California legislature of 1913 rivaled the session of 1911 in the amount of new legislation it considered and passed. A law creating a state conservation commission was passed in the face of increasing conservative opposition. Largely framed by Francis J. Heney and former Governor Pardee, the bill sought to regulate and control the remaining undeveloped water resources in the state. Among its most important provisions was the stipulation that any further exploitation of water or water power was to be based upon the three fundamental and far-reaching principles: (1) The state should receive just compensation for all future private development of water resources. (2) The old common-law doctrine of riparian rights should cease to be valid after a ten-year period. (3) The value of any water or power rights granted in the future by the state should not be reflected in the capital structure of any private corporation or company. Passed by administrative pressure after it had once been defeated, the water resources measure was immediately subjected to referendum by the private power interests. But by the vote of the people in 1914 it was duly enacted into law.

By other administrative-sponsored legislation a State Commissioner of Corporations was created to examine all public issues of securities for fraudulent practices. A state Immigration and Housing Commission and an Irrigation and Rural

152

Credits Commission were instituted, pipelines were brought under the authority of the railroad commission, real-estate dealers were licensed, and the state civil service was widely extended. The only serious progressive setback was the defeat of bills regulating insurance companies and the dredger mining of gold in the rivers of the state.

In the realm of social and labor legislation, the positive accomplishments of the 1913 legislature were somewhat less impressive than in the regulation of corporate affairs. A Red Light Abatement Act, looking to the suppression of prostitution, was passed, as was an act setting up an Industrial Welfare Commission with power to regulate the minimum wages, maximum hours, and standard working conditions for children and women. An amendment to the Workingman's Compensation Act made it compulsory for all employers, except those engaged in farming, to contribute to the state insurance fund against industrial accidents. A bill creating free state employment bureaus was approved, only to be vetoed by Governor Johnson. Other labor legislation set a minimum wage of three dollars a day for all contract work by the state, prevented assignment of wages to "loan sharks," required employers to include notice of a strike whenever they advertised for men during a period of labor trouble, and provided for better factory inspection.

But the progressive mentality, which sought to aid the underprivileged individual while it frowned upon the rise of organized labor as a bargaining social group, was still at work in the 1913 legislature. The anti-injunction bill, and measures for legalizing peaceful picketing and requiring jury trials for contempt cases growing out of labor disputes, were defeated for the second time. Even though the national Progressive party platform had included specific promises to limit the issue and scope of labor injunction, the anti-injunction bill was clearly defeated by the negative votes of Johnson's supporters in the senate. And once again the left wing of the California progressive movement complained bitterly against the "political and moral progressives" from the south who were reformers only when "reform was cheap enough." More than balancing these attacks from the left, however, were the conservative charges that the "Johnson Ring" had sold itself to the devils of radicalism. "The cunning of labor union bosses and agitators who seek to fill the statutes of California with fiery Red and anticapital laws," ran a typical news story, "is strikingly shown in the myriads of anarchistic measures offered by their legislative slaves. . . ." Assailed from all sides, the center position in California politics was becoming increasingly unpleasant. It remained to be seen how long the average progressive would stand there.[26]

The remainder of the California legislative session of 1913 was devoted to framing and defending the alien land bill against the national administration. This measure was directed against the estimated 45,000 Japanese in California, who by 1914 owned 331 California farms and leased 282 more. Generally, the California progressive was just as determined to exclude the Japanese from any participation in the life of the state as were the labor unions and the small farmer. Although the Los Angeles Chamber of Commerce passed a resolution in 1910 favoring the admission of enough Oriental laborers to pick the fruit crop, even the southern progressives were strongly in favor of exclusion. On the whole, progressive sentiment toward Japanese ownership of land was neatly phrased by the *California Weekly*. "Our legislature," said that progressive sheet in 1909, "should limit Mongolian ownership of soil to a space four feet by six. A white population and a brown population, regardless of nationality or ideals, can never occupy the same soil together with advantage to either. Let us dwell apart and in amity, for we cannot dwell together that way." [27] There were limits to competition. To the progressive mind, one of these limits should be set at the color line.

Supported by the administration, antialien land bills were introduced in both houses early in the session. But strong opposition developed to the bills, first among the backers of the Panama Pacific International Exposition to be held in San

Francisco, and secondly among the representatives of European-owned land and mining interests in the state, whose property was definitely threatened by provisions discriminating against aliens and even corporations whose stock was held by aliens. It was only after the bill had been amended to allow corporations of European ownership to hold state land that the bill was finally passed by both houses. But then the national government objected on the grounds that the measures violated treaty undertakings with Japan and threatened serious international friction with that nation. After Secretary of State William Jennings Bryan's personal visit to Sacramento, the Heney-Webb Bill was substituted for the original measure. This act, which at least partly met the objections of the national administration, provided that aliens not eligible for citizenship could hold land in California only to the extent that the existing treaties between this country and their home nations permitted. With a few further amendments pertaining to the leasing of land, the bill was passed and signed by the Governor.

In addition to the imposing list of reforms already discussed, the Johnson administration enacted a weights and measures act, a child-labor statute, an antiusury law, and legislation giving pensions to the aged and to school teachers. It provided for the reform of criminal procedure in the state's courts, and for the establishment of the state board of control, which for the first time assured California of a businesslike budget system. Altogether this League program constituted one of the most sweeping charters of reform ever passed by an American state.

No complete story of the early progressive years in California can be told without directing some attention to the administrative revolution that went on throughout the state government. Under the old machine politics before 1911, the state offices and bureaus were regularly staffed by the party faithful whose main job, it appears, was to turn out the vote on election day. What civil service procedures existed were systematically ignored, and indifferent, incompetent, and even fraudulent administration was often the rule instead of the exception. As a result, investigating bodies seldom investigated and regulatory commissions rarely regulated. What was true of the railroad commission was also true of almost every state bureau. When Johnson came into office, this state superintendent of banks found that illegal practices had been habitually tolerated by his department. In fact, the superintendent reported, laws had been so "consistently winked at" and "evasions so systematically conducted" over such a long period of time, that the state bankers resented any state control as "officious interference." [28] Admittedly, the superintendent was not an unbiased observer of his predecessor's practices. But according to other evidence, his report was not without much basis in fact.

Within a short time after Johnson and his friends took office it was apparent that the entire state administration had been enormously invigorated. Laws that had gathered dust for years on the statute books were suddenly enforced. The term "public interest," as applied by regulatory commissions, took on new life and new meaning. Perhaps two pieces of evidence will suffice to indicate this new vitality. Before 1911 the state Bureau of Labor Statistics had contented itself with examining a few hundred cases of alleged labor law violations a year; by 1914 the same body had completed almost ten thousand investigations in a twelve-month period. Whereas the old railroad commission had scarcely been known even to suggest a rate reduction, in the first year of its existence the new body had reduced the earnings of the Wells Fargo Express Company from 130 per cent annually to a modest 10 per cent.[29]

This efficient administration continued through the progressive period in California. But after the first three years of the Johnson administration, the springs of legislative reform dried up rapidly. By the end of the 1913 legislature, the fundamental reforms of the progressive program had been virtually completed. From then on, within the state at least, the current of the progressive movement ran perceptibly slower. The progressive mentality, it seemed, was reaching the nether edge of permissible reform, and Johnson and his lieutenants set their eyes on the greener and more important pastures of national politics.

CHAPTER VII

Goodbye, My Party, Goodbye!

*

From the very beginning of their reform movement many of the California progressive leaders had been aware that the ends they hoped to achieve could not be secured through state politics alone. As early as 1907 they chose to call themselves Lincoln-Roosevelt Republicans, a name implying qualification of their Republicanism throughout the nation as well as inside the state. Two years before their initial state victory they indicted both Nelson W. Aldrich and Uncle Joe Cannon, the Republican leaders in the Senate and the House, for their reactionary standpat policies. During the campaign of 1908, they were the original Taft men in California because they believed that the Ohio candidate would carry out the policies of Theodore Roosevelt. They seriously debated the advisability of running liberal Republicans against the incumbent conservative congressmen then representing California. Their final decision to avoid national politics at that time arose from their weakness as a group and not from disinclination.

During the next two years the Lincoln-Roosevelt League identified itself more and more with the insurgent-progressive bloc in Congress. All through his successful primary campaign of 1910 Hiram Johnson repeatedly declared himself an insurgent. As the President and the progressive congressional group drifted farther apart, the California progressives became eager to find another Republican candidate for the 1912 presidential elections. At one time or another League papers proposed Theodore Roosevelt, Robert LaFollette, Senator Cummins, or Gifford Pinchot as substitutes for Taft in 1912.[1] Until the summer of 1910, they preferred Roosevelt. In person and in his principles, the former President appealed to the majority

158

of California reformers. Besides, he looked like a sure winner. After his return from Europe in the spring of 1910, however, Roosevelt was something of a disappointment to the Californians. For one thing, they failed to secure his endorsement in the hot primary fight against the machine. Secondly, they disapproved of his studied attempt during the summer of 1910 to bring the Republican progressive and conservative wings together again in support of the President. The California progressives were jubilant over Roosevelt's speech at Osawatomie, Kansas, where he enunciated his New Nationalism. But they were "not at all satisfied with the New York platform," which Roosevelt later dictated in the interest of his friend Henry Stimson.[2] And, finally, any chance of Roosevelt as their candidate in 1912 seemed to go completely by the board when the Colonel himself declared repeatedly that he was not available. Much worse, he was writing at the same time that he expected to support Taft for renomination.

Contrary to the attitude of the man from whom they had taken their name, the California Leaguers were in no mood for compromise in the fall of 1910. Their appetites whetted by the victory over the old Republican state machine, they looked forward to extending their movement to the nation. This was implicit in Governor-elect Johnson's remarks before the Republican State Central Committee in December. The California progressive movement, he said, owed nothing to either the national Republican or Democratic party, but placed its allegiance "with the LaFollette type of insurgency." The same tendency to separate themselves from the traditional Republican party was also evident in the remarks of Meyer Lissner. The coming division in politics would not be between the Republicans and Democrats, he predicted, but rather "between the Insurgents and the Progressives on the one hand, and the reactionaries on the other."[3] Coming from the newly elected chairman of the Republican State Central Committee, this was a striking comment.

On January 23, 1911, the nation's press announced the formation of the National Progressive Republican League.

Among its charter members were Hiram Johnson, William Kent, and Francis J. Heney. Founded in the Washington home of Senator LaFollette of Wisconsin, the League, according to its creators, had been formed to propagate progressive doctrine throughout the country. But its real purpose, as every acute politician recognized, was to nominate and elect a progressive Republican president in 1912. With Theodore Roosevelt out of the running there was only one logical man for the League to support—Senator Robert Marion LaFollette, the unquestioned leader of Middle Western progressivism. A supreme example of an incorruptible individual in politics, Battle Bob had been fighting the progressive fight in Wisconsin and in the United States Senate since the turn of the century. LaFollette had the support of both the farmer and laborer in his native state. His faith in the people was axiomatic, as was his opposition to corporate influence in government. Probably the most advanced prominent progressive of his day, LaFollette was a foe worthy of any opposition.

The Wisconsin senator was no stranger to California and California progressives. During 1909 he had toured part of the state, speaking for insurgent ideas in the interest of the Lincoln-Roosevelt Republican League. Scheduled to speak on the tariff before the City Club of Los Angeles, he told Marshall Stimson, who met him at the train, that instead of speaking on the tariff he was prepared to read *Hamlet* to the crowd because he had an entirely new interpretation of the play that would keep everyone on the edge of their seats. Stimson vigorously remonstrated that the crowd had gathered to hear a political speech, and it was only after considerable persuasion, and another audience found for his *Hamlet*, that LaFollette agreed to talk on the tariff.[4] Kept at home by his own campaign in Wisconsin in 1910, LaFollette, unlike Roosevelt, sent a warm message of encouragement to the California progressives during their campaign against the railroad machine.

LaFollette formally announced his campaign for nomination against President Taft on June 17, 1911. Although Hiram Johnson felt that the campaign should be pushed immediately,

160

the united support of the California progressives was not forthcoming. Both William Kent and Rudolph Spreckels had already contributed substantial financial aid to LaFollette, but for many weeks the rest of the California progressives were strangely silent. A few of them had already decided to back the President, and many more hoped that Taft would so change his policies that their support would be warranted. That hope was completely dashed, however, by the President's trip across the nation in the early autumn. If he had not made it clear before that he was completely out of sympathy with the progressive wing of the party, Taft did so on this trip. He praised Nelson W. Aldrich and denounced the insurgents during the first days of his trip, and reaffirmed his conservative allegiances in California. "Politely refusing" Johnson's invitation to stay at the governor's house at Sacramento, Taft proceeded to surround himself with the old guard in California, his principal companion being the standpatter Duncan McKinley, whom Kent had defeated in 1910 for Congress. At the official banquet for Taft in San Francisco, every rat in the state of California was out of his hole and present to do homage, according to Hiram Johnson, while every man who believed in political righteousness was elbowed aside. The California governor had listened intently for one note in all of Taft's speeches "in consonance with humanity," but he heard none, he wrote. "There was never in his attitude any indication that he was governing for any but one class, and for one purpose—business." [5]

Though alienated from Taft, many California progressives were still reluctant to cast their lot with the LaFollette movement. The senator was too radical for many of the "political," as distinct from the "economic" progressives, and many of the reformers, including Johnson, still hoped that Theodore Roosevelt could be persuaded to run. For the average California progressive the former President had two great virtues: he was more moderate in his views than LaFollette; and even more important, under the banner of the dynamic and colorful Roosevelt, victory seemed far more certain. After waiting

161

through most of the autumn without word from Roosevelt, the Californians began to lose hope, and then in mid-October, Governor Johnson received a letter from the former President stating definitely that he was not a candidate. A few days later Meyer Lissner wrote to LaFollette's campaign manager, urging the senator to make a speaking trip in California in the near future. Simultaneously, at a Chicago progressive conference Francis Heney, Fremont Older, Edward A. Dickson, and Chester Rowell announced their support of the Wisconsin man.[6]

This California announcement for LaFollette was decidedly belated, coming almost four months to a day after the senator had opened his formal campaign, and it was only half-hearted. Johnson and his colleagues had not yet given up Theodore Roosevelt. On October 20, 1911, the governor again wrote the former President fervently urging him to enter the race. The last paragraph of that letter said volumes about the California progressive attitude toward the election. After paying his respects to LaFollette's sterling qualities, Johnson was most pessimistic about his ability to succeed. The nomination of Taft, the governor believed, was foreordained as against Senator LaFollette. The same mood was evident in Chester Rowell's first LaFollette editorial. Although he commended the Wisconsin senator, the article was less than enthusiastic. Between the lines, it clearly indicated that the progressives were behind LaFollette simply because there was nothing better to do.[7]

But with the LaFollette decision made, it was still not certain that the Johnson progressives would take up cudgels for the senator. Rudolph Spreckels was already unofficially heading the LaFollette movement in the state, and few of the Johnson inner group had any love for the San Francisco capitalist; besides, if they furnished the votes for a cause, they insisted upon leading it. When Spreckels jumped the gun and called a state-wide organization meeting under his own name, the LaFollette sentiment among the Johnsonites rapidly cooled. Rowell, who "could not be there," felt that Spreckels "should go ahead locally," but that a state meeting should be postponed until after the legislature had adjourned. Not one of the Los Angeles leaders could attend, and Lissner pointedly referred Spreckels to Governor Johnson, "whose lead we shall follow." The governor himself found it impossible to be at the Spreckels meeting and thought the situation relieved his friends of all responsibility for the campaign. He was glad, he wrote in a moment of pique, to resign any responsibility and leave it all with Spreckels.[8]

Johnson's resignation from the LaFollette movement, however, was but the thought of an irritated moment. The California conservatives had already thrown in their lot with President Taft. To join them in supporting the President was unthinkable. Yet the regulars and their candidate could not be beaten without a countercandidate, and in November, 1911, Robert LaFollette appeared to be the only hope, however poor. Politics being the game it was and is, the Johnson forces consequently set about capturing the movement for themselves. Soon Lissner was writing the Wisconsin senator that his campaign manager was making a big mistake in "not making up" to Governor Johnson. Since Spreckels had "no enthusiastic following," Lissner pointedly remarked, the best policy in California was "to get the governor into the fight." Robert LaFollette was no child politically; he could take a hint. Spreckels, he replied, was not managing his campaign but only trying to raise money. He was quite aware that Governor Johnson was the unquestioned leader of progressive thought and action in California. Californians and not he should decide "campaign matters," he concluded diplomatically. With that extremely satisfactory reply Chester Rowell, not waiting this time for the legislature to adjourn, announced a state-wide LaFollette organization meeting for November 25, 1911. Invitations were sent out to all members of the Lincoln-Roosevelt Republican League, but apparently the name of Rudolph Spreckels was overlooked.[9]

The San Francisco LaFollette meeting listened to speeches by former Governor Pardee and Lieutenant Governor Wallace, among others, and then proceeded to elect Chester Rowell president of the newly organized California LaFollette League. But in many ways the organization seemed stillborn. For weeks after the meeting there was no visible sign of any considerable activity for the Wisconsin senator, either by the organization or by ostensible friends. Throughout December and January the president of the League scarcely mentioned the LaFollette candidacy in his paper. In Los Angeles even a deeper silence prevailed, especially until after the Socialists had been defeated in the December 10 mayoralty election. Earl, Dickson, Stimson, Avery, and Lissner had agreed that neither they nor their followers would join the LaFollette movement until after Job Harriman had been defeated. They needed the aid of the conservative Republicans in that campaign, they confessed, and their endorsement of LaFollette might alienate them. Between a Socialist mayor in Los Angeles and a conservative in Washington, the Angeleño reform leaders left no doubt as to their preference.[10]

Contributing further to the weakness of the newly organized LaFollette League was the resignation of Rudolph Spreckels the day after the San Francisco meeting. Spreckles' irritation was understandable. He was one of the original La-Follette men in the state, and one who had contributed considerable money to the cause. After his own attempt to organize the state had been thoroughly ignored, the "Johnny-come-lately progressives" had obviously won LaFollette's blessing. Moreover, they had neither asked him to make a speech at their meeting nor appointed him to any office within the organization. It was a little thick even for an insensitive man, which the San Francisco capitalist definitely was not. It took weeks of Rowell's most persuasive ways to win back the affronted Spreckels. He had not been personally invited to the meeting, Rowell wrote, because no one had been invited. He had not been invited to make a speech or placed in office because of his absence. With that explanation Spreckels came back into the fold, choosing to ignore the fallacy in both the premise and the subsequent reasoning.[11]

By far the most potent handicap that the California La-Follette organization carried in December of 1911 and the following month, was the inclination of its leaders to desert to Theodore Roosevelt, provided there was the slightest chance that the former President would change his mind about entering the presidential list. During the first ten months of 1911, Roosevelt thought it was "sheer folly" for the progressives to oppose the President. In the fall he was certain that LaFollette had lost ground and that there was a reactionary wave in the nation spelling defeat for any progressive. Most of all he believed that his own candidacy would be a tragedy both for himself and for the progressive movement. Therefore, he wrote to Hiram Johnson in late October, he was asking every good friend of his "to do everything possible to prevent not merely my nomination, but any movement looking toward my nomination." It was on the basis of this and previous letters that Johnson and his California friends had regretfully turned to LaFollette.

Within a month, however, the variable Roosevelt had changed his opinion about the desirability of the nomination. Boredom with private life, pressure from political friends, and the Taft administration's suit against the United States Steel Corporation, which Roosevelt interpreted as a personal attack, were all instrumental in his shift. Without committing himself to candidacy, the former President by December 1, 1911, was at least permitting close personal friends to "sound out the country." He still protested that he did not wish the nomination. But five days later he wrote, if the American people wished "for *their* sake" to have him undertake the struggle, "that was a totally different question." No one who knew Roosevelt intimately could possibly misinterpret the drift of his thoughts.[12]

Hints of Roosevelt's changing attitude, of course, soon spread among the nation's progressives, causing uncertainty and anguish. The California progressives, in particular, were distinctly perturbed as they carefully watched the growing movement in the East. Not on intimate terms with the Colonel

165

at that time, they had received no specific word of the future direct from Oyster Bay. Was the Roosevelt movement valid and sponsored by the Colonel, or was it merely a flurry of the moment soon to be destroyed by the man who had so recently declared himself uninterested? Much depended upon the right answer to that question. The position of the progressives in California would be highly dubious at best if they continued to support LaFollette and Roosevelt later became a candidate. On the other hand, to throw over the Wisconsin senator without making sure of "a better 'ole" did not seem to be political wisdom. They could think of nothing better to do than wait for a reply to the rather agonizing letter of inquiry sent from Sacramento to Oyster Bay during the first week in January.

On January 14, 1912, Theodore Roosevelt, dodging Johnson's more direct questions, asked the governor to come East and "consult on the political situation." Johnson was further spurred to action by another Roosevelt communication four days later stating "that the movement has grown so that it would be nonsense to affect longer to ignore it." Hurriedly, the governor arranged for a conference with his most intimate advisors to "determine on a definite presidential plan" before he set out across the country. But as Earl, Stimson, and Avery could not attend on such short notice, and Dickson was in Washington, only Rowell, Brundige, and Lissner gathered at the governor's mansion. The day of earnest discussion apparently produced little more than the decision that Johnson would act for all of them in the East, and that meanwhile the leaders in California would sing LaFollette's praises in a decidedly low voice. On January 23 Johnson announced that he was going East to visit his son Archie at Columbia University; at the same time the governor's office declared there had been "no change in the plans of the Progressives of California. They intend to go forward with the LaFollette contest as originally planned." [13]

Johnson's trip East and its purpose was not unknown to the LaFollette organization. Rowell was painfully frank in answer to a query from the senator's campaign manager as to why there had not been more LaFollette publicity in California. It had been delayed, he wrote, partly because he was busy, and partly because they "were trying to avoid a separate Roosevelt candidacy." With LaFollette and Roosevelt competing for Progressive votes, Rowell predicted, there was little hope of carrying California. He was awaiting definite word from Governor Johnson, who was to arrive in New York that day, before taking any action whatever. On the same day Rowell wrote another LaFollette supporter that they had agreed before Johnson left that until further decisions were made "it would be best not to do much public agitating." Pending word from Oyster Bay, the chairman of the California LaFollette League was obviously determined to put the LaFollette campaign in very deep cold storage.[14]

Meanwhile, Johnson had talked with Francis Heney in Chicago. Heney was positive that the LaFollette campaign in the East was a losing one. The senator, Heney reported, had spent all his time writing his autobiography instead of campaigning, and his candidacy had lost all its vitality. From Chicago Johnson went on to New York, arriving there on January 30. He immediately sat in on a conference with the Pinchot brothers, George L. Record, Medill McCormick, and Gilson Gardner. The others had just come from LaFollette's headquarters in Washington where they had heard the senator's campaign manager, Walter L. Hauser, say on January 29 that the campaign was hopeless and that the only way to defeat Taft was for LaFollette to withdraw and turn his strength over to Theodore Roosevelt. With the exception of Johnson, who would not commit himself, the New York conferees substantially agreed with Hauser's sentiments.[15]

On February 2 Hiram Johnson had lunch with Theodore Roosevelt at Oyster Bay. Afterward, Johnson wired back to California that Roosevelt was an active candidate and had been since the middle of January. This news, which would have made the Californian supremely happy a few months before, was now somewhat disconcerting. For although the Colonel was quite willing to listen to any reasonable suggestion, Johnson did not like the people who were heading the new movement. They were not their kind of people, he wired to his friends in the West. And there was LaFollette, to whom they had pledged themselves. Johnson felt he could not make a decision until the following week, when he was to talk with the senator in Washington.[16]

But before the California governor arrived in the capital city, the issue as to whether most of the important national progressive leaders were to continue supporting the Wisconsin senator was practically decided. On the evening of the same day that Johnson talked with Roosevelt, LaFollette made a tragic speech at the Philadelphia periodical publishers' dinner. Worried about an illness of his daughter and the apparently wholesale defection among his supporters, he lost command of himself. For two hours he delivered a confused and bitter tirade against the nation's publishers. Then he sank into his seat, clearly an exhausted, if not a sick man. The following day the press carried stories of Senator LaFollette's "breakdown."

The incident at Philadelphia came like providential rain to many LaFollette supporters who had long since transferred their affection, though not their public allegiance, to Roosevelt. On Sunday, February 4, Senators Bourne, Bristow, and Clapp, Representative Lenroot of Wisconsin, and John D. Fackler, LaFollette's Ohio campaign manager, met with Walter Hauser. The latter apparently agreed with the majority of those present that LaFollette should withdraw immediately. The following day Hauser showed at least four men a typewritten announcement in which Battling Bob "specifically withdrew" and advised his friends to support any progressive who had a chance to beat Taft. The statement was to be issued, Hauser told the group, after LaFollette's state managers had had time to switch their support to Roosevelt. Whether the senator himself approved or even saw that fateful message is doubtful. But of its existence there can be no doubt. Senator Clapp saw it and told George L. Record about it in Jersey City that night. Gilson Gardner saw it, and John D. Fackler went home to Ohio with the understanding

Willie, the Bellman

San Francisco Call, November, 1910

"WILLIE THE BELLMAN"

LIKE FATHER LIKE SON.

San Francisco Examiner

"LIKE FATHER LIKE SON"

FRONT AND REAR.

San Francisco Examiner

"FRONT AND REAR"

that he was to switch the LaFollette forces in his state to Roosevelt after twenty-four hours unless he heard of a change in plan. When no different advice came within the allotted period, Fackler made the change. The Pinchots, Medill McCormick, William Flinn, and many others publicly announced their new allegiance. It was a blow from which the LaFollette candidacy never recovered. Since the senator and Hauser later denied that they had ever sanctioned or even thought of withdrawing, the entire episode created bitter feelings on both sides which were to last for years.[17]

Meanwhile, back in California, the progressive leaders were still in the dark and divided in opinion as to the best course to follow. On January 30 Lissner was opposed to taking a Roosevelt-LaFollette poll in the group because he felt that the great majority of California liberals would be for Roosevelt, and since in all probability they "will have to make a LaFollette campaign," the results would put them "in a hole." Six days later he agreed with Rowell that a Roosevelt stampede was probably inevitable. Lissner did not feel, however, that they should start a "Roosevelt-Johnson boom" as Rowell had suggested, until they heard something more definite from the governor. Instead, the two men secretly polled the progressive leadership in the state and found, as they had expected, an overwhelming majority in favor of swinging to Roosevelt. This information was promptly sent to Johnson, who was now in Washington.[18]

The tricornered correspondence between Johnson, Rowell, and Lissner now took on the air of the best international spy novels. Messages were broken in half and each part sent in code. Occasionally, one half of a message was not delivered to the right person and general confusion resulted. It was highly exciting. All three were now eager to declare themselves for Roosevelt but they were embarrassed about LaFollette, and each was reluctant to initiate California's swing to Roosevelt. Johnson was full of sympathy for LaFollette. Still, he wired, if their crowd was to be a factor, Roosevelt was the only choice. That decision, however, should first be made by the home people. Rowell and Lissner, also sorry for the senator, felt they had "gone the limit" with him. The time to make a clean break had come; but they fervently agreed that the first statement should come from Johnson.

For the next few days Johnson and the two men in California wired back and forth briskly, each suggesting that the announcement be made at the other end. On February 13 Rowell and Lissner concluded: "We may have to make an announcement at once, if the Governor does not." But finally, five days later, Johnson informed Lissner that he would speak the next day. He had been busy working on the declaration of principles that Roosevelt was soon to give before the Ohio constitutional convention, at which time he planned formally to announce his candidacy. Lissner in turn cryptically wired Rowell: "Expect issue black [statement] tomorrow speaking for our crimson [progressives]." On February 19, as Johnson declared himself in New York, Rowell called for a state-wide Roosevelt organization meeting to be held on February 28. LaFollette was being left, according to the progressive chorus, because his campaign was hopeless, because he had been supported only in the first instance as a "sacrifice for 1916," because he "was so seriously ill" that a further effort might even mean "murder," and because Roosevelt was a sure winner.[19]

When the California progressive leaders turned to Roosevelt they took with them practically all of LaFollette's supporters. The returns from a postcard poll taken by Rowell showed that among the party's local workers almost a six to one majority favored the Colonel. Rudolph Spreckels remained with the Wisconsin senator, and several leading progressives, including Kent and Hichborn, were not too enthusiastic about the new hope. But for the most part the delegates convening at the Roosevelt state organization meeting were fired with an almost religious zeal. Roosevelt was the man they had wanted all along, and Roosevelt was the one man they believed equal to the task of defeating Taft and thus saving the Republican party and California progressivism from certain defeat in November.

Taft and Roosevelt did not personally solicit votes in California as they did in the East. Only LaFollette stumped the state. But the absence of the two major candidates did not stop their followers from exchanging the violent abuse that characterized the 1912 contest elsewhere. In the conservative journals Roosevelt was depicted as a man on horseback, ready to sacrifice every fundamental principle of American democracy to sate his enormous ambition. If successful, this third term attempt, it was freely predicted, would result in a fourth and a fifth term and a consequent loss of the democratic system. This "furtive and treacherous" personal quality had been obvious in Roosevelt's entire career, one conservative paper observed.[20]

Johnson's progressives returned as good as they got in the campaign. To them this was the same struggle that had been waged in the state in 1910, now raised to the national scene. Pointing to the fact that former Senator Flint, former Governor Gillett, and Sam Shortridge were supporting Taft, the progressives charged that the old machine was attempting a comeback behind the more than ample back of the President. Once more the Southern Pacific was properly denounced, and once more the hustings sounded with the cry of fraud, dishonesty, and vice. Taft and his conservatives, however, did not worry the progressives in California nearly so much as did LaFollette. The reiterated charge by the LaFollette men that the progressives were apostates was irritating enough. Of far more weight in the Johnsonites' rising discomfort was the realization that the LaFollette vote in the state would not be negligible. Lissner was sure that he was going "to cut into" them, and Johnson himself admitted that he was worried about the senator's strength. There was no thought of the senator's winning the state, but the capital question was if he would take enough votes away from Roosevelt to permit Taft to win. Consequently, when LaFollette toured the state

175

in late April, both Johnson and Heney followed and answered him speech for speech.[21]

Hiram Johnson had the same penchant as Theodore Roosevelt for ascribing the basest intentions to an opponent even if that opponent had been a friend the day or so before. During the first few weeks after the California progressives had swapped presidential horses, the governor felt charitably inclined toward the Wisconsin senator. But his sense of charity wore increasingly thin during the heat of the rising struggle. It disappeared entirely when LaFollette and Spreckels bitterly described Johnson and his friends as "apostates." Johnson and Heney had agreed that they would not mention the senator personally in their campaign, but this was a position too moderate for either of these intensely partisan men to hold for long. And although Johnson did become incensed at Heney upon one occasion, for mentioning LaFollette by name, the governor himself could not resist branding the senator as a man "overcome with a sense of his own importance." Away from the public ear he was much more personal. In LaFollette's blind rage and intense egotism, Johnson charged, he was in reality seeking the destruction of the progressive movement and his continual lying was dissipating all the respect he had once earned. The conclusion Johnson felt forced to arrive at was that LaFollette was totally crooked. As someone has observed, the trouble with politicians as compared with other men is that politicians preserve their correspondence.[22]

The results of the primary election of May 14 for the selection of delegates to the Republican national convention indicated once again the powerful hold of progressivism on the state. The Roosevelt ticket, headed by Johnson, Rowell, Kent, Heney, Lissner, Stimson, and Eshleman, polled more votes than the Taft and LaFollette tickets combined. Only on the Democratic side of the struggle was there something of an upset. Supported by Theodore Bell, Champ Clark defeated Woodrow Wilson decisively. The progressive victory on the Republican ticket not only assured all but two of the state delegates for Roosevelt, but it also made Hiram Johnson a real contender for the vice-presidential nomination. The "Roosevelt-Johnson boom" that Rowell had proposed in early February had been assiduously fostered both in and out of California. If Roosevelt were nominated by the Republican convention, the New York *Times* speculated in early March, Hiram Johnson would probably be his choice for vice-president. After the successful primary election, Lissner and Rowell wondered whether they should go to Chicago early "to work up the Johnson spirit." The plan was discarded upon Johnson's own objections. The governor believed, Lissner wrote, that if Roosevelt was nominated he would dictate everything else, "and of course, there is much truth in that suggestion." [23]

Few preconvention periods in American political history have been so punctuated with personal recrimination and hatred as the one that ended in June, 1912. Roosevelt's unprecedented action in running against the man he had made president just four years before, his attacks upon the Supreme Court, the advanced radicalism of his New Nationalism, and the bitter personal feeling he held for Taft had excited tempers on both sides of the controversy to white heat. With the results still unknown in the first week in June because of the 254 contested delegates, all moderation departed in the rising tenseness. "Mark these words!" declared the usually temperate *Harper's Weekly*, "Roosevelt's election to the Presidency would spell revolution within ten years. And by revolution we do not mean mere political overturning of a system of government. We mean actual warfare by force of arms upon the rule of a despot. We mean bloodshed and carnage!" [24]

In such an air the Republican National Committee met in Chicago on June 7, to make up the temporary roll of the convention. Dominated by a majority favorable to the Taft administration, its decision would be crucial. If Theodore Roosevelt won as many as fifty of the contested seats his nomination appeared certain. If he did not his cause was doomed, irrespective of his being the unquestioned choice of Republican voters, as the returns from the direct primaries in thirteen states indicated. Two of these contested delegates came from California's fourth Congressional district in San Francisco. The fundamental point in the dispute arose over a conflict between state primary legislation and the rules of the national Republican party. In short, California law provided for the election of all delegates by the voters of the state at large, whereas the party rules directed that all except so-called designated delegates-at-large should be elected on the basis of the returns from Congressional districts. Since Roosevelt had won the state by an overwhelming majority at the same time that two Taft men had apparently won majorities in the San Francisco district, the conflict had to be resolved. Complicating the question was the recent change in the boundaries of the district which cut through the heart of fourteen precincts in the city. Although the Taft majorities were certified immediately after the election, the city registrar of voters later testified that it was impossible to say who had received the majorities in the disputed district.

Among the men representing the Roosevelt interests in the national committee meetings was Francis J. Heney. Characteristically, Heney pulled no punches in his attack upon the opposition during the hectic two-week session of that body. Apropos of the California squabble, he charged that the committee had framed a plot to steal the entire delegation. "I intend to hurl their crooked schemes right into their teeth," he announced before the question was argued. At one point, after the lie had been passed directly, Heney and a North Dakota member of the committee would have had a fist fight had they not been immediately surrounded. During the actual debate over the dispute, Heney told the committee, "Abe Ruef could learn more crooked business in ten minutes by watching you fellows than he acquired in a whole lifetime in California." Meanwhile, Hiram Johnson added to the festivities. Invited to attend the meetings while the California matter was under discussion, Johnson refused to attend anything that looked like the proceedings of the Calhoun machine. "I will not submit to a trial to the title of property by the thief who steals it," the governor snapped in true Roosevelt fashion. But personal zeal and aggressiveness were no match for a majority vote, and the Taft-dominated committee ruled against the two California progressive delegates just as they did in scores of other Roosevelt contests. Of the 254 contested seats, 235 were awarded to Taft and 19 to Roosevelt.[25]

In attempting to evaluate the justice of the California decision as well as all the other critical findings of the national committee, the historian is tempted to ask, like Pontius Pilate, "What is truth?" These things are clear about the controversies: Both sides were inconsistent in their claims; even the most just of men could not have made infallibly fair decisions on so many issues in the allotted time; the majority of the committee was unquestionably pro-Taft before the meeting; the committee, in seating enough Taft delegates to control the convention, was acting on the basis of good political precedent, dutifully adhered to by Theodore Roosevelt in 1908.

Roosevelt and his followers were not men to take a licking lying down. They argued that in the face of popular sentiment this was a bare-faced fraud upon the people of the United States, and the air was filled with righteously indignant cries of thievery. Concerning the California decision, the Roosevelt Chicago office issued the following example of what passed on both sides in 1912 for reasoned statements: "The saturnalia of fraud and larceny now in progress under the auspices of the national committee took on new repulsiveness today with the announcement of the committee's action in the case of California. . . . Hitherto it was supposed that the national committee was content with the political emoluments of pocket picking and porch climbing. Today, however, it essayed the role of the apache and the garroteer." [26]

In California, tempers were just as high at this action of the national committee. More than 2,000 people met at the Santa Fe Station in Los Angeles to see the delegates off to Chicago and to protest the stealing of the two California delegates. They cheered excitedly as Lee C. Gates roundly denounced the Chicago proceedings and ended with a significant promise. "You'll have a chance to vote for Roosevelt," he said as the train was pulling out. "If you don't have it by the convention of hand-picked delegates, you'll have it by another convention." That Gates was not speaking for himself alone was indicated by an editorial in the Earl-controlled Los Angeles *Tribune*. The piece called upon the California delegates to stand by their principles. If these were overridden, the paper trumpeted, "Republicans of the state of California call upon you to unite with delegates from other states and found the Progressive party. . . ." Of even more significance was Johnson's last letter to Meyer Lissner before he left for the East. "I think we may preside at the Historic Birth of the Progressive Party," the governor wrote on June 9, 1912. While still on the way to Chicago, the California delegation passed a resolution empowering Governor Johnson to commit it to any plan that would insure the submission of Theodore Roosevelt to the electorate in the fall election. In the convention city, Johnson became the first prominent progressive leader to demand the founding of a new party. Before the Republican convention met, California's governor had already proposed a walk away from the old party. Thus, in a very real sense, Hiram Johnson became one of the fathers of the Progressive party.[27]

The convention met on Tuesday, June 18, amid wild rumors of violence and disorder. As conservative papers gave credence to mythical reports that Roosevelt had organized a strong-arm squad equipped with firearms and led by the "hoodlum Heney," the California delegation marched into the convention hall breathing defiance to anyone who tried to remove Charles S. Wheeler and Philip Bancroft, the two delegates discredited by the national committee. The two California Taft delegates were finally escorted into the hall by the police and seated as far away as possible from the main body of Californians, who had publicly threatened to throw them out if they tried to sit with the rest of the state delegation. From that first moment, members of the California delegation were in the midst of the Donnybrook Fair that followed. Gaining the rostrum on the opening day, Heney, his finger pointed at a member from Colorado, shouted that the only difference between him and Abe Ruef was that Ruef was in the penitentiary while he, as a member of the national committee, had helped to make the temporary roll of the convention. Fist fights broke out on the floor in the resulting uproar, and Heney had to leave the speaker's stand, his speech unfinished, but unable to make himself heard.[28]

Beaten by a bare majority of twenty-nine votes in the election of the temporary chairman, the Roosevelt forces turned to the credentials committee as the court of last appeal. There Hiram Johnson led the Roosevelt forces, and there again they were met by the stubborn Taft majority. Twice in twenty-four hours Johnson led the Roosevelt men out of the room in protest against an unfavorable decision. The credentials committee, Mr. Dooley remarked, "was interrupted from time to time be th' usual routine bolt iv th' Rosenfelt dillygates, led be Guviner Johnson iv California. I like that man. He can get out iv a convention an' back in again as quick as any man iv his weight I iver see." [29]

The next day Johnson was to lead his Californians out of the convention again, this time for good. When it became clear that the committee would seat enough delegates to insure Roosevelt's defeat, the Colonel called his leaders together for a fateful conference. There, in the rooms of the Congress Hotel, on the night of June 20, the Progressive party was born. After the decision for the great secession was made, Governor Johnson confessed that he would have preferred to walk out of the Republican party many days before.

On the following day, the Republican convention nominated William Howard Taft by a vote of 561 to 107 for Roosevelt, and 41 for LaFollette. But 344 of the delegates had refused to vote. Most of them were at Orchestra Hall that night, listening to Hiram Johnson give the opening speech of the new Progressive party. Shortly thereafter, Theodore Roosevelt announced that he would accept nomination by the new party if it were offered to him by a convention called and elected in the traditional fashion. As the California delegation entrained for home, they were a happy group. Two years before they had won California; the stakes were now nationwide. They stood with Theodore Roosevelt at Armageddon and they battled for the Lord.

From the moment of the birth of the new party, the California progressives were among its most prominent leaders. Governor Johnson was made chairman of the national organizing committee, and his suggestions on the proposed platform weighed heavily with Roosevelt. The platform should be radical, Johnson advised Roosevelt, by which he meant the radicalism that had obtained in such states as California, rather than the radicalism of Debs.[30] The Californians were much in evidence at the first Progressive party convention that opened in Chicago on August 5. There Francis J. Heney worked out the compromise in the provisional national committee for settling the vexing color question among the southern delegations. There Johnson, Rowell, and Lissner led the fight against the influence of George W. Perkins who, with the multimillionaire newspaper publisher, Frank Munsey, was supplying most of the money for Roosevelt's campaign. In fact, at one time during the convention, the battle grew so bitter between Johnson and former Senator Beveridge and Perkins, that it threatened to disrupt the party before the nominations were even made. Beveridge became so enraged at Johnson that during a great demonstration for Roosevelt he alternated between leading the cheers and telephoning Roosevelt to urge him to give up the whole thing and threatening to walk out himself.[31]

The first quarrel of the Californians with George Perkins opened a schism in the party that was never to heal. Perkins was a Morgan partner, a one-time executive of the New York Life Insurance Company, and a director of the International Harvester and the United States Steel corporations. Because of his power and money—he contributed over a quarter of a million dollars to the 1912 campaign—he took a commanding position in the new party from its very origins. Moreover, he used that position to decry a fundamental progressive principle of trust busting and to praise the stabilizing influence of the great corporations and the men who ran them. Perkins' prescription for the industrial ills of the nation was not a return to the competitive system but rather the institution of a persuasive system of paternalistic governmental regulation of both industry and labor. Obviously, he was a strange political companion for the self-styled "rank individualists" from the west. Johnson, Lissner, and Rowell disagreed not only with Perkins' economic doctrines; they also distrusted the man himself. Was he not the perfect example of the "men in broadcloth" whom Johnson had so recently arraigned in California? They joined the brothers Pinchot in their opposition to Perkins' platform proposals. Later, the same combination objected to Perkins' appointment as chairman of the national committee. On both points they were beaten. Consistently supported by Roosevelt, Perkins not only had the famous "missing antitrust plank" deleted from the platform, but also, according to Chester Rowell, insisted that the sociological part of the document be "changed back into the bad English in which he had originally written it." To make the pill even more bitter, the day after the convention adjourned the New York capitalist was elected chairman of the national committee.[32]

But the California delegation did not come away from the August convention empty-handed. Aside from the trust plank, they had seen their desires and more written into a platform, the most progressive political document presented to the American people by a major party since the days of the Populists. In fact, the California progressives who had objected strenuously to the regulation of working conditions and hours and to the limitation of labor injunctions in their own state, must have been a little uncomfortable with the advanced social position of this national Progressive platform. Of even more importance to the Californians was Roosevelt's personal selection of Hiram Johnson as his running mate. Johnson refused to be considered for the vice-presidency unless several other aspirants for that honor withdrew, an act of abnegation for which they showed little inclination. It was only after Roosevelt's personal intercession that the ambitious contestants retired, and the touchy Johnson was persuaded to accept the honor.[33]

Meanwhile, in California the newly self-designated Progressives had met and solved, at least to their own satisfaction, an extremely important question. Immediately after the organization of the new party, the California leaders were forced to decide whether they would organize a new state Progressive party or cling to their control of the existing Republican machine. The problem was delicate, perplexing, and withal exceedingly embarrassing. Consistency and perhaps honor called for the construction of a new party. But more material considerations argued the other way. A careful examination of the California election laws, Johnson wrote most confidentially, indicated that if a new party were formed both its candidates for the legislature and presidential electors would have to run as independent candidates and thus be mixed in with a list of prohibitionists and other splinter party nominees. To acquire its own separate ticket, a party had to poll at least 3 per cent of the vote in the previous election. Admixture with all these independent candidates, Johnson thought, meant defeat. The governor had no other comment on the situation except that it looked "damn bad." [34]

On July 6 twenty progressive leaders met at Sacramento to consider the problem. After hours of argument they decided to be Republicans within the state and Progressives nationally. Under the election law of California the men nominated for presidential electors were selected at party conventions comprised of the nominees for the state offices and the holdover senators. All the Progressives had to do, apparently, to retain their hold on the state Republican party, was to nominate at the September Republican primary a majority of the eighty assemblymen and twenty senators pledged to name Roosevelt electors. When the Progressives' decision became known a roar went up from the regular Republicans. Describing the strategy as bald-faced robbery and sheer dishonesty, the old guard demanded that Meyer Lissner resign as chairman of the Republican state committee, and that the Progressives clear out of the Republican party entirely. Lissner, of course, refused and pointed out that the primary offered them a chance to win. If they won the party was theirs; if they lost they still retained the "right to squeal as usual." And since the old guard had no power within the organization, they had to acquiesce, however unwillingly.[35]

The outcome of the September 3 primaries was never in doubt. Of the one hundred legislators elected at least eighty had pledged themselves to vote for Roosevelt electors. At the state convention held at Sacramento later in the month, the thirteen "Taft Republicans" could do nothing better than bolt the meeting and hold a rump convention, at which they drew up a list of Taft electors and appointed a Republican State Central Committee in opposition to the already existing party machinery. Subsequently, they petitioned the state Supreme Court for a writ of mandamus directing the Secretary of State to place the Taft electors on the Republican ballot and refuse that designation to the Progressive nominees supporting Roosevelt. But the court held that the electors had been selected legally and that the judiciary could not concern itself with their opinions. Since the Taft men refused to place electors on the ballot by petition, Californians wishing to vote for the Republican President had to write his name in on the ballot in the November elections. To all intents and purposes the Republican party had removed itself from the 1912 California elections.

If the Progressives had won easily over their old enemies, the standpatters, they realized that success in the final election was far from assured. For one thing, they had suffered serious defections in their own ranks. Rudolph Spreckels and the men who had supported LaFollette had neither forgotten nor forgiven. William Kent had refused to become a national

Progressive, preferring to run for Congress as an independent candidate. Senator Works, former Senator Bard, and Assemblyman Drew, all former Lincoln-Roosevelt members, flatly refused to leave the Republican party either nationally or in the state. Drew may have been prompted by a sense of party regularity. Bard and Works, however, were vehemently opposed to the "radicalism" of the new party, a feeling shared by not a few of the old Lincoln-Roosevelt Leaguers. When Works publicly attacked his old comrades for their "treachery" to the party of "sound conservative principles," the Los Angeles group, headed by Lissner, formally asked him to resign his seat in the Senate since he no longer represented the opinion of those who had elected him.

But perhaps the greatest blow to Progressive hopes for victory in California, as in the nation, lay in the nomination of Woodrow Wilson by the Democratic party. Acclaimed by the Johnson forces in the past as one of the most "advanced progressives in the country," Wilson was a formidable opponent. If only Clark had been nominated, Johnson moaned, the California progressive movement would have remained unified and obtained support from both reform-minded Republicans and Democrats. Now, as the governor diagnosed, Wilson was in the fortunate position of having both the crooked and progressive wing of his party to espouse his candidacy. Johnson, in 1912, apparently saw little difference between a conservative and a crook.

For the Democratic candidate to wean away the Democratic progressives was bad enough. What hurt more was his support from former Republicans. "I don't like the way many are talking since the Democratic nomination," Lissner wired to Johnson. These apprehensions became fully realized fears when one after another former LaFollette supporter followed Rudolph Spreckels into the Wilson camp. "It is too bad," Lissner wrote, compounding irritation with regret, "to find a man with such potentialities, so arrogant, aristocratic and strabismic, he will never learn the value of teamwork." Exactly what Spreckels' ocular contortions had to do with his politics, Lissner never explained.[36]

Meanwhile the campaign had got under way. From the first the new national Progressives in California were under fire from both the conservative Republicans and the Wilsonian Democrats. By the Taftites they were assailed for their radicalism, their lack of party loyalty, and their "unscrupulous methods in clinging to the Republican party." To the San Francisco *Chronicle,* the Roosevelt party was the party of "muckrakers—those who besmirch honest men; the liars . . . and the thieves—those who would steal the name of a party which they do not belong to. . . ." By the Democrats, Johnson and his colleagues were accused of being frauds as reformers and in reality representing George Perkins, United States Steel, and the House of Morgan. In the words of Wilson, the Progressives were supporting the great industrial combinations in their attempt to dominate the country, by the setting up of an industrial commission which actually would be controlled by the very concerns which they were supposed to regulate. As palpable proof of these charges, Wilson, Brandeis, and other Democratic campaigners in California pointed to the missing antitrust plank and the "pervasive" influence of George W. Perkins in the new party.[37]

Since Hiram Johnson as the vice-presidential candidate had to spend most of his time campaigning outside California, he made only a few speeches in his native state, the most important of these being at the Dreamland Rink in San Francisco immediately after his return from the Progressive national convention. Before the 12,000 cheering people welcoming him home, Johnson seemed like a new man. The governor had been deeply affected by the spirit of that remarkable body which he described as "carrying a Bible in one hand and a claymore in the other." Instead of the pugnacious warrior of two years before, full of "fighting guts" and smiting the foe hip and thigh, he appeared now as an evangelical pleader for righteousness and social justice. The old fire was still there occasionally as he blasted at his old enemies, the standpatters, but most of his time he spent in defense of the Progressive platform designed "to bridge this awful chasm that exists in our country between those who are ever growing richer, and those who are ever growing poorer." In that great social crusade he asked for the enlistment of "all that is best in humanity, all that fever, all that enthusiasm that makes men grasp each other in warm embrace with tears running down their faces." [38]

Ten days later Johnson left the state on a cross-country tour. During the next ten weeks he made 500 speeches in twenty-two states from Utah to Maine. And following Roosevelt's lead, scarcely once did he depart far from the general tenor of his opening notes in San Francisco. At Madison Square Garden in New York City at the end of October, he was still talking generalities about morality and public conscience. Such labor in the vineyard of righteousness, however, did not improve the governor's temper. As grueling weeks piled up, he became increasingly irritable. This time most of his spleen was taken out against Perkins, Munsey, and the New York Progressive headquarters. Whereas Roosevelt had a private car and was surrounded with newspaper correspondents, Johnson was afforded only a public Pullman and, he complained, at times he even had to make his own reservations. Nor did the party headquarters think enough of his efforts to send along even one publicity man. Then too, he felt they were "making him somewhat of a goat" by working him to death. Johnson finally exploded when the New York office scheduled several speeches without first consulting him. The whole campaign, he wrote to Perkins, had been horribly mismanaged. He threatened to quit the campaign, and those at Progressive headquarters were only able to persuade him to meet many of his engagements with "considerable difficulty." To an entreaty from home he replied with emphasis that he would not campaign in California after his return; he was too weary and disgusted. Eight years later Johnson was to be offered the vice-presidential nomination again. This time, had he accepted, he would have become President of the United States. It is more than possible that a good deal of the painful experience of 1912, when Johnson was the number-two man on the ticket, dictated his brusque refusal of Harding's offer in 1920.[39]

Other things contributed to Johnson's testiness during the campaign. After Roosevelt was shot at in Milwaukee in mid-October, the national committee expected Johnson to stay in the East until the day before the election, filling the Colonel's speaking dates. Despite the fact that the attorney general of California declared that he might legally stay out of the state for more than sixty days, he was worried that his enemies might bring court action against him. Assured that "the fear of God is in the courts," he was nevertheless troubled, and at one time thought of making the trip to California and coming back to the East just to have an anchor to the wind. On top of this, Johnson never once dreamed of the possibility of winning. From the first to the last he was convinced that it was a losing cause, at least for 1912. And then the frightening thought occurred that they might lose California. Lissner tried to be cheerful in his letters, but again and again the governor wired that all of his advices and estimates placed the state either in the Wilson or in the doubtful column. The worst news coming to him, he wrote in mid-October, was from California. Later, on the eve of the election, he was a little more optimistic about California, but believed that the Roosevelt-Johnson ticket would carry only eleven other states.[40]

Even this gloomy prediction proved to be too hopeful. The Progressive party outside of California won just Pennsylvania, Michigan, South Dakota, and Washington. Wilson had carried San Francisco by more than 10,000 votes but was beaten in the state by the substantial Roosevelt-Johnson majority rolled up in Los Angeles. In a long analysis of the vote, Lissner judged that their failure in San Francisco was due to the opposition of organized labor. The Progressives, he observed, had not carried a single district south of Market Street. And although the state legislature was safe, the Progressive candidates in the congressional elections had fared worse than had the Lincoln-Roosevelt Leaguers in 1910. In all California only three certain Progressives, William D. Stephens, William Kent, and John I. Nolan were successful. The south had done wonderfully well by them in the election; the north had been simply hell, was Johnson's final observation on his unsuccessful vice-presidential campaign.[41]

A month after the dismal returns of 1912 had been counted, Governor Johnson wrote that he was completely on edge. "Every dog was in full cry," it seemed, demanding that the would-be progressives either get out of the Republican party or renounce their national Progressive connections. And yet the trouble with making such a decision was that there were great drawbacks for the California Progressives whichever way they went. Johnson and his associates could not very well call themselves Republicans after the Chicago convention. Still, as a matter of practical politics, their control of California might depend upon their remaining Republicans within the state. They were not happy either with the state of the Progressive party. As the months went by, many of them grew conspicuously less happy. Johnson, Lissner, Heney, and Rowell had been opposed to Perkins' position in the party before the election; they were even more so now. Perkins was not the man, Johnson felt, to be the public exponent of the progressive movement. But since Johnson did not have the heart to add to Roosevelt's troubles just then, Lissner and Heney spoke for the California progressives on the subject. Lissner wrote to Perkins and Roosevelt that he was sorry to say he was still of the opinion that he had held when he opposed Perkins' election as chairman of the national committee. Francis J. Heney added his voice to the protest against Perkins. But when Roosevelt replied that he "was outraged at these attacks upon Perkins" by men ready "to sacrifice every principle of fair dealing and every question of the welfare of the party to the gratification of personal animosity," the Californians subsided for awhile. Heney attended the December Chicago conference of the party as Lissner's proxy. There the much disputed antitrust plank was reinserted into the platform as a gesture to the rebels. But Roosevelt himself was so angry at these "foolish and intemperate radicals" that he would not even talk to them about Perkins. At a later meeting of the national committee an anti-Perkins resolution to remove the party national headquarters from New York to Chicago was easily beaten. Perkins' influence in the party was increased rather than diminished, and the committee proceeded by a substantial majority to empower the chairman to issue statements at any time on any subject in the name of the committee and the party. Whether the Californians liked it or not George W. Perkins was, and would remain for some time, the official voice of the party. It was a particularly bitter decision to Johnson and his associates. In California they had opposed and defeated the control of politics by great wealth. Now in the house of their friends they feared they might be forced to succumb to it.[42]

Other considerations also added to the California reformers' indecisiveness as to whether or not they should cut loose from the old party. During the first months of 1913 it appeared to some observers that the less than year-old Roosevelt party was already disintegrating. The Progressive leaders had hoped after the election that many of the so-called prominent progressive Republicans would soon join their ranks. Instead of becoming converts, George Norris, Joseph Bristow, Herbert Hadley, William E. Borah, William S. Kenyon, and Albert B. Cummins were more cool to the new movement than they had been before. And instead of gaining members, the Bull Moosers appeared to be losing them. William Kent, for one, announced that he would not join the Progressive congressional caucus when he arrived in Washington. Throughout the country other so-called Progressives were acting "extremely queer." Moreover, the Progressive political machine, jerry-built as it was in the space of weeks, had practically folded up within six months after the election. Without money, patronage, or influence except in a few states like California, there was little adhesive power in the Progressive party to hold its members together.

Of all the blows struck at the continued vitality of the party in 1913, the desertion of Frank A. Munsey was by far the worst. This wealthy personal friend of Roosevelt had contributed more than $200,000 to the party in 1912, besides support in his chain of powerful newspapers. Munsey had never been very interested in progressive reforms; the principles of the old Republican party, by his own admission, satisfied him perfectly. Now he was through with subsidizing "uplift." In a series of articles beginning in the February, 1913, issue of *Munsey's Magazine*, he proposed to return to the Republican party through "an amalgamation process." After this, from time to time there were even rumors that Roosevelt was willing to come back to the old Republican fold. Returning to Los Angeles in July after a talk with the Colonel, Francis J. Heney reported Roosevelt as saying that if the Republicans threw out the reactionaries and adopted the Progressive platform, nothing but himself stood in the way of a reconciliation. And if the Republicans demanded that he not be a candidate again as a prerequisite to fusion he would agree to that.[43] Grave doubt, apparently, existed all along the party's ranks as to whether the Progressive party would continue much longer as a going concern.

The California progressive leaders, meanwhile, had long debated if it was wise to leave their comfortable position in the state Republican party and embark upon this hazardous new political venture. Most of them agreed that national success was improbable until a breakup occurred in the Democratic party between liberals and conservatives. But no man in January, 1913, could with certainty predict that such an event would or would not occur. Likewise, no one could know whether they, as Progressives, could maintain their hold on the state they had won as Republicans. There was also a danger of the disintegration of the Progressive party itself. Theodore Roosevelt's letter to Hiram Johnson on the point was not reassuring. Asked whether he approved of the Munsey fusion movement, Roosevelt had refused to answer the governor yes or no. Munsey, he wrote, while acting "unwisely," had been prompted by very natural and "entirely proper motives." As for himself, he hoped "that things will shape themselves so that these principles will triumph through the Progressive party, and within a reasonable period of time. . . . I shall fight as strongly as I know how for the perpetuation of this party exactly in its present shape and with no more attempt at fusion with one of the old machines than with the other." The letter included neither a strong indictment of Munsey's actions nor a hard and fast promise to maintain the Progressive party indefinitely as a separate political entity.[44]

Among the more prominent members of the party, Kent, Heney, Earl, Dickson, and Stimson were most opposed to leaving the Republican fold. Heney told Johnson that Roosevelt himself had urged him to remain a Republican in California, and Kent felt that "it would be suicide" not only for Heney but for Johnson and all the rest to try to carry the state as Progressives. Kent was sure that Woodrow Wilson was "going to get away with the Progressive movement," and that would leave the California reformers "isolated." Even Rowell, who personally preferred to be a Progressive both inside and outside California, had grave doubts about leaving his comfortable position. If the new 1913 election law, he wrote, permitted candidates to seek nominations on two or more party tickets, then why not maintain their Progressive organization and "grab the Republican party also . . . ?" He had "no squeamishness" about that plan, he said, "provided the law permits." [45]

On the other hand, Meyer Lissner was most determined to break away from the state Republican party. He told Joseph M. Dixon that he felt at home politically for the first time in years because the new party squared exactly with his "innermost convictions." Governor Johnson also felt the impulse to organize the new party in the state. But the difficulty was that a majority of important state leaders and almost all their friends in the legislature were opposed. There were three

193

types of these near-progressives, Johnson wrote: first, the pussyfooted politicians who had been progressives because they had had to be to keep their jobs; second, the more timid of their friends who wanted to "maintain an anchor to the windward;" and third, the conscientious men who felt honor bound to remain Republicans because they had been elected on that ticket. It was a most troublesome question, and Johnson felt that it demanded a thorough discussion at his home in Sacramento.

Angry words punctuated that important conference held about the middle of November. Lissner led the fight for the new state party and Rowell, having changed his mind, now supported him. But Earl and Dickson felt that they should keep control of the Republican party for at least another year "to see which way the cat jumped." Lissner was "so surprised and provoked" at their attitude that he felt called upon to apologize later for what he had said in rebuttal.[46] In the end, of course, it was Johnson's decision, and finally after many an uneasy movement, the governor decided with Lissner and Rowell. To become Progressives in the state as well as the nation, he felt, was the only consistent action they could take.[47] On December 5, 1913, the progressive-dominated Republican State Central Committee disbanded as a group. And on the following day, at the Palace Hotel in San Francisco, the California State Progressive party was organized.

CHAPTER VIII

Depression and Division

*

The two years following the formation of the new state party were a time of trouble for the California Progressives, not confined to the uncertainties of politics. By the summer of 1913 the prosperity of the past few years seemed to have vanished, and industrial depression settled on the state as well as the rest of the nation. With wages and unemployment increasing, tension between labor and capital mounted rapidly through the state. When it threatened to explode into outright strife, the Progressives, occupying a middle position between the two groups, were bound to be affected individually and as a party.

The first large skirmish between capital and labor occurred in 1913, and not on the city streets but on the land. On August 3 some 2,800 migratory farm laborers and their families were camped on the Durst hop ranch near Wheatland. They had gathered there in response to an advertisement for 2,700 workers to pick fruit and found the general living and sanitary conditions so filthy that, as one of them said, even the dogs turned up their noses. Far more discouraging was the information that the owner could use only some 1,500 hands, a fact he was aware of, he later admitted, at the time he advertised. The majority of the laborers toiled for a wage of between seventy-eight cents and a dollar per day, many were entirely without work, and half of those actually employed were so poor they had to cash their chits regularly after a day's labor for food.

Among these hapless human beings were a score or more members of the International Workers of the World. Led by

Blackie Ford, the I.W.W. leaders called a mass meeting to protest against the conditions on the Durst Ranch. Almost immediately, however, a sheriff's posse appeared. When the district attorney started toward the assembled workers to arrest Ford, a shot was fired. After a few minutes of confused struggle four men, including the district attorney, a deputy sheriff, and two workers, were dead. Many more were injured. Within hours, four companies of the National Guard were maintaining order over the surrounding countryside.[1]

Sometime before the bloody Wheatland outbreak the Wobblies had staged "free speech campaigns" in Fresno and San Diego. In both cities the reaction had been fast and violent. With clubs and whips, law-and-order vigilantes started a wave of lawlessness which a state commission appointed by Governor Johnson to investigate the disturbance, later characterized as approaching the tyranny of tsarist Russia. Declaring that constitutional liberties had obviously been restricted, Johnson immediately sent the attorney general to San Diego to see that free speech and the right to free assembly were preserved. That was in 1912.

In 1914 the governor acted with similar dispatch, but this time to call out the National Guard whose obvious purpose was to overawe any labor demonstration and to protect private property. The migrant workers were dispersed in short order, and many of them arrested. Blackie Ford and a fellow I.W.W. leader were eventually caught and sentenced to life imprisonment on the legal charge of murder, although the court records would seem to indicate that they were really tried and found guilty because of their membership in the Wobblies.[2]

From a political standpoint at least, Johnson's intervention in the Wheatland riot was wise. The California fruit farmers reacted to this first brush with migrant labor as if they had been touched by a glowing wire. Seasonally confronted with the necessity of harvesting his crop within a matter of hours or seeing it spoil, the fruit farmer needed amenable and low-cost labor for a few days of the year, which he then wanted to disappear quietly until the next harvest. Labor trouble at harvest time was thus a disaster, the extent of which no urban industrialist could appreciate. And when a strike was joined to the I.W.W. antiproperty brand of radicalism, this was catastrophe compounded. Within a year after the Durst Ranch riot the state fruit growers had formed the Farmers' Protective League, devoted to destroying agricultural unions and to defeating prolabor legislation of the type that many progressives had proposed.[3]

Meanwhile, many urban laborers were walking city streets looking for work and a paycheck. By the late fall of 1913 the state board of immigration estimated that 75,000 men were unemployed in San Francisco and Los Angeles alone. All through the dark winter breadlines and resentment grew, and in the spring the talk of an unemployed march on the national capital rapidly spread the length of the state. As one such army gathered in San Francisco in early March, another in Los Angeles, and still another in Redding, it looked as though the dreary days of the early 'nineties would be repeated.

The San Francisco division of this latter day "Coxey's Army" was organized under the inevitable "General," Charles T. Kelley. Given a free ferry ride across the bay to Oakland, the army's journey was hastened by gifts of transportation from cities and towns anxious to see the last of it. But when the men arrived in Sacramento, 1,500 strong, their journey was brought to an abrupt stop by the threat of Governor Oddie of Nevada that they would be turned back by force when and if they arrived at Reno. Faced with this, the union army decided to settle down for a while in Sacramento. Embarrassed by their camp along the Southern Pacific tracks and by their insistent demand for food, Sacramento officials offered the jobless men free transportation back to San Francisco or to any other California city they designated. But the members of the union army wanted no part of this proposed backhauling. Parading the streets of the capital, they voiced their demands for food, shelter, and shipment in song:

The unemployed refuse to go to Frisco
The unemployed are doing mighty fine
The unemployed refuse to leave the city
We want to go to Reno on the S.P. line.

Perhaps this determination to move east was reinforced by news from Contra Costa County. There the sheriff, mobilizing three hundred special deputies, threatened to "shoot them down in rows" if they entered his county again.

For a time the army was fed by the city of Sacramento, but after its leaders refused to board a special San Francisco–bound train, official patience began to wear thin. Eventually, amid much talk of an I.W.W. conspiracy, "General" Kelley was arrested and his army beaten back and dispersed with much brutality across the Sacramento River by volunteer deputies armed with clubs and firehoses. Governor Johnson remained remarkably quiet during the excitement, but there is no question that his sympathies were with the city officials. Although many progressives undoubtedly approved of his course, a good minority questioned whether a more enlightened solution to the problem could not be found than the "club and water method." [4]

While the disturbing scenes at Wheatland and in the streets of Sacramento were reflecting the rising class tensions in the state, another even more important movement began in those days of deepening depression. On March 26, 1914, the San Francisco Merchants and Manufacturers' Association was organized. Similar organizations mushroomed in Oakland, across the bay, and in the near-by valley city of Stockton. A month later a broader organization, the Citizens' Alliance of Northern California, made its appearance, the purpose of which was "to foster and protect the industrial and business interests of San Francisco and the state," and "to prevent all overt industrial disturbances." Noting the business groups' similarity in nomenclature and stated purpose to the powerful Los Angeles open-shop forces, organized labor prepared for battle.[5]

The interval between the birth of these imposing industrial organizations and the outbreak of a labor war was short. On July 11 the 403 members of the Stockton Merchants, Manufacturers and Employers' Association voted unanimously for the creation of an open-shop town. To achieve that goal each member pledged himself to bar all union labels and cards in his establishment and to deal only with individual workingmen and not with any collective group. This much was made public. Held in secrecy until a congressional investigating committee made it public information, was the further agreement to pay a tax into the association's treasury of twenty-five cents a month per employee, to be used for the protection of property and to indemnify members whose business establishments had been closed through labor difficulties. A secret understanding was also made between Stockton's mayor and C. G. Bird, the president of the association, permitting the latter to name enough special policemen "to maintain order" during the course of a strike.[6]

Fully mobilized, the Stockton businessmen opened their assault on union labor within two weeks. At the outbreak of labor difficulties in late July the association's strike committee imported strikebreakers from San Francisco armed with guns and blackjacks, who were promptly added to the city's official police. At the same time, the committee called a meeting of the town's three newspaper editors and asked for "fair publicity." In particular, they objected to the news stories printed in the Stockton *Record* describing the importation of strikebreakers and armed guards into the town. Its progressive owner, Irving Martin, was informed that unless such unfavorable stories were killed in the future, the newspaper's credit at the local banks and its advertising would be curtailed. When Martin refused to stop printing stories containing "both sides" of the open violence occurring daily on the city streets, he began to feel "the squeeze." The employers' association, he wrote to a fellow progressive, "has succeeded in controlling employment, finance and credit, but has not succeeded in controlling either the press or the pulpit . . ." and he did not know how long he could hold out because the local merchants were "withdrawing advertising from the two evening papers and concentrating it in the morning paper. . . ." [7]

The perplexing position of Irving Martin, one of the original founders of the Lincoln-Roosevelt Republican League in California, clearly illustrated not only a personal dilemma but also one for the entire Progressive party. It raised the disquieting question of whether early twentieth-century progressivism could long endure in an atmosphere of increasing hostility between organized capital and organized labor. Martin sincerely thought of himself as representing a middle way. Testifying before the Wilsonian Commission on Industrial Relations, he made it clear that he had no wish to ally himself either with the pro- or the antiunion movement. He was in the uncomfortable position of having his credit and advertising threatened by organized business, and the wages of his employees raised by the unions without his consent. Martin made the point that the conflict in Stockton was not simply one between unions and antiunion factions. It was class warfare, and it permeated all the town's social institutions. "The class lines," he said, "are just as absolutely drawn as anything can be." [8] At that juncture Martin, and in fact all of his fellow Progressives, might well have wondered whether they could sustain their isolated, individualistic attitude in the conduct of their business, their social life, or their politics.

Indications of growing strains also existed within the Progressive party structure. Much of this tension was far removed from ideological and economic questions. But to a degree, at least, it reflected in the party something of the struggle that was going on between capital and labor throughout the state. In the northern part of California, outside of Governor Johnson's own immediate circle of supporters, the strongest elements in the party were clustered around Francis J. Heney, Congressman William Kent, and Fremont Older, editor of the San Francisco *Bulletin*. Collectively, the three men constituted much of the Progressive party's left wing, as their stand on labor and economic issues in the 1911 and 1913 sessions

200

of the legislature indicates. Relations between Johnson and Heney had never been very cordial, and in the next two years they were to grow rapidly worse. Kent had been irritated at the changes in the boundaries of his Congressional district in the fall of 1911, which were made, he felt, with Johnson's consent to run him "out of a job." And although Dickson and Lissner assured him that they had made the changes solely "to get" standpatters Knowland and Needham in adjoining districts, Johnson's lack of support for his renomination in the following spring confirmed Kent in his first belief. In the spring of 1912 Johnson blamed Kent for the bad feeling between LaFollette and his Progressives. The congressman further incurred the governor's ire in the fall elections by running as an independent instead of a Progressive. Kent, in turn, carefully noted that whereas Older and Lissner supported him in that contest, Johnson and Rowell were silent. By the fall of 1913, the personal relations between the two men were so strained that a mutual friend had to arrange a meeting between them.[9]

Fremont Older had long been "sore" at Johnson and his "political progressives" for not passing any significant labor legislation, William Allen White reported to Progressive headquarters. And in 1913 Older began a campaign to free Abraham Ruef from the penitentiary, a course of action that brought him into direct conflict with Hiram Johnson. By 1914 the *Bulletin* was printing refutations of the governor's arguments on the Ruef case, and Johnson never forgot Older's effrontery. From that time on he repeatedly referred to him as a prime troublemaker.[10]

In the south, relations between the party leaders were worse than in the north. In the spring of 1913 Los Angeles faced another municipal election and with it again the threat of a Socialist victory. In March the Socialist party again nominated Job Harriman, who had come so close to victory in 1911. By that time both conservative and Progressive leaders in the city had a bad case of nerves. Their jumpiness was clearly reflected in their readiness to indict each other for the impending disaster at the same time they were pleading for "unity" to avoid a Socialist-labor triumph. In the face of the greater enemy, however, as in 1911, they temporarily resolved their differences. On March 28 the Progressives, old guard Republicans, conservative Democrats, and businessmen met in a closed meeting and heard their chairman Stoddard Jess call for united action, "to follow the example of San Francisco when businessmen organized to expell McCarthyism." The result of this ex-officio meeting of the Los Angeles Chamber of Commerce was the formation of the Los Angeles Municipal Conference of 1913.[11]

At a later meeting of the conference, John W. Schenk, an honest but otherwise undistinguished conservative, was nominated for mayor on a nonpartisan ticket, along with a list of councilmen of approximately the same political hue. With Meyer Lissner heading the campaign committee, and the nonpartisan ticket supported by practically all of the non-labor press, success seemed assured. At the end of March only two factors disturbed conservative complacency. One was the critical attitude of Edwin T. Earl and his two progressive papers, the *Express* and the *Tribune,* and the other was the unexpected entrance into the race of a second nonsocialist, independent candidate. From the Progressive viewpoint, Earl's defection was by far the more serious development, bearing as it did on the continued success or failure of progressivism in both local and state governments.

For some time before 1913 personal relations between Lissner and Earl had not been of the best. Both were strong-willed, fond of power, and inclined to be intolerant of opposition. Since Johnson's first victory in 1910 Lissner had represented him in Los Angeles. With Chester Rowell, Lissner had also dominated the important state party machinery. In Sacramento Lissner's and Rowell's suggestions invariably seemed to weigh more heavily with the governor than those from other quarters. Earl resented Lissner's position at the Statehouse, and a clash between the two men was probably inevitable. When it came, it was over proposed strategy in the 1913 municipal campaign. At a meeting of Earl, Lissner, Stimson, and Avery in February, the wealthy publisher argued against any plan that would smack of a coalition with the Otis-dominated crowd of Republicans. Instead, Earl wanted to junk the non-partisan scheme and run a straight Progressive ticket. He further advocated the selection of councilmen by wards instead of at large, so as to give a better representation to the labor districts of the city. It was only through labor's support, he believed, that socialism could be defeated and the city government prevented from falling into the hands of the Otis conservatives.

Outvoted by Lissner, Avery, and Stimson in the conference, Earl supported his "middle way" in his two newspapers at the same time that the three were making overtures to the Otis-Republicans for a coalition. Earl's refusal to abide with the decision of the three brought fire from Lissner. "I am satisfied," he snapped in a letter, "that this will throw our city council absolutely into the hands of the Socialists. If this is what you desire to bring about, of course you are going about it in the right way." Earl's curt reply was in the same personal tone, and it not too subtly threw into question his continued financial support of the nonpartisan movement.[12]

Declaring that the most vital issue of the coming campaign was the extension of public-owned utilities, Earl had first proposed the nomination for mayor of William Mulholland, who had conceived and built the Owens River aqueduct. But despite Marshall Stimson's plea for this nomination in the Municipal Conference, the conservative majority ignored the engineer and agreed upon Schenk. Earl turned a hot fire of criticism upon the conference and upon Lissner, the Progressive most responsible for engineering the coalition, although he eventually supported Schenk. At the end of March both the *Express* and the *Tribune* were charging Lissner, Avery, and Stimson with an attempt to deliver the Progressive party in Los Angeles into the hands of the reactionaries. "This alliance with the First National Bank and other corporate interests," the Earl papers declared, "to deliver the city

203

government into the hands of the money power is a most amazing act of treachery to the people." Lissner's justification of the coalition, that it was to save the city from the menace of socialism, was entirely trumped up, the *Express* charged. The real menace to Los Angeles was the money power and the corporation interests, which were "desperately seeking to defeat the distribution of surplus Owens River water, aqueduct power, and completion of the harbor." To support this charge, the *Express* triumphantly printed the conference platform, which cautioned against the "too rapid" development of public utilities and of public ownership. In addition, the Earl papers tellingly pointed out that every councilman nominated by the Municipal Conference lived west of Figueroa Street, in the wealthier part of the city, leaving the great workingmen's districts to the east entirely unrepresented. The district west of Figueroa, the *Express* clinched its argument, was precisely the part of the city that had defeated the last bond issue for the development of public power. Since they had no choice they would stand by Schenk, the Earl papers declared, but they would not support the reactionary council slate hand-picked by the "foes of the people" (a category which patently included Lissner and his associates). Soon after, Earl announced the formation of the Taxpayers' Progressive League, to fight for "a decent, progressive, and representative council." [13]

Meanwhile, the violent feud between Earl and Lissner had broadened to include other Progressives, and eventually spilled over into the public print. When Lissner received a personal letter from Dickson asking him to support the Taxpayers' League, Lissner replied to his old friend with a public letter in Otis' *Times!* It was a strange place, indeed, in which to place a Progressive communication and it succeeded in enraging Earl. The following day Dickson issued a public reply, denying Lissner's open charges that Earl sought to become the dictator of the Progressive party and accusing Lissner of ruining the party's prestige in the south. Lissner replied again in the *Times* with the charge that Earl and the Tax-

payers' League, of which Dickson was president, were array-
ing "class against class and section against section" in their
effort to elect Earl's personally selected ticket.[14] The private
schism in the Progressive ranks had thus become a public feud.
In the election, both the candidate of the Municipal Conference, Schenk, and Rose, the independent, ran well ahead
of the Socialist, giving substance to Earl's charges that the
Socialist bogey had been devised by the reactionaries for their
own purposes. But in the enforced runoff election, Rose
soundly beat the candidate of the coalition, thanks to the
votes of the embittered Socialists and a surprisingly large
number of businessmen who deserted the Good Government-
ites once the Socialist threat had been removed. This was
the first serious defeat for Lissner's reformers and the Los
Angeles Progressives since they had recalled Mayor Harper in
1909. So chagrined was Russ Avery at the results, that this
cofounder of the progressive movement in Los Angeles declared his political activity in municipal affairs was now at an
end.[15]

Of far more importance than the local results was the effect
of the Earl-Lissner quarrel on the Progressive party and the
future shape of state politics. Lissner and Dickson patched up
their differences with mutually courteous regrets, but something had been lost from the old camaraderie. No reconciliation was possible between Earl and Lissner, nor between the
Los Angeles publisher and Chester Rowell, who had supported Lissner's antisocialist moves in his Fresno *Republican*.
During the critical political events of 1916, Rowell wrote that
Earl was one of the two "violent progressives" in the state who
still did not speak to him because of his part in the 1913
affair.[16]

Governor Johnson, who had refused to take any part in
the quarrel, was critical of both sides. Rowell wrote that there
was no truth to the rumor that Johnson would replace Lissner
with Earl as his representative in Los Angeles. The governor,
however, was intensely displeased at Lissner's public reply
to Earl, and felt that the election results demonstrated the

naïveté in making an alliance with the "reactionary higher-ups" unless one expected to be sold out in the end.[17] But the fact that Johnson stuck with Lissner after the election did not endear the governor to Earl. After the 1913 fiasco a large group of Los Angeles Progressives distrusted the state administration and its local representatives. This feeling, when added to the split in the north between the conservatives and radicals, foreshadowed the disintegration of California progressivism.

As long as men are men, personalities as well as principles will continue to be issues in politics. Whether the progressive division in the 1913 Los Angeles elections was mainly a conflict between personalities or principles is hard to determine. Considering Earl's strong opposition to labor proposals in the legislature, it is probable that both factors were present. The same may be said about the far more significant struggle in the Progressive party some months later, when Hiram Johnson and Francis J. Heney were the principal, but by no means the only, contestants.

Ever since Johnson had taken Heney's place as head graft prosecutor in San Francisco, the two men had not been friendly. Some friction had already existed between them at the time Johnson was selected to lead the Lincoln-Roosevelt ticket in 1910. This had increased during the campaign, when Heney was asked to stay out of the state during the campaign because Lissner, and presumably Johnson, believed Heney's presence would frighten the more conservative members of the League. After the election, Johnson's presence at the Heney banquet was obtained "only by bitter pressure." The governor had few kind words for the fiery graft prosecutor. In 1911 he strongly objected to the part of a recall bill that Heney had prepared and during the campaign of the following year he was critical of Heney's electioneering methods. Later he spoke of an impertinent letter he had received from Heney, offering what to all intents and purposes seemed to be honest and indeed farsighted political advice.

Reflecting on the quarrel, Marshall Stimson, who never

was unfriendly to the governor, thought that it was largely a product of Johnson's wife, who dreamed of the Senate for her husband and saw Heney as the chief obstruction to that ambition.[18] When Heney was proposed for the United States Senate in 1911 in the event that the ailing Perkins died, the proposal received an extremely cool reception from Johnson. It is probable, however, that Hiram Johnson needed little encouragement to dislike the former graft prosecutor. The simple fact was that Hiram Johnson throughout his life was constitutionally unable to play a coördinate, much less a minor role, in any drama. Whether as prosecutor, governor, or senator, he had to stalk the center of the stage. If he could not be the hero of a piece, he seemed compelled to be the hero's chief antagonist. He had been acutely unhappy as a vice-presidential candidate in 1912; eight years later he abruptly refused to be the second figure again in a national campaign, and thus lost his chance to become President. Unable to lead in the Senate, he became the great rebel there. All through the progressive years he was apparently determined to be "The Boss," the number-one man in California. Whoever threatened that position was likely to incur his wrath. William Kent was probably right when he commented in 1912 that Johnson was "thoroughly jealous of Heney and intends keeping him down." [19]

This personal conflict between Johnson and Heney burst into the open during the spring and summer of 1914. In that year California was to elect both a senator and a governor. Instead of running for a second term as governor, Johnson would have preferred to run for the Senate. That had been his ambition in 1910, and that was his admitted ambition three years later.[20] But the decision was so delicate, and involved so many considerations bound to affect the party's future, that the governor debated the question with his intimate advisors for months and delayed his decision. As early as June, 1913, Lissner and Rowell had "gone over the whole subject" with Johnson. Six months later he still had not made up his mind. During that uncertain and vexing period, two main obstacles apparently prevented him from arriving at a decision. The first was Article 5, Section 20, of the constitution, which prohibited a governor from running for the Senate during his term of office; the second was Heney's aspirations.[21]

In mid-summer of 1913 Heney talked with Johnson and made it clear that he was determined to run either for the senatorship or the governor's chair in 1914, but that he had no intention of opposing Johnson in either race. Heney later reported that he quite distinctly invited the governor to state his preference but that he got no satisfaction on that point. This was quite understandable. Johnson was thoroughly opposed to Heney's running for either office and expressed himself explicitly to that effect to intimate friends. Caught between Heney and the state constitution, he delayed a decision, probably in the hope of freezing Heney out of both contests.[22]

From mid-summer until September Heney awaited the governor's painful decision. When no word came, he formally announced his senatorial candidacy without consulting the silent Statehouse. This "independent action" was certainly not in the California progressive tradition of hand-picking candidates for the primaries, and what Johnson felt about it can be left to the imagination. Even more shocking to Johnson than Heney's "self-announcement" was the public support given his candidacy by Earl, Dickson, Stimson, Kent, Older, C. K. McClatchey, Irving Martin, E. W. Scripps, and former Governor Pardee. Heney thus had the backing of powerful newspapers in the six largest cities of the state. To Johnson this support of Heney by his old friends was akin to personal treachery.

After Heney's announcement, the governor was sorely tempted to run against him in the primaries. The senatorial office seemed more inviting now than it had before, but there was still that uncomfortable clause in the constitution. There were also other factors, as Rowell, Lissner, and Eshleman pointed out. Like Johnson, they were against Heney's candidacy for any office but, they argued, if Johnson now announced for the Senate, Heney might well change his ambitions and run for the governor's office. "Our calculations might go amiss, and Heney might get nominated," Rowell wrote. "That would not smash things if he were nominated for senator. But in his present mood he would smash things utterly if he were nominated for governor." [23]

It was a most perplexing situation and Johnson continued to waver. Then Heney did what Rowell had feared. Without warning, the former prosecutor announced publicly that if Johnson ran for the Senate, he would become a formal candidate for the governorship. Astounded, his supporters nevertheless quickly informed the public that they would back him for either office. Heney later told his friends that he had had to make the second announcement to prevent his being frozen off the Progressive primary ticket altogether by the Johnson faction. Just before the December conference of the party, he explained, Johnson, Rowell, and Eshleman had planned to refuse to run for any office, with the explanation to the party members that Johnson preferred the senatorial candidacy, but that in the interest of party harmony he was willing to retire to private life. That would have branded him, Heney, as an obstructionist, Heney continued, and would have set in motion great pressure on him to withdraw. Then, when Heney was thoroughly tarred with this brush, Johnson and Eshleman would announce their candidacies for the Senate and the governorship respectively.[24]

Whatever the truth of the foregoing story, Heney's either-or announcement brought about a final rupture in the personal relations between him and Johnson. At Rowell's insistence the two men had met in November and had patched up a "superficial truce." A month later Rowell reported that the bitterness between them "was unbridgeable." [25] Heney's provisional announcement for the governorship also persuaded an unwilling Johnson to seek a second term. On January 6 the governor made the news public, stating as he did so that he would have preferred to run for the Senate. On the same day he wrote a letter to Lissner that was fairly saturated with bitterness: he had restrained himself mightily from elbowing Heney out of the senatorship and supporting Eshleman for governor. Heney's course all through their relations had been one of duplicity and treachery. Heney would never appreciate the intensity of the struggle that Johnson and his friends had endured in reaching their final and disagreeable decision. Heney was sure to interpret it as an action born of fear.

Of more importance for the future of the Progressive party was Johnson's wrath at Dickson, Stimson, Kent, Older, and all who launched the Heney boom without even a by-your-leave from Sacramento. He felt a great resentment against those people, Johnson wrote, who had created all the difficulty by trying to make Heney the central figure in the California progressive movement. How differently it had all turned out, Governor Johnson wistfully concluded, from what they had planned and hoped.[26]

Although Johnson had apparently removed himself from the Senate contest, he was in no mood to see Heney win the prize unopposed. During the fall, in fact, when he himself was still playing with the idea of entering the race, he had occasionally encouraged both Rowell and Eshleman to think about running against Heney. Of the two men he preferred Rowell for the Senate. In mid-October Rowell wrote that he was "looking toward a possible senatorial candidacy." This was not at Johnson's specific request, Rowell told Russ Avery, for outwardly the governor had to be neutral. But Johnson had said that something must be done "to meet the one-candidate movement." At the very least, Rowell ended, Johnson "wanted it known that the field is open." [27]

With the governor still a possible candidate, Rowell's "tentative candidacy" could not be made public. He and Lissner worked hard behind the scenes, however, to gather support. One of their objectives was to get provisional endorsement from the Los Angeles group. This project, however, was blocked by Dickson, who insisted upon calling a meeting of the leading members of the party in the south to discuss the senatorial affair and vote on preferred candidates. This conference overwhelmingly favored Heney.[28] Lissner had better luck with a poll taken among the subscribers to the *California Outlook*, the result of which favored Rowell. But Heney objected to the publication of Rowell's poll victory on the grounds that the count was taken without his consent and without any of his followers present to participate in the administration of the poll.[29]

As Johnson still refused to count himself out of the Senate contest, and his personal relations with Heney grew more tense, Rowell decided that his candidacy was not worth the candle. In view of the rising personal bitterness and the kind of campaign he would be expected to make against Heney, he wrote to both Governor Johnson and Lissner, "I regard my former tentative candidacy as having already definitely ceased. . . ." Even after Johnson's decision to run again for governor was made known, Rowell stated that he would do nothing more in an active way but leave the question of his candidacy "up to those who are responsible for the guidance of the party." If they considered it "a serious party emergency" and asked him to run, he would do so. "But," he ended, "that has to be the evident judgment of all leaders." [30]

For the next month the curious situation continued. Rowell stubbornly refused to announce his candidacy without specific encouragement from Johnson and the governor, though insisting that Heney should be opposed, refused to make any definite commitments. In fact, as the pressure mounted on Johnson to indicate his views, "he became quite violent against any person" who even attempted to interpret his views. In the end Rowell had to announce his candidacy without a specific pledge of support. However, he later stated that he entered the contest "to help Governor Johnson fight off Francis J. Heney." [31]

Because of the most scrupulous conduct of the two principal contestants, the following campaign was comfortably quiet. Only Lissner's charges against Earl for not mentioning Rowell in his papers, and the demand by Fremont Older that Rowell withdraw from the contest, disturbed the already taut relations within the party. The restraint of the contestants was fortunate because the primary returns seemed to predict a dismal future for progressivism in California. Heney's 78,351 votes easily beat Rowell's 33,575. But even their combined vote was embarrassingly small when compared with the total number of Democratic and Republican ballots.

The summer of 1914 was gloomy for the Progressives and Hiram Johnson. Just as they had completed their separation from the Republican party, elsewhere in the country the movement of Progressives back into the Republican party was noticeable. In New York Theodore Roosevelt himself seemed to have blessed this new development by advocating a fusion of the Progressives and Republicans to support the Republican Hinman for governor. Answering Johnson's sharp criticism of this proposal, Roosevelt pointed out that even in California, if the spring registration figures could be believed, the Progressive party was not a majority party.[32] Johnson was painfully aware of this. He was also aware that general economic conditions in California were far from good. The depression which had settled over the state had not let up. Everywhere in the commonwealth there was deep concern over the future.

Seizing upon the prevailing conditions as campaign material, Captain John D. Fredericks of Los Angeles, the Republican nominee for governor, began a militant campaign against Johnson and the Progressives for the "extravagance" and "socialist tendencies" that had frightened capital and enterprise away from the state. Although he accepted the Progressive political reforms, Fredericks turned all of his criticism on Johnson's "freak legislation" and appealed for the reestablishment of the sane Republican party and prosperity. Consistently ignoring the Democratic nominee, John B. Curtin, Johnson focused his attention on Fredericks. In answering the Republican, however, the Progressive leader had little new to propose. With the exception of demands for nonpartisan state elections and conservation measures, the Progressive platform had been silent on additional reform. In his opening speech of the campaign, Hiram Johnson emphasized that he would run on his record of accomplishments during the past four years. "Our main objective in the future," he said, "will be to preserve and perpetuate those great policies of political and social justice." [33] But this time he spoke before a social backdrop of depression and unemployment.

If the governor had run through his store of reform ideas, he had not lost his old aptitude for excoriating an opponent. When Fredericks wavered in his support of past political reforms in the middle of the campaign, Johnson compared him to the Texas politician who, after advancing his program of buncombe, remarked in closing: "Those are my sentiments. But if you don't like them, Ladies and Gentlemen, I can damn soon change them." The governor also enlivened his campaign by his vociferous attacks upon "the three militant, marauding millionaire publishers" who were supporting Fredericks— Harrison Gray Otis, Mike de Young, and John D. Spreckels. His cause was aided by Fredericks' acknowledged conservatism and his reputation as an enemy of organized labor. From the time Fredericks had headed the prosecution of the Los Angeles *Times* bombers, he had been a foe of the unions, a fact labor publications in Los Angeles and San Francisco reiterated throughout the contest.[34]

In contrast to the rather flat tenor of Johnson's campaign, Francis J. Heney's speeches consistently hit hard for a long list of reforms. Opposed by two able vote getters, James D. Phelan, the liberal Democrat, and Joseph R. Knowland, the conservative Republican, Heney made it clear that he belonged to the radical wing of the Progressive forces. He endorsed a steeply graduated income tax, an inheritance tax, government ownership of telephone, telegraph, and energy-producing natural resources (including coal, lumber, oil, gas, and water), a measure to take all profits out of war, and woman suffrage.

During the campaign relations between Johnson and Heney were a little less strained on the surface than they had been previously. They exchanged mutual compliments from the stump, but nowhere in their letters or in their private remarks was there the slightest indication of any real reconciliation. In fact, when Marshall Stimson tried to persuade the governor to speak with the senatorial candidate, Johnson was profane in his refusal. Only after the most strenuous efforts did mutual friends, including Rowell, succeed in getting them together in Los Angeles.[35] Nor were the supporters of the two men any more gracious. Both the Los Angeles *Express*, supporting Heney, and the *California Outlook*, the Johnson organ, were conspicuously cautious in the amount of space they lent to the opposing faction's candidates. Only a few individual leaders seemed enthusiastically interested in the success of the progressive ticket as a whole.

Sometime before the election it became common gossip in the state that certain elements in the Johnson camp were decidedly hostile to Heney. During the first week in October the nonpartisan *Sunset Magazine* predicted the possibility of a Heney victory. He was handicapped, however, the article pointed out, "by the silent hostility of Governor Johnson's well-oiled organization." By election time the rumors had grown until the Los Angeles *Examiner*, supporting Knowland, flatly predicted that Heney, "was undergoing a delicate surgical operation known in politics as being knifed," with the Johnson faction of the Progressives acting as the "operating surgeons." These published stories and others more explicit circulated by word of mouth seemed to be verified by the November election results.[36]

The 1914 balloting all but ended the life of the young Progressive party nationally. Everywhere their leading candidates were overwhelmingly defeated—everywhere, that is, except in California. Johnson, carrying all but four counties in the state, became the first California governor to be reelected since 1853. Most of the Progressive candidates for the minor state officers were swept along in the tide. Even in California, however, indications of the ebbing Progressive strength were apparent. So many reform-minded candidates

214

for the legislature had been defeated that control of that body was in doubt. And although the people by referendum had approved the Red Light Abatement Act and the Blue Sky Law, they turned down a state-wide eight-hour law and a minimum-wage law for women and minors.[37] Moreover, the Progressives had failed to defeat a single conservative incumbent in the national House of Representatives. But by far the greatest blow to Progressive prestige in California was Heney's defeat. In the hot, three-cornered race for senator, James D. Phelan, the Democrat, had received some 279,000 votes to Heney's 255,000 and Knowland's 254,000.[38]

Hiram Johnson had polled more than 460,000 votes compared with Republican Fredericks' 271,000 and Democratic Curtin's 116,000. When these totals were compared with the senatorial figures, the bitter charges that Johnson had "knifed" his running mate were multiplied. More specifically, it was charged that Johnson had traded with Phelan and San Francisco labor at the expense of both Heney and Curtin. Offered as evidence to support the indictment were Heney's defeat in San Francisco, Johnson's large majority in the city and his great influence with labor there, and Phelan's antiunion reputation.

Surface evidence for such a charge is one thing, proof another. Although Johnson and many of his supporters were unquestionably hostile to Heney, no evidence has been found that suggests a trade either with Phelan or with San Francisco labor. Heney's defeat in San Francisco can be rationally explained on other grounds. He was not liked there in many quarters. His attack on both union labor leaders and corporation representatives in the graft trials had not been forgotten. The town had defeated him before in 1909 when he ran for district attorney. His aggressive personality and his swing to the left of the progressive movement had made him many enemies. After the election Theodore Roosevelt wrote that he had been "surprised and concerned" to find how many Progressives had intimated to him that they would not support

215

Heney "because he was an extremist." [39] Finally, San Francisco was a strongly Democratic town, especially in national elections. Despite Hiram Johnson's popularity there, he had been unable to persuade the city to favor Theodore Roosevelt in 1912. What the magnetic Roosevelt could not do against Woodrow Wilson, Heney had little hope of doing against a Wilson Democrat.

One other point is relevant. If Heney lost the election by the vote in San Francisco, it might be argued that he lost it in the rest of the state too. Thousands of people voted for Hiram Johnson and then either cast their ballot for Heney's opponents or refused to vote for any senatorial candidate (as did some 50,000). A good number of these people outside of San Francisco were probably Progressives, and although it may have been that they were reacting to the known attitude of Johnson and his friends toward Heney, they might simply have been exercising their preferences. Newspapers, labor leaders, and politicians, as the historian knows, have invariably overestimated their ability to deliver a vote for or against any man.

Reason and politics are seldom brothers. Whatever the facts of the 1914 election, Heney's friends felt that Johnson and his allies had betrayed them. "Damn those leaders who threw him down," one of them wrote. Dickson, Earl, Older, Stimson, and Kent were more reticent but they fully subscribed to those sentiments.[40] As for the unfortunate Heney, he was certain that Johnson and Phelan had formally agreed to bilk him. That agreement, he wrote, had been sealed two weeks before the election and had included the city administration, the saloons, the gamblers, and the criminal element generally. Johnson owed more to him for his political advancement, Heney thought, than to any other man, and this made his defeat doubly hard to bear. The more Heney thought about the election, the more he disliked Hiram Johnson. A year later he was asked whether he would run for the Senate again in 1916. "No," he replied sharply, "not unless Johnson does." [41] Although Heney's supporters were not quite that bitter, the atmosphere within the Progressive party after the election of 1914 boded ill for solidarity and victory in the future.

"The Progressive party has come a cropper," Theodore Roosevelt remarked, after sadly surveying the national election returns in November, 1914. Ruin had come about, Roosevelt felt, because the party had gotten a reputation for radicalism from its "lunatic fringe" at the same time that the nation was rapidly swinging away from liberalism. This swing had been due, he thought, to the excesses of the radicals in the progressive movement, as well as to the current economic depression. The people had changed their interest from reform to bread-and-butter issues. They were "tired of all reformers" and especially of him.[42] These were revealing statements, not only about Roosevelt's reform ideology, but also about many California Progressives. It never occurred to them, as it did not occur to Roosevelt, that the bread-and-butter issue could be a reform issue in itself. They thought of social justice almost entirely in a political context. When the phrase was translated into economic terms it entailed "class legislation," an anathema to the average California Progressive. Heney's economic progressivism, as he called it, was to them Socialism, and something to be fought at whatever cost.

Certainly during 1914 and 1915, even in progressive California, it appeared as if Roosevelt's estimate of the political swing might be right. In 1914 San Francisco recalled a reformer from the state legislature who had proposed that the projected world's fair be dry. Shortly afterward former Mayor Schmitz was given an enthusiastic welcome to the city by a huge and cheering crowd. Elsewhere throughout the state there were subtle indications that the temper of public opinion was changing. Even the most staunchly progressive organs were admitting, "Probably we are beginning a period of political reaction." [43]

Early in January of the following year Governor Johnson sent his annual message to the new legislature. The message was nothing if not moderate. True to his campaign promise,

217

the governor asked for few new enactments. Despite the fact that the state was still in the slough of a depression, that unemployment was high, and that capital seemed to be organizing for an all-out struggle with the unions, Johnson proposed that the legislative body confine itself to considering his proposals for state-operated labor exchanges, a revision of the state tax laws, a system of rural credits, and a scheme for making all state elective offices nonpartisan except for United States senators and representatives.

With the governor's steady support, bills for creating free state unemployment offices and submitting nonpartisan proposals to a referendum, were easily passed. But taxation was a horse of another hue. Up until 1905, California had gotten most of its money from taxes on real property, the assessment of such taxes being left to local officials. The existence of local discrimination in assessments, and the heavy burden upon real estate under this plan led to a demand for reform by the state Grange and real-estate interests. Before the reform victory in 1910, a tax plan had been approved to separate the sources of revenue of the state and local governmental units. For state funds a tax was placed upon the gross receipts of railroads and other public utilities, and upon the capital stock of banks. The local units of government drew their revenues from real property within their respective districts. The bill also provided that no increase could be made in the state assessments except by a three-fourths vote of both houses of the legislature.

By 1913 experience had shown that the old inequities had not been removed under the new taxation system. In addition, the greatly expanded functions of the state government were demanding more funds than those produced by the old gross receipts tax. Largely at the governor's insistence, the rates on corporate gross receipts had been raised in 1913 and again in 1915, but each time the legislature balked at attempting a total revision of the old tax system. In 1917, when the State Tax Commission recommended a state income tax, it got no support of any kind from Governor Johnson. California, like most states dominated by Progressives, continued to tax without consideration of the citizens' abilities to pay.[44]

Only once during the rest of the session did Johnson look like the reformer of old. When the Western Pacific Railroad went into bankruptcy, a movement for its purchase by the state was led by Rudolph Spreckels and the Hearst papers. Johnson was briefly intrigued by the idea. "A transcontinental railroad owned by a state is a most alluring picture," he announced as he let it be known that he was seriously considering the proposal.[45] But then his growing caution asserted itself and the project was allowed to lapse. From then on the governor's voice was scarcely heard in the legislature. Progressive attempts to regulate insurance concerns and small loan companies got no response from the Statehouse. A renewed attempt to limit labor injunctions even met with some hostility.

Few progressive papers were entirely enthusiastic when they surveyed the work of the legislature at the end of the session. About the best the San Francisco *Bulletin* could do was to call the body "respectable." "If it did not take us very far forward," Fremont Older's paper concluded, "at least it did not thrust us very far backward." [46] But no progressive organ conceded the obvious fact that California progressivism, and in particular its leading exponent, Hiram Johnson, had run out of reform ideas, and therefore had served its purpose and fulfilled most of its excuse for being. Just as the 1915 legislature adjourned *sine die,* an inquiring reporter asked the governor what further reforms he felt were needed in the state. Johnson thought for a moment and then replied that if he were governor for the next three years, he would press for action on rural credits and land colonization legislation. Beyond that, he said, "little remains to be done." As a possible corollary to this revealing statement, Johnson remarked to the departing members of the assembly: "This is my last public office in this state." But before the conservatives could properly celebrate their impending delivery, a rude shock came from another quarter. On the same day that Johnson renounced further ambitions in the state, Harris Weinstock opened a campaign in San Francisco to nominate the governor for President in 1916.[47] The timing of the two events was so obvious that no one, not even the most hopeful member of the old guard, could miss the connection.

CHAPTER IX

National Politics

That Hiram Johnson had national aspirations for 1916 was evident in almost every move the California Progressive party made after 1914. But the road to the national capitol was to be a rough one. Outside of California the Progressive defeat in 1914 had been almost total, and the movement to return to the Republican party, started by Frank Munsey in 1913, was accelerated after the disheartening elections. There was even talk that the National Executive Committee, scheduled to meet in December, 1914, would vote to abandon the Progressive party altogether. Such a confession of defeat less than a year after the Californians had formally left the Republican party would have been extremely embarrassing for Johnson and his followers. To jump back into the Republican party so soon after they had so resolutely left it might strike the voting public as more than ludicrous. If a return had to be made—which even the stubborn Johnson was later to admit might be desirable—it had to be done with the dignity befitting a righteous cause. For this, much time and forgetfulness were required. The California Progressives insisted, Johnson wrote to Roosevelt, that nothing be done that would even suggest amalgamation or consolidation with the Republican party.[1]

The governor need not have worried, however, about Roosevelt committing himself precipitously to a public confession of failure. The Colonel was much too proud a man and much too good a politician for that. The 2,000,000 Progressive votes cast in 1914 still might have much trading value, and Johnson was not the only Progressive who had national ambitions for 1916. But if Rowell and Lissner at the Chicago conference did help to compose flat instructions to the Progressive National Committee to arrange for a 1916 nominating convention, they had very little else cheerful to report when they returned to Sacramento. There had been considerable sentiment among the Chicago group for accepting a "straight return ticket" to the Republican party. Other members of the group proposed that they wait and endorse either the Republican or Democratic candidate in 1916, depending upon their relative progressiveness. Only a very few delegates, except the Californians as one observer noted, were really enthusiastic "for the maintenance of the Progressive party nationally. . . ." [2]

Rowell and Lissner brought back more bad news from Chicago. Once again the California delegation had been defeated in their attempt to curtail the power of George W. Perkins in the party. If anything, the former Morgan partner left the meeting in a stronger position than ever. Notwithstanding Meyer Lissner's protesting letters to Roosevelt, letters which undoubtedly Johnson approved, Perkins continued to act as the party's chief financial supporter and director. This was bad enough, but even worse in its implications for the continued life of the California Progressive party was Theodore Roosevelt's sudden change in sailing directions during the early part of 1915. Ever since the Progressive convention of 1912, whenever Roosevelt had concerned himself with public politics, he had blasted at the old guard and championed the cause of social justice. Now, with the elections of 1914 behind him and with the spread of the World War, the Colonel did a sharp about-face. Where once stood the crusader, now stood the nationalist. Gone were the appeals to humanity and the attacks upon the malefactors of great wealth. In their place were fervent calls for patriotism, national defense, and possible action against the barbaric German and backward Mexican. Roosevelt had abandoned the conservative Republican party as his chief domestic target and now spent most of his energy lashing out at President Wilson's "effete foreign policy," at the American pacifists, at the pro-Germans, and at people who were opposed to an immediate invasion of Mexico. As Roosevelt became almost hysterical in his demand for a venturesome foreign policy, he became increasingly conservative in domestic affairs. By 1915 one could scarcely distinguish his domestic utterances from those of the old guard. In October, 1915, he declared that the strike situation in the United States was "a scandal" and demanded that all labor disturbances cease "in the interest of patriotism." [3]

Neither Roosevelt's decided swing to the right nor his indictments of Woodrow Wilson greatly bothered the California Progressives. Johnson and his lieutenants had been taking much the same course. By the early spring of 1915 practically all of the California inner group were ready to agree with Roosevelt that the future of the Progressive party was dim. Hiram Johnson's own attitude toward the national party was reported accurately and succinctly to Roosevelt by a mutual friend after a conference in Sacramento. "He holds," Dwight B. Heard wrote, "that we should maintain a bold front and keep our organizations throughout the country . . . we should do so with the firm knowledge that we would have little or no opportunity for success as a third party in 1916, but by maintaining as much unity as possible . . . we would be able to force one of the old parties—preferably the Republican party—to adopt a progressive platform and nominate progressive candidates." [4]

Holding such views, Johnson and the group around him could not have quarreled much with Roosevelt's new policy of friendliness toward the conservative Republicans. But the Colonel's belligerent nationalism was cloth of another weave. With few exceptions, the California Progressive leadership was ardently devoted to peace with both Mexico and Germany. Though they supported a moderate preparedness program, the great majority of them was firmly against anything that smacked of militarism. As for Mexican invasion, Rowell, Older, and Kent, with Johnson's blessings, combined in indicting "the deliberate conspiracy to force this country into war" with that hapless nation.[5] Moreover, after the outbreak of the World War, the average California Progressive desired a policy of strict neutrality and argued that both sides to the struggle were guilty of perpetrating this offense against mankind. "Neither German barbarism nor English Philistinism," the *California Outlook* stated, "furnish us an excuse as Americans for running amuck when all the world is mad." Consequently, except for Meyer Lissner, the Californians increasingly praised Wilson's policy and criticized the warlike "bloviations" of Theodore Roosevelt. After returning from a California tour in the summer of 1915, Roosevelt wrote his friend Henry Cabot Lodge that he was willing to sacrifice the support of a great many of his Progressive friends there. On the coast he had found that "the two strongest anti-preparedness papers were the two leading Progressive papers." What was probably more important to the Colonel was that they were both highly critical of his political "new departure." [6]

Late in 1915 Meyer Lissner sent out an interesting letter to every state Progressive chairman. In it he asked two questions: (1) How many previously enrolled Progressives had returned to the Republican party? (2) What chance did Theodore Roosevelt have to win control of the state's delegation to the 1916 Republican national convention? The answer to the first question was the dismal one that large numbers of Progressives had returned to the Republican party. About half of the state chairmen thought that Roosevelt had a good chance of winning Republican delegates for the 1916 nomination. These answers were eventually forwarded to Roosevelt, but not before their meaning had been thrashed out at a conference in Sacramento. There, the news that the Progressive party had practically ceased to exist except in California was properly digested. The conference met shortly after Governor Johnson's cherished nonpartisan plan for all California elections had been defeated in a special state-wide referendum. This reverse plus Lissner's report served to change many minds about the desirability of maintaining the

Progressive party in California. Returning from Sacramento, Lissner wrote to Rowell that, "quite a few leaders" felt no further obligation to the national party and were in favor of "looking out for ourselves by grabbing the Republican machine in California and reorganizing it." [7]

Sensing the possible disintegration of the national party, the California Progressives were, of course, acutely concerned with what would happen inside their own state. But from another viewpoint the shifting sands of national politics interested them just as much. The fate of California progressivism and that of Hiram Johnson were almost inextricably joined by 1915, and Johnson had announced that his second term as governor would be his last public office in California. That could have meant either a farewell to politics or an ambition to move to Washington. Remembering Johnson's preference for the Senate in 1910 a good many people concluded that with his little speech to the legislature, he was staking his claim to the senatorial nomination in 1916.

As a matter of fact, in the months before the June conventions, the governor had his eye fixed upon the possibility of much bigger game than a mere senatorship. For that Theodore Roosevelt was partly responsible. Back in the summer of 1914, after Roosevelt had despaired of the Progressive party and discounted his own political future, he wrote to Johnson that he did not suppose the voters had been "gotten up to the point" where Johnson could be nominated for President. However, he continued, if a chance of that eventuality developed, he would begin at once to do his part "in organizing a Johnson movement." He was certain that the governor would let him know if he thought there was such a chance.[8] No sweeter words could have come to an aspiring politician, for the suggestion of four years' residence on Pennsylvania Avenue is the final accolade. Yet it was a cruel thing to suggest to Hiram Johnson two years before the nominating convention. Presidential ambition has often had a way of making trimmers of the most courageous, and connivers of the most straightforward. The mere suggestion of the presidency has changed more than one man's life and composure. To the ambitious, pessimistic Johnson, it could do nothing less.

Johnson replied to that fateful letter from Roosevelt with a thin veneer of self-depreciation. He did not have sufficient egotism to believe that the highest gift of the American people could come to him. He understood the situation perfectly, he continued, and more than that, he understood himself. The very mentioning of the office was flattering, but he had always been a realist about political situations, and about this one he had no illusions. On the surface, that seemed to be that. But in politics, as in diplomacy, the surface is often incidental. Two things are clear about Johnson's letter. The presidential office was the highest gift he could imagine, and he did not refuse it. One other fact is relevant. Within a month there was real talk among Johnson's friends of nominating him for the Progressive and possibly the Republican candidacy for President.[9]

It is probable that Hiram Johnson himself never had very much hope of the presidential nomination, but after reading one of Roosevelt's later letters, a copy of which was conveniently forwarded to Sacramento, his spirits must have risen. Roosevelt had written a friend that if he could select the next Republican nominee, it would be Johnson. On the other hand, still later he wrote that he did not think the Progressives could get the Republicans to accept the governor. Even more dispiriting was the lack of enthusiasm among the Progressives outside of California. Within the state there was even blunt opposition. "The people of California," former Governor Pardee's paper brutally stated, "do not regard Johnson as Presidential timber." [10]

If the nation's first office proved to be out of reach, what about the second? If the Progressive and Republican parties were to combine in 1916, what better way of achieving unity was there than by nominating a Progressive for vice-president? To the minds of the Californians the logical Progressive nominee was Johnson, and the only possible presidential run-

ning mate for the Progressive Johnson among the more prominent Republican candidates was Charles Evans Hughes.

Once this plan was decided upon in the early spring of
1915, the next step was to get Roosevelt's approval. Consequently, after a trip to California, Dwight B. Heard, a political
intimate of the Colonel, reported back to Oyster Bay that
Johnson had suggested a coalition ticket against Wilson, of
Hughes for the first position and himself for the second. Heard
wanted Roosevelt's frank opinion on that combination.[11] The
Colonel was noncommittal but on his mid-summer trip to
California he discussed the proposal as a possibility, a discussion which Meyer Lissner possibly assumed was equivalent
to Roosevelt's support. At any rate, Lissner was soon writing
eastern friends that the best thing that could happen in 1916
was for both the Republicans and the Progressives to nominate the same ticket, and that since the Republicans would not
accept Roosevelt as the number-one man, the best alternative
was a Hughes-Johnson slate. Johnson had agreed that "the
plan sounds well as a tentative proposition," and Lissner was
sure that the Republicans would have to accept if Roosevelt
made known that it was Johnson for the vice-presidency or
a fight. "We should all plug, I think, for Hughes and Johnson,"
Lissner advised.[12]

A similar campaign launched in California had better luck
than the ill-fated one to make Johnson president. After the
story was planted over the state, the San Francisco *Bulletin*
reported that the suggestion was meeting with the hearty approval of many California Progressives. When Chester Rowell
left for the East to attend the January, 1916, meeting of the
Progressive National Committee, the Johnson-for-vice-president movement was already well under way.

On the whole, the strategy accepted by the National Committee for the coming campaign had the full approval of the
California group. This was, in short, to maintain the Progressive organization and hold a nominating convention simultaneously with the Republican party in the hope that through

a process of barter and compromise the old enemies would nominate the same candidates. Therefore the committee "reaffirmed" in one sentence the advanced liberal program of 1912, and devoted the remainder of a public statement it gave out to an attack upon the Wilson administration and a demand for a stronger foreign policy. The committee also voiced the hope that both the Progressive and the Republican parties "would choose the same standard-bearer and the same principles."

On only two counts did the Johnson group differ with the national body in that January session. The first was in their characterization of the Wilson foreign policy as "futile, cowardly, and unrighteous." But Roosevelt and his aide, George W. Perkins, were still running the Progressive show, and if the hopes for Johnson were to materialize in 1916, Roosevelt's help seemed to be imperative. For that reason Rowell went along on the foreign policy statement even though he had been writing editorials of a vastly different nature in his home town newspaper. The second point bore more directly on Hiram Johnson's future. Notified that Roosevelt was opposed to entering his name in the primary contests of either the Progressive or the Republican parties, the Progressive executive committee decided to urge Hiram Johnson to file in both primaries, not only in California, but in various other states as well. When Rowell wired the suggestion to California, however, Johnson refused to concur. Whatever might be the final decision in California, Johnson telegraphed back, he was opposed to entering the primaries of any other state. That decision had been agreed to, Johnson affirmed, by all of his advisors at Sacramento.[13]

Just why Hiram Johnson refused to enter either the Republican or Progressive primaries outside of California must remain a matter of speculation. Perhaps he felt that to compete with Republican presidential candidates for Republican delegates was not the best road to the vice-presidency. Or perhaps the decided defeat he had taken in the autumn of 1915 on the nonpartisan measure led him to think that he could better gain his objective by trusting to negotiation rather than to an uncertain electorate. One thing is sure: his desire for a place on the national ticket increased rather than diminished in the early part of 1916.

Ten days after the meeting of the Progressive National Committee, a part of a telephone conversation held between Johnson and the Republican governor of New York was quoted in a San Francisco paper. "We will all be together again in June," Johnson was reported as saying. On the following day a public statement amplifying that remark came from Sacramento. He was not abating his progressive ideas "one jot," the governor declared, but if the Republicans selected candidates in sympathy with progressive principles, he assumed that the two parties would "unite and go forward together." [14] This was not only a vague hope of the governor, but in the light of immediate events a direct invitation to the Republicans for a compromise. Two days later in San Francisco, the governor's private secretary, Al McCabe, and Meyer Lissner "accidently" met Walter R. Bacon, chairman of the State Republican Executive Committee. Before the pleasantries of that accidental meeting were through, Lissner and McCabe made a most interesting proposal, the core of which was an offer to combine the Progressive and the Republican parties in the state through a joint delegation to the Republican National Convention, one-half of the delegates to be selected by the old guard, one-half by the Progressives. A Progressive condition to the offer was that the hybrid delegation be uninstructed for the presidential nomination but bound to Hiram Johnson for the vice-presidency.

Keeping the matter strictly confidential, Chairman Bacon called a meeting of the state Republican Executive Committee. There the plan was debated and turned down without a vote, a procedure which probably indicated some support for the movement within that body. Only after the meeting were the negotiations made public. Johnson immediately denied all personal knowledge of the maneuvers. He had never "heard of such a proposition." Furthermore, the angry opposition of the Republican press to the plan clearly made further negotiations impossible. The Los Angeles *Times'* final words on the subject on March 4, 1916, reflected its united opinion: "Republicans welcome to their ranks all men without distinction of race, color, or previous condition of servitude to Hiram Johnson. Whenever a crook or a Toopious Earl, a lying trickster or a Meyer Lissner, a Progressive band or a Chet Rowell, or any member of the Johnson plunderbund shall make an appearance at a Republican Club banquet, let us receive him courteously, welcome him warmly, and tell the steward to keep his eye on the spoons." [15]

The dreary end of the February negotiations constituted a serious rebuff to the Progressives. But there are, indeed, many ways to recite tribal lays. Even before the direct negotiations had broken down Lissner and Dickson, among others, had pulled the wires for the calling of a conference of prominent Republicans of "forward-looking tendencies," some of whom still shied at the word progressive in either lower or upper case letters. Headed by Guy C. Earl, vice-president and general counsel of the Great Western Power Corporation, Robert N. Bulla, a former president of the Los Angeles Chamber of Commerce, Thomas E. Hughes, president of the Union League of Los Angeles, and Victor Metcalf, Secretary of the Navy in Roosevelt's cabinet, this group of "Our Crowd" Republicans, as Lissner called them, announced intentions to preserve the political advances made in the state victory in 1916 by combining all the "former elements of the Republican party." [16]

Originally, it had been the intention of Johnson's advisors to hold a joint meeting between the "Our Crowd" Republicans and the Progressives, with the purpose of selecting identical delegates pledged to Johnson for the Progressive and Republican June conventions. But both Johnson and some of the new-departure Republicans objected to this direct use of his name. At the conference held in San Francisco on February 27 these "United Republicans," as they now called themselves, officially selected a list of uninstructed delegates pledged to support some candidate upon whom agreement could be had. Although they did not designate Hiram Johnson outright, few politicians were confused by the evasion. As the Los Angeles *Times* remarked, the list of twenty-six delegates included five real Republicans and twenty-one men who would vote for Johnson for anything.[17]

Meanwhile, another attempt to strike a bargain was initiated, this time according to Progressive papers, by the regular Republicans. Afraid, perhaps, that a list of delegates supported by the combined Progressives and "United Republicans" might sweep to victory, representatives of the United Republicans were invited to meet with the Republican State Central Committee. Here they were offered the same proposal that the Progressives had made originally, except for the pledging of the delegation to Johnson for the vice-presidential nomination. But by this time the Johnson price had gone up, and when the "United Republicans" countered with an offer to place only four of the old guard leaders on their ticket, the negotiations broke down after three fruitless meetings. On March 5 a straight Republican convention gathered and named a straight Republican list of delegates to present to the voters in the May primaries. Through the "United Republicans," Johnson and his fellow Progressives had at least a foot in the door of the Republican party again. Whether or not the prodigal sons would be taken completely to the old family bosom would depend upon the voters.

Since the Progressive ticket had only one slate of delegates in the May primaries, the only interesting struggle was the one between the two opposing sets of Republicans. Here the fight was on a pro- and anti-Johnson basis. Progressive leaders and their papers, without actually announcing the death of their own party, prayerfully asked their followers to enroll as Republicans and support the "united" ticket. To make the plea official Hiram Johnson published a letter of recommendation. "I hope," he wrote, "that you will win. I trust that every forward-looking man and woman in the Republican party *and every man and woman not of that party in the past, but*

expecting to affiliate with it in the immediate future, will vote
with you. . . ." [18] In spite of all the blessings of Progressive
leadership it was a difficult task to convince the faithful that
they should return to the camp of their old enemies. Mourn-
fully, Johnson admitted that the Progressive vote could not
be directed or controlled. To obtain a Progressive majority
within the Republican party while many of his most ardent
followers were still within the Progressive party, was an almost
impossible task, he wrote Roosevelt. If Roosevelt's name were
to head the ticket, the governor suggested hopefully, then
the job could be pulled off. But the Colonel would give no
aid on that score. Cannily refusing to do what Johnson himself
had refused to do, all that Roosevelt would say was that he
hoped "the hard and fast Progressives of California would go
right into this Republican contest. . . ." [19] That was not
enough.

In an extremely light election during the first week in May,
the United Republicans were soundly beaten, and Johnson
received his second serious defeat within a matter of a few
months. This was extremely unfortunate for the pugnacious
governor's aspirations and, as it turned out, for the Republican
party and the hopes of Charles Evans Hughes. Though the
defeat did not entirely stop the Johnson-for-vice-president
movement, it did slow it up considerably. On the assumption
that Johnson was no longer a force in California politics, the
California old guard drew a totally unwarranted but heartfelt
conclusion that he could be ignored in the future with complete impunity. The taste of victory was so sweet after the
long years of defeat that they ceased to be realists. Jubilantly
they welcomed back into the party the Progressive rank and
file, "without any embarrassing reminders." They made it
clear, however, that there would be no such consideration for
the leaders. Most of all there was to be no welcome for Hiram
Johnson. According to the regular newspapers, he was "in
discard," "through," and "decapitated," and "might as well
forget any further political ambitions." These misapprehen-
sions help explain the stiff-necked attitude of the California

232

regulars that was to prove so costly during the campaign of 1916. This same attitude aided in Hughes' loss of California and thus the presidency.[20]

Hiram Johnson had too much partisan spirit and personal vanity to take defeat easily. After the United Republican defeat he was grim indeed, and the immediate future merely emphasized his bitterness. By the middle of May it was apparent that Roosevelt, despite his refusal to permit his name to go on the ballot in California, was a candidate for the Republican nomination. A public letter to an old cabinet member on May 23, 1916, made definite what had been probable for weeks—that the Colonel was trying for the Republican nomination on a platform of Americanism and preparedness. In addition to slighting the California Progressives, Roosevelt's action was fatal to Johnson's hopes of the vice-presidential nomination. If Roosevelt won the nomination the second place on the ticket would necessarily be given to a conservative Republican. Besides, Roosevelt's recent flirting with pronounced conservatives and his belligerent militarism were already creating havoc in the ranks of the Progressive party in California. As Roosevelt went rapidly to the right, he suddenly acquired new friends in California as in the rest of the nation. The most steady reactionary voice in the state perhaps, the San Francisco *Argonaut,* was now full of praise for his "genuine patriotism." In rejoinder, a good many old Progressives were also suddenly changing their allegiance. It was an uncommonly strange day when one could read in the San Francisco *Bulletin,* "Even Bryan is truer to democratic principles than Theodore Roosevelt." More important for California politics was the *Bulletin*'s later comment that the only issue that separated the Democratic party from the now combined Progressives and Republicans was that of "militarism." That charge, as Johnson well knew, could betoken only trouble for his continued control of California.[21]

When Hiram Johnson arrived in Chicago to help complete the plans for the Progressive convention, he was decidedly not in an amiable mood. The events of the week before the meeting of that body served only to sharpen his resentment of friends and foes alike. For one thing, he found George W. Perkins more in control of the party than he had been in 1912. Johnson had never been fond of the Wall Street man. Sourly he wired the sick Lissner, who had been left behind in California, that the situation was much confused by Perkins' pussyfooting tactics. The governor's disaffection turned to rage, however, when he found that the strategy of the convention as planned by Perkins was not to nominate anyone on the Progressive ticket until the Republicans had acted, in the hope that they would be coerced into accepting Roosevelt. Having tried the same game in California and been rebuffed, Johnson was in no mood for further bargaining and insults. Besides, that strategy ended all hope of Johnson's securing the vice-presidential nomination. On June 4 he publicly indicated his dissatisfaction with Perkins' leadership by announcing that he was through compromising and wanted Roosevelt's immediate nomination.[22]

For the next two days he rowed with Perkins. Then, with Henry Allen of Kansas and Gifford Pinchot, he threatened to issue a public statement denouncing the "stall and dicker" strategy. It was then that the intransigent governor first learned that Roosevelt was supporting Perkins' strategy to the hilt. On the following day an even more painful blow fell. When the convention opened, Johnson was defeated for permanent chairman of the body by Raymond Robbins. It was obvious that Johnson no longer had a decisive voice in the party's inner circle, and that his running mate of 1912 had partly deserted him for other men. It was cruel even for the cruel game of politics, and Hiram Johnson was not notorious for his thick skin. From that moment he became one of the acknowledged leaders of the so-called radicals within the convention. Had this group had its way, it would have overthrown Perkins and nominated Roosevelt immediately.

However, when the convention opened Perkins, with Roosevelt's steady support, was in control. The demands for Roosevelt's immediate nomination were swept aside and

Raymond Robbins, Roosevelt's personally chosen temporary chairman, gave a keynote speech that promised coöperation with the Republican convention then in session at the Coliseum. The Progressive platform adopted shortly afterward was innocuous enough to please the most devout of the old guard. And after these developments Johnson, seeing the inevitability of playing the game as Roosevelt wanted it, changed his tactics again. For the next two days, even though he did not agree with the policy, he helped to keep the delegates in line for the "stall and dicker" scheme. Accordingly, he publicly endorsed Roosevelt's open letter asking the convention to coöperate with the Republican party, and supported the action of the delegates in appointing a conference committee to meet with a similar Republican group for the purpose of agreeing upon a compromise candidate.[23]

That was on a Thursday. All that night and until three o'clock the next morning the Progressive conference committee, of which Johnson was one of five members, fruitlessly debated the question of possible candidates with their Republican comembers. The Progressives argued for Roosevelt; the Republicans said "no," and then refused to advance an alternate choice. The next day it was apparent that Roosevelt had little chance for the Republican nomination. On the second ballot he got 81 votes against a total of 328½ for Charles Evans Hughes.

Meanwhile, the Progressive convention again threatened to revolt from their leaders. In answer to Perkins' request on Friday morning for a further delay in action, boos and catcalls echoed through the hall. At the convention meeting that night a large body of delegates loudly expressed their loss of confidence in Perkins' strategy. "Why not, why not nominate him now?" they shouted in unison as the disorder grew. It took a speech from Hiram Johnson to restore order among the increasingly suspicious body of delegates. Though Johnson still supported the leadership of the party in his speech, he plainly did not agree with it. If it were not for Roosevelt's expressed wishes, Johnson stated, he would support an immediate nomination. He was not in accord with "the few who have been keeping this splendid body of men from the action they wished to take with respect to the men who robbed them in 1912." In fact, he demanded "the right to protest with all my soul against what's been done today and tonight with the Progressive party." Amid great cheering he promised the delegates: "After we've cleansed our soul and taken a moral bath, we'll stand together again and act like men united to fight and preserve the Progressive party of America." In a report of the meeting to Roosevelt, Charles J. Bonaparte succinctly remarked: "Some of the more prominent members of the convention, including Governor Johnson, Mr. Parker, and Victor Murdock were critical and obstructive. . . ." [24]

At eleven o'clock on Friday night the conferees from the two conventions met again. Once more the Republican members declared that they would not support Roosevelt under any consideration. This time two of them at least had a tentative alternative—Charles Evans Hughes. But since the Progressives would accept nothing less than a unanimous suggestion, the conference adjourned at three o'clock in the morning with no agreement. Then Theodore Roosevelt talked with a leading member of the Republican conference committee and suggested the names of Major General Leonard Wood and Henry Cabot Lodge as compromise candidates. When Nicholas Murray Butler indicated that only Lodge could be considered, Roosevelt later recommended the Massachusetts senator to both conventions as a patriot and "a staunch fighter for different measures of economic reform in the direction of social justice." [25]

The suggestion of Lodge for the nomination caused Johnson and his California Progressives indescribable anguish. General Wood was bad enough to the peace-inclined Californians, but Lodge was definitely worse. Cold, haughty, and bleakly conservative, Lodge was far removed from the spirit of California progressivism. To have supported him for any office would have meant denying practically every word the Progressives had spoken for the past eight years. Johnson could not possibly have missed the fact that the Colonel had not even mentioned his running mate in 1912 as a possible compromise, and if Lodge were accepted by both parties, the Johnson dream for the vice-presidential office was gone. For Johnson to be paired with Lodge would have been the ultimate stultification. "He will never do," Johnson snapped when he first heard the bleak news. "We will tell the Colonel in language so direct that he will understand it." [26]

When the Progressive conferees met at nine o'clock on Saturday morning to present the name of Lodge to their Republican colleagues, Hiram Johnson was conspicuously absent. He and John Parker of Louisiana had quit the body in disgust, even though the remaining three Progressives had agreed to present Lodge as Roosevelt's choice and not their own. Consequently, Johnson had no part in the discussion which led to the agreement that the Progressives would offer Hughes to their convention as a possible compromise. The California delegation helped to table the Hughes suggestion when it was made to the Progressive convention, and from there went on to participate in the open rebellion against George W. Perkins which marked the end of the convention and of the Progressive party.

With the Republican meeting already on its third ballot, Perkins still attempted to stall off any action. In the roar of disapproval from the delegates the chairman refused to countenance Perkins' motion and acknowledged Bainbridge Colby, who nominated Roosevelt. But before Johnson could make the seconding speech, Perkins was again on his feet with an objection. What he had to say was never heard. The thoroughly angry delegates shouted him down, permitting Johnson to give his seconding speech. Three minutes after the Republicans had chosen Charles Evans Hughes, Roosevelt was nominated unanimously.

The weary story had not yet come to an end. During the recess called for lunch, the leaders of the convention heard what most of them had known, that Roosevelt would decline a nomination which favored him over Hughes. Now they debated whether it would be best to publish the Roosevelt statement before or after the convention adjourned. Perkins, with Roosevelt's approval, suggested that they keep silent about Roosevelt's refusal until after the delegates had left the city. This would have ended any possibility of a rebellion and another nomination, and it is probable that the plan would have been followed, had it not been for Hiram Johnson's determination that the leadership in the meeting for once should be frank with the rank and file. Thanks to Johnson's insistence the Roosevelt telegram provisionally declining the nomination and placing the whole matter into the hands of the national committee, was read to the convention shortly after the nomination of John W. Parker for vice-president.[27]

"It was pitiful and tragic," Chester Rowell wrote afterward, "to see that great convention . . . held in leash to the very end, and loosed only to jump down an empty hole." As Roosevelt's message was read, the heart visibly went out of the body. There was no rebellion. Dumbly a majority voted to refer the matter to the national committee as Roosevelt had requested. And dumbly the same majority slowly got to their feet and walked to the door as the band played "America." Only here and there among the members did one hear the grim word, "traitor." Rowell remarked that most of them were "too broken hearted and disillusioned" for immediate bitterness. That would come later. That and a sense of guilt in some of the leaders. When he arrived home a month later Chester Rowell was still not at peace with himself. "Much of the tactical policy adopted in the convention," he wrote by the way of public confession, "I disapproved and protested against in private. But publicly I accepted it, and was a part of the steam-roller crew. If it was wrong—and it was—I was a party to that wrong, and I do not want to shirk responsibility." Hiram Johnson, however, felt nothing but sharp resentment against the leadership of the Progressive party. Interviewed the day following the convention, Johnson would not even talk about Hughes. About the outcome of the Progressive convention, Johnson's only words were that he would not "presume to criticize Roosevelt." [28]

After the Progressive convention had ended with this "dull sickening thud," the California Progressive leaders set off for the East. Dickson was on his way to Washington, where he proposed a plan to Hughes to place Rowell and one Progressive from each state on the Republican campaign committee. After much persuasion, Johnson accompanied Rowell to New York, where the latter was still hopeful of doing something for his disappointed chief. Never, Rowell wrote, had he seen Johnson in a more peevish mood. Invited to see Hughes the day of his arrival, the California governor declined in a huff. Roosevelt was soon given to understand that Johnson did not even want to talk to him, to say nothing of making a visit to Oyster Bay. When Roosevelt asked Rowell why the Johnsons had declined to visit him, all the Fresno man could say was that the governor was "thinking with his liver." Although Roosevelt snapped back that he did not want anyone to think that he cared one way or another about the slight, later in the summer he wrote a warm letter of congratulations to Johnson on the occasion of his senatorial primary victory. But nothing came from Sacramento in reply except a long, cold silence. Much later, Rowell tried to read Johnson one of Roosevelt's letters expressing confidence in the governor. By reading rapidly, he told Lissner, he managed to get over twenty words of it before Johnson stopped him with the remark that he was completely indifferent to whether Roosevelt "was friendly or hostile." And thus a friendship came to an end. The touchy and perhaps oversensitive Hiram Johnson characteristically never forgot nor forgave the events of June, 1916.

Johnson's only apparent pleasure in the trip to New York was gathering with a group of Progressives who had a "terrible bitter resentment against Roosevelt." Amos Pinchot and his friends, Rowell wrote Lissner, were busy gathering a group "of historic traitors." Pinchot's brother was telling everyone who would listen that the Progressives "had been used for bait." Johnson, Rowell concluded, was in perfect agreement with both Pinchots.[29]

Rowell, at least, was on more specific business in New York than to join in an anti-Roosevelt chorus. His first and most cherished hope still was to obtain the vice-presidential nomination for the California governor, even though Fairbanks had been selected by the Chicago convention. For three days, Rowell reported, he had been "trying to engineer Fairbanks off the ticket and Johnson on. That is what he [Johnson] really wants," Rowell stated emphatically. He had to report later that the slightly fantastic scheme "is not working very well," even though it had been carried clear up to Hughes. Consequently, Johnson was in "one of his black dumps." But Rowell had more than one string to his bow. When the vice-presidential matter fell through, he and Perkins began a concerted campaign among the Republican national bosses to "get a let-up on Johnson in California so that he would have a walkover for the Senate." According to Rowell, Senators Murray Crane and John C. King were impressed with the idea that if Heney ran as a Democrat, he could probably beat any Republican except Johnson because of the latter's appeal to the radical vote. But they also were aware of Johnson's recent defeats and were afraid that Johnson might lose in the Republican primary. Therefore, King was looking into the possibility of giving Johnson a clear field. King, Rowell added with a new-found cynicism, had been given "the job of picking in the various states the men whom the people are to elect senators. . . ."[30]

At first Johnson was not interested in this scheme. "He does not care much about being senator," wrote Rowell. Also, Johnson neither trusted the honesty of the Republican leaders nor believed "they could deliver the goods" in California even if they tried. Time and ambition apparently changed the governor's mind. Rowell later wrote that he had been "definitely promised" by Senators Crane, Penrose, and King on

behalf of the Republican steering committee, then in inter-
regnum authority, that they would do everything they could
to clear the way for Johnson in California, even to the extent
"of enlisting the influence of Mr. Hughes." This was later attested to by George Perkins, who knew of the delicate negotiations. To facilitate the agreement, Rowell was made a joint
national committeeman from California to serve with the
regular Republican, William H. Crocker. California thus enjoyed the honor of being represented during the campaign by
two national committeemen, one a Progressive, the other a
regular Republican.[31]

Several points are extremely interesting about this agreement that was to cause so much trouble in the future. Rowell
himself wrote that it was made only "on behalf of" and not
by the Republican steering committee. The question arises by
what authority this group made a promise that would be
binding upon the as yet unselected national campaign leaders.
Although Rowell had had two long conferences with him, it
was never suggested that the one man who could have given
the strongest pledge of performance, Charles Evans Hughes,
had personally approved of the bargain. Finally, the regular
Republican leaders in California clearly did not approve and
probably had had no previous knowledge of the agreement.
Rowell and Johnson, however, had apparently accepted the
promises of Crane, King, and Penrose as a commitment, for
on June 27, at the final riotous meeting of the Progressive National Committee at Chicago, Rowell gave a long account of
his meetings with the Republicans in the East and fervently
pleaded for a unanimous acceptance of the Republican nominee. On the same day, Hiram Johnson grudgingly announced
his support of the former Chief Justice. Inasmuch as Hughes'
nomination had been the only Progressive achievement at
Chicago, he said, and because his record warranted it, Johnson had made his individual choice and would support
Hughes. Each member of the party, he concluded, would have
to decide for himself, "basing the decision solely upon his

sense of duty and love of country." As the disgruntled Johnson traveled the bitter road to Canossa, he went alone by preference. The San Francisco *Bulletin* pointed out that Johnson had not undertaken to deliver a single vote to the Republican candidate, other than his own.[32]

CHAPTER X

1916 and the Lost Election

*

Hiram Johnson's indifferent support of Charles Evans Hughes in late June, 1916, might be explained by the fact that he was still "thinking with his liver," but the demands of practical politics offer a better explanation. Before his return to California, the governor had determined to run for the senatorial nomination in the Republican primaries. Viewed against the background of recent Progressive defeats in the state, this was a hazardous venture at best. Johnson was aware that he could ill afford to alienate the many Democrats who had supported him in the past, either by too much pumping for Hughes or by too much criticism of Woodrow Wilson. The call that went out on June 29 for a state-wide gathering of the Progressive clan was most diplomatically phrased. The conference, this form letter ran, was being called to discuss the future plans of all Progressives. Whether they expected to affiliate either with the Republican or with the Democratic party, the need of further organization was essential so that they might keep their unity and perpetuate the progressive movement in the state.

On July 8, between five hundred and a thousand party members gathered at the Palace Hotel in San Francisco to hear Johnson give an address to the last official gathering of the Progressive party. Sadly, the governor confessed that the national party had committed suicide in Chicago by "dallying." But whatever that convention had done, Johnson belligerently stated, it had done in a trusting spirit, at the behest of Theodore Roosevelt, but never with full knowledge of what had been planned for it. Roosevelt and "his five personal representatives from the East directed every action, just as it

243

was done and just when it was done." Leaving the painful past, the governor turned to the future. He would support Hughes, he declared, but he would not attempt to dictate the actions of any fellow Progressives. All he asked was that they organize within the party of their choice so that the California progressive movement might endure. This was imperative, Johnson emphasized, because even then the California reactionaries were organized for an onslaught against liberalism. He shouted that de Young, Hearst, Otis, John D. Spreckels, and Joe Knowland, "in a pretended hysteria for preparedness, all lie in wait to undo the progressive achievements of the past decade." In contrast to these wolves in patriotic clothing, Johnson went on, the California Progressives stood for a real preparedness—one which would protect the national honor and the national shores, but would also protect the individual citizen from rapacious private greed. The end of that kind of preparedness was "to make the state so loyal to the citizens that the citizens will be loyal to the state." To secure these ideals, the governor promised, he stood ready to run for senator on the Progressive as well as on the Republican ticket.

After thirty minutes of uproarious celebration, a move to endorse Johnson's candidacy was carried by acclamation. But a motion by Chester Rowell to endorse Hughes encountered so much opposition that it was withdrawn. Then, as planned, the delegates divided into two meetings, where they organized for Hughes and for Wilson. The members of both meetings thereupon reaffirmed their endorsement of Hiram Johnson for United States senator.[1]

Even Johnson's most optimistic followers conceded this was to be his hardest fight; and the more pessimistic, with whom the candidate agreed, were sure that the obstacles to success were almost insurmountable. Because of Johnson's unsuccessful attempt in 1915 to make all state elections nonpartisan, plus his rather tortuous course before the national nominating conventions, there were still 45,000 voters in the state registered as Progressives and 300,000 more without party

designation. None of these people was eligible to participate
in the Republican contest unless they reregistered. Despite
all the Progressive leaders could do, many of these potential
supporters had not yet returned to the Republican fold by
election day.

Other liabilities as grave threatened. Gone was the Progressive unity of 1910. The bitterness of the 1914 Heney campaign would not disappear. For a while it looked as if Heney
himself might announce his candidacy for the Democratic
nomination. "Carr told Lewinsohn last Saturday," Lissner
frantically wired to Johnson, "that he did not see how he
could keep Francis from running if you did." Both Lissner and
Johnson knew that not a few Progressives would prefer to
support Heney on a Democratic ticket than Johnson on a Republican slate. The Progressive party's recent swing to the nationalistic right, and the juggling of the last national convention, influenced many California Progressives to announce
for Wilson. Older had already pointed the way in the *Bulletin*.
Kent and Heney were soon to follow. In view of this group's
patent disgust with Johnson, the large question that arose
was whether their followers would cross party lines and support the governor in the Republican primary contest.[2]

Of one thing, however, the Progressive leaders were assured—the implacable opposition of the regular Republican
organization and of most Republican papers. The Los Angeles
Times made this clear immediately after the closing of the
twin conventions in Chicago. The party would welcome all
the Progressive followers, Otis' journal stated, but not the
leaders. "For its own protection," the paper continued, the
Republican party must never let Johnson, Lissner, Rowell,
and about "fifty other of these mischief makers" return. So
that there would be no mistake, the paper promised soon to
print a black list of the untouchables. The decision of the
Progressive leaders to support Hughes did nothing to soften
this hard-chinned attitude. Republicans viewed this development, declared the Oakland *Tribune*, "without emotion." But
neither the *Tribune* nor the other important journals could say

the same for Rowell's appointment to the national committee and the announcement of Johnson's candidacy. Otis was beside himself both in private letters and in print. "Rowell," he was quoted as writing to Senator Smoot in protest, "is one of the most odious of Progressives in California." The San Francisco *Argonaut* went even further. Johnson had not only been a "traitor to the party" in the past, he now stood "among its most persistent and malignant enemies." If Rowell's agreement with the Republican steering committee to "clear the way" for Johnson in California was to be effective, not a little fervent missionary work needed to be accomplished.[3]

Rowell, in fact, had busily set to the work of conversion as soon as he had come home from Chicago. Instead of softening the opposition, his activities seemed to harden it, and he was soon burdening the wires to Perkins and William R. Willcox, Hughes' campaign manager, with requests for the help that had been promised him. On July 7 he heard the disheartening news from Perkins that "Crane and King say they have done everything they can from this end of the line to prepare matters as per their conversations with you here." The only thing they had left to suggest, according to Perkins, was that Rowell hold a conference with William H. Crocker, the regular Republican member of the National Committee, "and talk frankly with him." Especially disquieting to Rowell was the fact that both King and Crane seemed reluctant to communicate with him directly. All Hughes' campaign manager felt called upon to do was to wire Crocker complaining of the friction. Harmony in California was essential, Willcox suggested weakly, if the national ticket was to be successful.[4]

Willcox's vague telegram was scarcely designed to stop the determined regular attack upon Johnson. When Rowell met with Crocker, as Perkins had asked him to do, he found that the Republican leaders in California had never heard of the eastern arrangement to clear the way for Johnson. Instead of clearing the way, Crocker told Rowell, he was determined to defeat Johnson and nominate Willis H. Booth of Los Angeles, who had already announced his candidacy. A few days later,

after another Republican, Walter Bordwell, had announced
his intention to enter the senatorial primaries, Rowell heard
the alarming rumor that Crocker and the chairman of the
Republican State Central Committee, Francis V. Keesling,
were intent upon forcing one of the Republicans from the
list so as to concentrate the entire regular strength against
Johnson. Since this was exactly the reverse of what he had
bargained for, Rowell telegraphed John C. King to come to
California and settle the question in accordance with their
agreement. King was too cagey a politician to enter the tangle,
and promptly wired back that it "was too late to get there
to be effective." His one hope was that "the Bordwell situation
should be held as it is as long as possible or until something
concrete develops here." [5]

After confirming that Crocker and Keesling had gone to
Los Angeles to force Bordwell off the primary ballot, Rowell
telegraphed a bitter protest to Crocker and asked for a second
conference. In this message, which he published in the daily
papers, Rowell demanded that instead of an anti-Johnson
elimination a pro-Johnson elimination be approved. "Position
of national leaders, as I know, is definitely favorable to Johnson," he added. At the same time, Rowell appealed to Perkins
to remind the national headquarters of their previous commitment. "Apparently," he complained bitterly, "not one word
definitely favorable to Johnson has been sent from there to
Crocker. I was specifically promised this." [6]

Soon afterward, the two California national committeemen met for another discussion. But before entering into the
conversations, Crocker and Keesling demanded the facts from
national headquarters about Rowell's "understanding" with
them. Although Willcox obviously knew about Rowell's conversations with King, Crane, and Penrose, he chose to be ignorant of the matter. "I have no knowledge of eastern leaders
as stated in your message," he replied to Keesling. In a second
telegram he wired: "The national committee has taken no
action of any kind favoring the candidacy of any person for
United States Senator. . . ." By refusing to mention the

so-called steering committee, Willcox in effect repudiated the agreement Rowell had made. With this assurance, Crocker and his regular colleagues entered the meeting with Rowell determined not to modify by one iota their plans to rid California of the Johnson influence. "California must have a Republican Senator," Crocker telegraphed to Willcox. "My efforts will be judiciously and unreservedly so directed." Lest there be any further doubt about the matter in the minds of the campaign committee, the Republican press threatened that if Rowell's pretensions were not limited, "There will be a storm of revolt led by the Republican press which will put California in the assured list of Democratic states." [7]

Feeling that he had been "sold out" and "made to appear a liar" by the national Republican leaders, Rowell told Perkins that he would make no further attempt to influence the organization in California until the Republican national leaders were ready to deliver the help they had promised. The regular leaders were not even "regarding the problem of getting progressive votes as serious." Crocker was "obdurate," he was convinced, in the belief that the entire future of California Republicanism lay in the absolute defeat of Johnson. Moreover, Crocker felt that if any deal had been arranged, then he should have been consulted. In that claim the fair-minded Rowell conceded that he was eminently right.

Sensing the disgust and hopelessness in Rowell's message, Perkins urged him to continue asking aid for Johnson both in New York and in California. His own inability to get support for the governor in New York, Perkins intimated, was not because of Willcox, but because of Charles Evans Hughes. "I personally feel," Perkins wrote, "that the difficulty lies in a place where we seem unable to smoke it out, namely with the Gentleman who gave Governor Johnson some cigars." Perkins then asked Rowell to telegraph Hughes for help. [8]

For some reason, Rowell decided instead to write one last letter of appeal to Hughes' campaign manager, Willcox. And in writing this sixteen-page letter, Rowell contributed immeasurably to the defeat of his immediate plans in California and ultimately perhaps to the defeat of Hughes himself. Replying first to a telegraphic plea from Willcox that the two sides of the California scrap get together and settle their differences, Rowell insisted that such a settlement was impossible because the two viewpoints in conflict were utterly irreconcilable. Although Crocker was extremely likable and a personal friend, Rowell wrote, he was "a standpatter of the extreme sort," and his advisors were even worse. Rowell listed in this group Supreme Court Justice Henshaw, "the ablest, the narrowest, and the bitterest representative of the old Southern Pacific machine still surviving in the public life of California"; Alfred Holman, editor of the *Argonaut,* "the most snobbish journalistic flunkey in California, whose function for years has been to translate into good English and plausible logic the stupidities and ignorances of California's reactionary rich"; and S. Fred Hogue, "editor of the San Francisco *Globe* during the time it was Patrick Calhoun's hired prostitute. . . ." Between these men and the followers of Johnson, Rowell was certain, there never could be a meeting of minds.

Rowell went on to give the details of his agreement with King and the other members of the Republican steering committee. And then, in the very last part of his long letter, he made what was probably his fatal error; he confessed that if the situation in California was not changed from the outside, Johnson and his Progressives would probably lose the primary election. "With 300,000 voters, practically all of the Progressive faction now registered without stating any party affiliation," he wrote, "and therefore not qualified to vote this year in any party primary, the primary is of course loaded on the standpat end, and it can be carried by the Progressives this year only by a landslide." By suggesting the strong possibility of a Progressive defeat in the primaries, the Fresno editor confirmed the predictions Willcox had been receiving from practically every regular Republican in California.[9]

Probably never have a harassed campaign manager and a presidential candidate been confronted by a more perplexing situation. Their main interest, of course, was in the success of the national ticket. But just how success was to be achieved in California must have been the subject of long debates between Hughes, Willcox, and their advisors. And in the end Charles Evans Hughes must have made, or at least approved, the decision on a matter of such major importance. That decision was to disregard the promises made to Rowell by the group of national leaders whose authority to make such an agreement was admittedly dubious, and to permit the Republican organization in California to conduct its affairs as it would, even to the extent of ganging up on Johnson and his Progressives.

Considering all the factors involved, it is difficult to see how Hughes and his advisors could have come to any other decision. Even had they wanted to help Johnson, there was no assurance that the California Republicans could be moved either by threat or by persuasion. All the California regular leaders had made it obvious that Johnson's defeat was as much of a consideration with them as the success of the national ticket, and perhaps more so. With so much at stake, Republican national headquarters undoubtedly read California newspapers most discerningly. They probably did not miss Congressman Joseph R. Knowland's remark that it was far better to elect a Democrat than to have Johnson for senator. Nor is it probable that either William Crocker's public remarks about Johnson or Alfred Holman's editorial comment in the *Argonaut* went unnoticed in New York. In introducing Nicholas Murray Butler, who had come to open Hughes' campaign in the state, Crocker labeled Johnson as "the party's most prominent and intolerant enemy in the state." Holman had written in turn on July 29, that even if Johnson obtained a mandate from the national party, it would not be honored in California. "It could not bind the Republican party of California in a matter of local concern," was his flat statement.[10]

In July, 1916, Johnson's power seemed to be waning in the state, and the cards appeared to be stacked against him in the August Republican primary. Rowell had felt this, and

Rowell's statements in his letter of July 29 must have counted heavily in Hughes' and Willcox's final decision not to honor Rowell's June arrangement with the Republican steering committee. Since any action was calculated to alienate one side or the other, it must have seemed the better part of politics to play with what looked to be the winning side. At national headquarters, as in the regular organization in California, there were also many conservatives who delighted in letting the old Progressives know that their day was over in the Republican party. Finally, by not taking any action in California and thus favoring the regulars, Hughes could be made to appear as a champion of local autonomy.

Thanks to this hands-off policy, the California regulars had forced an unwilling Bordwell off the primary ballot in a matter of days. Regular strength was fully mobilized against Hiram Johnson, and any hope of the fusion of all Republicans in California was clearly gone. From that time on the gauntlet was down between the two factions. Anyone who got in the way was in clear danger of being hurt. And unfortunately for the success of the Republican party, Charles Evans Hughes was scheduled to make a speaking tour of the state only ten days before the tempestuous contest between regulars and Progressives was to be settled at the August primaries.

Preparing for Hughes' visit to the state, the regular organization was intent upon one thing: that Johnson's candidacy should in no way be aided by the presidential candidate. For eight long years the California regulars had suffered without either honor or office. They had watched Johnson and his cohorts pass a great reform program which had violated practically all of their basic political instincts. In 1912 the Progressives had defeated the party that had elected them in 1910, and two years later deserted the Republican standard completely. It was too much to expect that they should be welcomed back in 1916 as friends and equals when their power appeared to be waning, and especially since they came demanding the senatorship. From the very start of the national campaign, the regulars made all the arrangements and grimly insisted on ignoring these unrepentant prodigals. Chester Rowell, the conational chairman of California, was neither consulted in the arrangements for, nor invited to, the speeches of Nicholas Murray Butler, the first national campaign orator to invade the state. But he was asked to sit on the stage "as a vice-president" during Hughes' speech at Los Angeles.

When Rowell received this invitation, he and the rest of the Progressive command responded with anger and bitterness. "As a member of the Hughes national campaign committee," he tartly replied to William H. Crocker, "it seems to me I should be giving, not receiving invitations." Rowell followed this with a demand and an ultimatum. He wanted to know immediately whether a "joint committee" of Progressives and Republicans could be agreed upon to make arrangements, or whether the regulars had decided to monopolize the affair. If monopoly was the order of the day, then any participation by him and the Progressives could be discounted. "I will accept no invitation in Hughes' campaign which I do not participate in giving and cannot urge any Progressives to accept any invitation unless some Progressive participates in issuing it and in arranging for the occasion on which it is issued," he concluded his telegram. For the eyes of Hughes' campaign manager, he fired an equally angry telegram to the East. The regular organization, Rowell wired to Perkins, was not disposed to grant the Progressives anything but perfunctory participation, or "to tolerate Johnson in any position which as governor he could accept." The governor already had a full schedule of speaking dates arranged for the period Hughes would be in California. Without an immediate and radical change in the California organization's attitude, Rowell declared, he probably would find it "difficult" to induce Johnson to cancel those dates and meet the candidate. Unless this "anti-Progressive ostracism" were stopped, he ended, there was no excuse for his remaining on the national committee.[11]

By this telegram intended for Willcox, Rowell made it clear

three weeks before Hughes came to California that Hiram Johnson was in no mood to be treated like a country cousin either by the presidential candidate or by the men who represented him in California. The message did not indicate that Johnson would cease his support of the Republican candidate in the event that he and his followers were slighted in California, but Willcox had every reason to believe after reading it that there would be no "Hail Caesar" unless Caesar was ready to hail back.

Rowell's telegram did accomplish one thing. As a result of pressure from the national organization, Crocker invited him to still another conference on July 27 where the whole matter might be talked over again. But that was as far as Willcox would go at the time in trying to pacify the Progressives. The California matter was so complicated, Perkins informed Rowell, that Willcox was afraid to do anything further, "lest he get the national organization in wrong all around." The Rowell-Crocker conference soon proved, however, that a California solution to the difficulties was impossible. At the meeting Rowell made two demands: first, that all arrangements for the Hughes trip be planned by a joint committee equally divided in membership between the Progressives and the regulars; and second, that Johnson be permitted to meet Hughes at the state line, welcome him to the state, and then preside over his meetings in San Francisco. In return for these concessions, Rowell was willing to permit Booth, Johnson's senatorial opponent, to preside over the Hughes Los Angeles meetings. Crocker and Francis Keesling refused to consider the proposal. Johnson might be permitted to welcome Hughes to the state, they tentatively agreed, but they were adamantly opposed to his further participation in the Hughes tour. As Crocker later wrote, they could not recognize Johnson because he was not a Republican. Inasmuch as they had agreed to keep Willis Booth away from the Hughes gatherings, they did not intend to see them converted into revival meetings for Hiram Johnson.[12]

Hopelessly deadlocked, the conferees did agree to advise

253

Willcox to delay the Hughes visit until after the Republican primary. When the campaign manager wired back that that was impossible, a solution to the impasse seemed as far away as ever. For the next two weeks the three men wrangled both in and out of numerous conferences, with both sides making demands and Rowell in particular appealing for support from the national headquarters. Under such pressure, Willcox did at one point cautiously suggest to Crocker: "There is some force in the governor of a state supporting the presidential candidate having the privilege of presiding at one of the meetings." But he suggested this "personally and not officially," and when Crocker refused to consider it, the Republican campaign manager hastily retreated and pleaded in the midst of frantic appeals for unity that the matter be settled in California.[13]

On July 31 it appeared that a compromise might be arranged by permitting Rowell to chair the meeting at Los Angeles and Crocker to head the ceremonies at San Francisco. Rowell apparently tentatively accepted the suggestion and then repudiated it after a conference with his colleagues. The plan was "wholly theoretical," Rowell wired to Willcox, and did not meet the "practical situation." The inference was clear. If Johnson were not permitted to preside, then neither Rowell nor any other Progressive leader would lend the prestige of his position by presiding over a Hughes gathering.

When the July 31 proposals were turned down by the Progressives, Crocker lost all patience with them. He wired Willcox to ignore advice from other people, and at the same time assured the Republican campaign boss that the California regulars would arrange things so as to safeguard against any embarrassment to Mr. Hughes. With that, Crocker turned over all authority to make the arrangements to Francis V. Keesling, chairman of the Republican State Central Committee. The latter showed even less of a disposition to coöperate with the Progressives than had Crocker. He was willing to coöperate with the Progressives, Keesling stated in a public letter, by naming them vice-presidents of all Hughes' meetings, but in nothing else. Rowell and other Progressives were only appointed to the national committee "to the extent they are and may become Republicans," the state chairman held, and this could not be construed as a recognition of the Progressive organization either in California or elsewhere. Nothing would be sanctioned, Keesling ended, which would "permit of that construction." Three days later the national campaign manager was informed that all arrangements for Hughes' visit had been completed.[14]

Rowell wired Perkins that he was ready to resign, but again entreaties from Willcox and Perkins prevented this public confession of an open break. After the strongest urging from New York, and with the California regulars now promising to coöperate and appoint joint-arrangement committees, Rowell again tried for a compromise. But Crocker had also wired to Willcox the flat statement: "We will not concede to recognition of Governor Johnson by Hughes." This determined regular stand actually made all further California efforts for conciliation worthless. The regulars would not do business with Johnson, and the Progressives would do nothing without his recognition by the Republican presidential candidate. Confronted with this dilemma, the harassed campaign manager could only propose that the tangled situation might be straightened out at the last moment in a personal conference with Hughes. Rowell, Crocker, and Keesling were therefore invited to meet the candidate on August 16 at Portland, Oregon, and ride south with him. Willcox hoped that somewhere between Portland and San Francisco a peace formula might be found. In the meantime, according to Rowell, Willcox requested that no "firm and final" arrangements be made for the Hughes visit until the controversy could be settled at the Portland conference.[15]

Unfortunately for the cause of peace in California, the proposed Portland meeting never took place. Rowell left for Portland as scheduled on August 15, but at the last moment Crocker, Keesling, and other members of the state committee delayed their journey and did not meet Hughes until the morning of the 17th at Gerber, California, a point less than six hours from San Francisco. With the candidate scheduled to speak that afternoon in the city by the bay, little time was left to alter any of the arrangements previously made by the chairman of the Republican State Central Committee; and so, whether by design or accident, the regular leaders did avoid making any serious change in their plans. Until evidence is produced to the contrary, it seems probable that Crocker and Keesling missed the Portland meeting with full malice aforethought.[16]

All the way from Portland to Gerber, Rowell presented the progressive case to Hughes and his immediate advisors. Several of these people were apparently impressed, and urged Hughes to give Johnson some recognition. But the prudent candidate, made even more cautious perhaps by Crocker and Keesling's absence from Portland, remained silent. Once in San Francisco, Rowell held a last bitter talk with Crocker during which the two men came near to a personal break. Since Crocker still insisted that Johnson be kept away from all the Hughes meetings, Rowell wired to Willcox that the governor could not possibly meet Hughes unless he were personally invited by the candidate himself. Evidently the national campaign manager made one last try at breaking the deadlock. For just a few hours before Hughes was to leave San Francisco, his advisors, in Rowell's words, were able "to extort the proposition from him" that if Johnson were to greet him in Sacramento, he would invite the governor to come with him to an extra speech in the capital city. Johnson, however, refused to entertain this "death-bed repentance." Consequently, all direct negotiations between Hughes and the Progressive leaders were thereby broken off until the dramatic happenings of Long Beach.[17]

During Hughes' stay in San Francisco, Crocker and Keesling took almost complete possession of him. Although the candidate in his first major address remarked that he had "no concern" with local differences, his actions, as most commentators pointed out, seemed to belie that remark. He saluted Crocker as "San Francisco's favorite son," and otherwise made it apparent that he found the company of the regulars most congenial. Except for Chester Rowell, scarcely a Progressive of any stature occupied a prominent place in his entourage. Rowell, who confessed to feeling lonesome, was carefully kept a proper distance from the throne. At the end of two days, both regulars and Progressives for once agreed: "Hughes had allowed himself to be completely identified with Johnson's enemies." When this became hopelessly obvious, Rowell changed his plans to accompany the candidate's party throughout the state and retired to Fresno, ostensibly to be near his ailing wife. But before he took a train south, Rowell sent one more telegram to Hughes' campaign manager in the East: "Open war to depose Crocker and Keesling from Republican organization . . . begins the day after Hughes leaves the state." To Willcox the implications of that grim message were plain.[18]

Charles Evans Hughes was in San Francisco for only two days. It is possible that no presidential candidate ever managed to alienate so many voters in one region within so short a time. By the time he boarded the ferry and said farewell, he had lost not only the support of many Progressives, but almost the entire labor vote as well. Here again it is probable that the candidate's great prestige was used to help determine the fate of a palpable local issue by some of the same men who were using his visit to defeat the ambitions of Hiram Johnson.

Hughes' relations with organized labor in San Francisco began months before the candidate entered the state. After a violent longshoreman's strike in the early summer, the San Francisco Chamber of Commerce first announced its comprehensive plan to crush organized labor in northern California. For years the San Francisco employers had battled labor in the city only to see it grow stronger. For years they had watched the increasing disparity in the wage-scale standard between Los Angeles and their own city as labor was repeatedly repulsed in its attempt to organize the southern city. Now in 1916, with liberalism apparently on the wane and the regular Republican chances of victory bright in both the nation and the state, a majority of the city's businessmen determined to fight a conclusive battle with the unions. If the Republican presidential candidate's visit to California could be made to serve their economic, as well as their political purposes within the state, so much the better.

At the end of June the San Francisco Chamber passed a resolution favoring the open shop. A week later, a mass meeting of a thousand businessmen was held to raise funds for the showdown struggle. It was an enthusiastic meeting from the first. Time and time again the audience broke out in vociferous cheers as Robert Dollar related how the unions had been beaten on the waterfront. Peace had returned to the docks, the old shipowner exclaimed, only when the union men "went to the hospital in ambulances." After an hour of appeals to "fight" by Dollar and William Sproule, president of the Southern Pacific Railroad, $200,000 was pledged as a start on a war chest of one million. A law-and-order committee was appointed and a program of principles adopted, calling for "the end of labor's tyranny by the establishment of open shops and by the abolition of all union violence, coercion, and intimidation including all forms of picketing." Lest any businessman misinterpret the spirit of the meeting and seek a separate peace with labor, a resolution had been previously adopted, "to oppose any attempt on the part of any interest, business, or organization which tries to throttle the commercial freedom of San Francisco." [19]

These were words uttered many times before, but this time action came sure and swift. Following a strike and a lockout of the culinary union in the city, the law-and-order committee promptly stepped into the struggle to stop the concession of an eight-hour day which some of the larger restaurants were willing to make. Thereafter the committee used every weapon from persuasion to coercion to place an open-shop card in the window of every restaurant in San Francisco. Against reluctant establishments were brought to bear the power of credit and the influence of wholesalers. For the more amenable, financial help was given, including free rent when necessary to keep an establishment operating. Finally, coupon books good only in open-shop restaurants were sold to all coöperating business houses in the city. Against this regimented capital, labor itself mobilized on a city-wide basis. As Charles Evans Hughes neared San Francisco, the blue chips were down again in the apparently never ending struggle between capital and labor.[20]

On July 22, 1916, three weeks before Hughes entered the city, San Francisco's businessmen held a huge preparedness parade. One hundred and fifteen divisions of the parade had been organized, representing practically every industry in the city, the Union League Club, and the usual patriotic societies. But in that long line of march not one division was given over to labor. On the contrary, a good many labor leaders had met with more than 4,000 citizens to protest against the parade the night before at the Dreamland Rink, where Rudolph Spreckels, Rabbi J. Nieto, and Sarah Bard Field had denounced militarism. On the morning of the parade the city newspapers received a penciled note warning of direct action against the patriotic demonstration. The note also contained a challenge to the San Francisco Chamber of Commerce, daring its members to march together in a group if they wished to show their courage. Later in the day a bomb exploded along the line of march, killing ten people and injuring forty more.

Denouncing this ruthless act, the law-and-order committee of the Chamber of Commerce demanded immediate apprehension of the criminals, and intimated that the peace meeting and the city's labor leaders were in part responsible. Without adequate investigation, Charles Fickert, the district attorney, quickly arrested two admitted labor radicals, Tom Mooney and Warren K. Billings, Mooney's wife, and two well-known union officials, Israel Weinberg and Edward D. Nolan. Mooney, a friend of Emma Goldman, had been associated with the bombers of the Los Angeles *Times*, and Billings had a prior criminal record. But irrespective of their guilt or innocence in the preparedness day atrocity, one of the major issues from the time of their arrest was their labor connection. Chester Rowell observed that again law versus violence and murder was not on trial at San Francisco, but rather capital versus labor. Almost from the first moment of the bloody episode it was plain that certain business elements were quite willing to use it as an instrument to fan antiunionism in their campaign for an open shop. What had started as a patriotic exhibition was now a class crusade full of mutual, irrational name calling, passionate hatred, and group vindictiveness.[21]

In the midst of this class struggle, the California Republican State Central Committee announced on August 16 that Hughes would dine and speak at the Commercial Club, one of the restaurants in the city which displayed an open-shop card in its windows. Hugo Ernst, president of the striking Cooks and Waiters' Union, protested in an open letter against "this placing of Mr. Hughes in the position of endorsing the open-shop policy." The union then requested that other arrangements be made to entertain the candidate in a way that would not "constitute an affront to organized labor in San Francisco." In reply, Francis V. Keesling agreed that the situation was unfortunate, but that he felt nothing could be done at this late date. Pressed further by enraged labor, the Republican official defended his position by announcing that the invitation to Mr. Hughes had been made directly to Mr. Willcox in New York, and that it had been accepted five days before the open-shop card had been posted in the club.[22]

Looking back upon the incident, it seems probable that Keesling knew of the open-shop card eight days before Hughes was to arrive, and that it was extraordinary for such an invitation not to have been cleared through local party officials. Because of the extreme delicacy of the California political situation and Willcox's reiterated insistence that all arrangements in California be made locally, it is almost beyond belief that Keesling himself did not make the final decisions as to where the candidate should be received. At any rate, labor chose to treat Keesling's reply as an evasion of the real issue, and to interpret the incident as an open declaration that the Republican state committee and Charles Evans Hughes approved of the open shop. Both the committee and the candidate, the official American Federation of Labor paper stated, were completely aware of what was at stake, and both had had plenty of time to make other arrangements. Instead, the paper concluded, "Charles Evans Hughes sat down to an open-shop banquet and was served by strike breakers." [23] Thus within forty-eight hours, the Republican candidate had managed to incur the enmity of both San Francisco labor and the middle-class progressive. Come November, this was to be a heavy liability.

As he left the hill-cradled San Francisco Bay, Hughes must have sighed with relief at putting the tangled political situation there behind him. For a time his tour of southern California seemed to promise more heartening results. The crowds there were larger and more enthusiastic than in the north, and after an initially ugly situation in Los Angeles, the meeting at the Shrine auditorium went off exceedingly well. In the beginning, the regulars had attempted to bar Edward A. Dickson, Meyer Lissner, Marshall Stimson, and Lieutenant Governor Stephens from the Los Angeles reception committee. And at one time in the resulting arguments over who should receive the candidate, Francis Keesling felt called upon again to warn Rowell that if Hughes made any personal move either to recognize or commend Johnson and his Progressives, California Republicans would vote for Wilson. But a compromise was worked out, and as the candidate basked in the good conservative cheer of Harrison Gray Otis throughout his stay in Los Angeles, even the most hard-shelled regular was completely happy. There and at San Diego, however, the Progressives had to admit that they were given "a better shake" than they had gotten in the north. [24] Then, on a pleasant Sunday morning at the Virginia Hotel in Long Beach, the dramatic and well-known incident occurred which historians have seized upon as the reason for Hughes' loss of California and the national election.

The story of Long Beach began when Hiram Johnson, who

had been campaigning in Bakersfield, arrived at the Virginia Hotel for a much needed week-end rest. Accompanied by Edward A. Dickson, Johnson was in a good mood as he saw crowds on the street and mistakenly thought they were there to greet him. But once inside the hotel lobby, which was sprinkled with regular politicians, he saw that this was not "his crowd." He and Dickson retired to their rooms, realizing for the first time that Hughes was under the same roof. Inadvertently, on that Sunday morning, the presidential candidate had also chosen to rest for a few hours in the Virginia Hotel. After an interval during which no invitation came from Hughes, Johnson and Dickson left their rooms and sat upon the hotel terrace. It was not until the candidate had returned to Los Angeles later in the day that Hughes' train manager, Charles W. Farnham, telephoned. Farnham apologized for the oversight, explained that Hughes had been unaware of Johnson's presence in the hotel, and asked him to have dinner with Hughes in Pasadena that evening. Angry because Hughes had not called him personally, Johnson refused the invitation on the grounds that he had a previous engagement. Then, after arranging for a conference with Farnham later, Johnson coolly put down the receiver and asked Dickson to have dinner with him at the Virginia. If not, he said, he would eat alone.

Later that evening, as Johnson sat in the lobby, Farnham appeared for the fateful conference. Unfortunately for the cause of peace, he was accompanied by Francis Keesling, the one man Johnson held most accountable for the regulars' policy toward the Progressives. He was incensed, he later told Dickson, that Keesling of all people should have been selected by Hughes as his personal representative on the delicate mission. When Farnham asked that Keesling be present at the conference, Johnson insisted that his private secretary also sit in on the discussions to be held in his room.[25]

For a peace meeting this was an unhappy start. Nor did the hour and a half discussion that followed prove to be much more auspicious. Farnham again assured Johnson that Hughes had not known of his presence in the hotel. The former Chief Justice later wrote Johnson that had he known, "Nothing could have prevented me from seeing you." In return, the governor pointed out that many of Hughes' associates were perfectly aware where he was, but that after all, "the affront to individual Progressives" was not important compared with the character of the Republican campaign which had up to that time been carried on in California by the regular organization leaders. Instead of seeking success for the party as a whole, Johnson emphasized, these men had been interested only in two things: the defeat of progressivism, and the return of the state to the hands of the "corrupt elements which had controlled California prior to 1911." But worst of all, the governor insisted, was the use the regulars had made of Charles Evans Hughes in this campaign.

Since Francis Keesling was obviously one of the men to whom Johnson had referred in his indictment, it is little wonder that he objected to Farnham's proposal that Johnson come to Sacramento and preside there over the Hughes meeting. The chairman of the Republican State Central Committee wanted the night to think over the proposition. And at that point the conference adjourned. Early the next morning Johnson received a telephone call from Farnham, then at San Diego. This time Hughes' emissary apparently did not repeat the invitation to come to Sacramento, but he did suggest that Johnson wire Hughes a message of greeting and support. In return Farnham promised that the presidential candidate would reciprocate with a message equally cordial. Now Johnson wanted time to think over a proposal. Perhaps because the invitation to Sacramento had not been repeated, perhaps because Hughes did not call in person, or perhaps because the governor had already made up his mind his eventual reply was a flat negative. Ignoring Dickson's advice to accept Hughes' invitation for a meeting, Johnson declined either to participate in a joint appearance in Sacramento or to enter into the mutual exchange of greetings by telegraph. He would have been very glad, he wired Farnham, to have welcomed Hughes to the state and to have presented him to his fellow citizens as a person worthy of their support. But that had been made impossible by the men placed in charge of Hughes' interests in the state. They had made it clear that if the slightest courtesies were exchanged between Hughes and himself, they would switch their support to Wilson. At this late date, when Hughes was about to leave the state, Johnson was sure that any action he took would be misinterpreted and distorted. He therefore sent his kindest regards to Hughes and best wishes for his success. That was the last communication between the governor and the Hughes party in California. That night the Sacramento meeting was presided over by an old line regular politician whom Johnson had fired from office. By the following morning the presidential candidate was east of the Sierra Nevada.[26]

Looking back over Hughes' trip through California, it is evident that it was punctuated by one serious mistake after another. What is not so clear is where the responsibility for the mistakes should be placed. In fact, one might well doubt whether they could have been avoided. Both the Progressive and regular leaders were understandably more interested in local issues than they were in the success of the national ticket. To have expected them to compromise without outside compulsion was to have asked too much from human flesh and blood. Moreover, it is reasonable to assume that thousands of conservative San Francisco businessmen would have preferred to win their war against labor than to elect a Republican President, if that hard alternative had to be faced. And in either case, any coercion from the Hughes headquarters for compromise probably would have alienated many supporters. Perhaps a more skilled politician than Hughes might have forced understanding, but a man versed in settling disputes by judicial mandate is far removed from the elusive art of politics. Perhaps Hughes thought it was beneath his dignity to intervene in a local quarrel. Or perhaps faced with a potential loss either way, he decided to string along with the regularly constituted Republican officials in the state, with whom he was unquestionably closer in principle and spirit than with Johnson and his followers. This would seem consistent with both his judicial bent of mind and his own political inclinations.

Whatever Hughes' reasons for his actions in California, it does appear that the Long Beach episode was not really the decisive factor in weaning many Progressives away from him. What happened at Long Beach was but the most dramatic of a logical sequence of events begun when Willcox refused to intervene in the arrangements for the reception of the candidate. A Hughes-Johnson meeting there might have patched up a façade of harmony, but it would have been only that. At that late date, nothing less than a complete endorsement would have mollified Johnson's Progressives. Even had Hughes desired to make this recommendation, which is questionable, he could not afford to, because of its possible effects upon his regular supporters both in California and in the nation at large. The fact that after the hotel incident, the Hughes headquarters did not renew the invitation to Johnson to preside at Sacramento, indicates the impossibility of a real compromise. The hardness of the Progressive heart was not the result of Hughes' unwitting oversight at Long Beach, but rather of his obvious preference for the regular Republican leaders and his coolness toward the Progressives from the first moment he had entered California. Because of the "seething resentment" among Progressives and their feeling that they had "been buncoed," California was no longer a certain Republican state, Lissner wired. "Hope Hughes personally is fully advised. The responsibility is his." [27]

Meanwhile, with the all-important Republican primaries a week away, Johnson and his associates had been barnstorming the state for weeks in their effort to regain power within the Republican party. In doing so, the former Progressives pulled no stops in their attack upon the regulars. He was still a Progressive, Johnson shouted to the crowds at the hustings, and if elected to the Senate he would continue to be one. He would support Hughes for the election and as long as his

politics warranted Progressive support. The governor reiterated that he was just as much interested in "preparedness for
peace" as he was in military preparedness. At this point in
his speeches he invariably blasted at his old enemies, the
Republican reactionaries, who were seeking to destroy in
this single campaign all the reform work that had been done
over the past seven years. There was not room, the Governor
declared, in the "same political house in California," for himself and for de Young, Otis, John D. Spreckels, and William
H. Crocker with his "inherited Southern Pacific millions."

The Republican regulars were equally vocal in calling for
a decisive rebuke to these Progressive upstarts. Willis H.
Booth, a former president of the Associated Chambers of
Commerce of the Pacific coast, was a formidable candidate.
He had never been tarred with the Southern Pacific brush,
and he was able. A most effective speaker, Booth pictured
the fight between himself and Johnson as a contest "between
real and bogus Republicans." In that charge he was strongly
supported by the entire Republican regular organization.[28]
On the day of the election William H. Crocker defined the
issue for the last time as the simple one of whether California
was to be represented by a Republican senator or by an
enemy of the party. No cards were under the table on August
29, and by a majority of 20,000 the Republican voters of the
state indicated their preference for Johnson's Republicanism
to that of Charles Evans Hughes' associates, William H.
Crocker and Francis V. Keesling.[29]

After the returns were in, Chester Rowell wired East ad-
vising Hughes to send a telegram unreservedly congratulating
Johnson and expressing hope for his election. "Even that,"
he felt obliged to add, "won't undo many things that have
been done." In answer, the Chief Justice salvaged what he
could from the painful situation by rejoicing in Johnson's
victory and trusting that there would now be "complete union
of forces, insuring a thoroughgoing victory." The word "trust"
was well chosen by the national candidate. Unquestionably,
the California Progressives felt that Hughes' long-belated

courtesy had a decidedly hollow ring. Chester Rowell expressed something of this a few weeks later in the Republican state convention when he was elected to succeed Francis V. Keesling as chairman of the Republican State Central Committee, and therefore responsible for the Hughes campaign in the state. The whole process, Rowell wryly observed, was like the Methodist church admitting a blackened sinner on probation one day and electing him bishop the next.[30]

In describing the subsequent campaign, historians have usually assumed that Johnson gave little more than lip service to the support of Hughes and thus indirectly encouraged his supporters to vote for Wilson.[31] This was the charge made by California conservatives after the election and this has been the popularly held verdict ever since. The documents of the campaign, however, do not justify that judgment. True, in his primary campaign Johnson did little except mention the national candidate's name, but in view of Hughes' conduct in the state, scarcely more could have been asked of the governor. It is equally true that Johnson went at the task of winning California for Hughes with no great personal conviction. Urging a colleague to strengthen the Republican forces in Orange and San Diego counties, he remarked acidly that if it could not be done in any other way, it might be accomplished by the celebrated Hughes-Johnson alliance. Furthermore, throughout his campaign Johnson did not once attack Woodrow Wilson. One has to remember that much of Johnson's support in the past had come from progressive Democrats, whom he was careful not to alienate. But campaign for Hughes he did, and in his customary energetic fashion. Again and again, he described the former Justice as a "champion of the people" and a man who warranted the support of every Progressive. In one of his last speeches he referred to Hughes as, "a progressive pioneer who had fought in New York for the very things which we now have in California." Even the Oakland *Tribune* had to admit that Johnson should be given full credit for his "direct support of Hughes and the Republican ticket." If that were not sufficient evidence of Johnson's good works, the request of the national campaign committee that he speak for the national ticket in the progressive Middle West should close the question.[32]

Although Johnson supported Hughes warmly in public, the same cannot be said of the regular press support of Johnson. Bitter and vindictive indeed were the regular papers after the surprising primary election. The governor's victory did not make him a Republican, the *Argonaut* sourly observed, nor were Republican voters under "obligation to vote for a Progressive or a Democrat because such a one has contrived through dishonest courses to win an 'official' nomination." No less muted in its attack was the Los Angeles *Times*. The Republican party, it told its readers, after Rowell became the state central committee chairman, was now controlled by "renegades" and "mongrels." Other regular Republican sheets ignored the governor and his speeches entirely, while the more reconcilable ones gave in only during the last few days of the campaign. It was not until the day before the election that the Oakland *Tribune* and the San Francisco *Chronicle* finally endorsed the Republican senatorial candidate by saying that they were Republican papers and therefore supported all Republican nominees, including the one for senator. Even then the *Tribune* did not mention Johnson by name. The Progressive charge after the election that if there was treason to the Republican ticket in California, much of it was inspired and directed by the regular Republican press, contained more than a little truth.[33]

Late in August, after Hughes had concluded his visit to the state, the Progressive leaders were almost unanimously gloomy about the prospects for a Republican victory. By November they had changed their opinion. Although they conceded that labor and the majority of the women in the state were for Wilson, they were confident that Hughes would carry the state. Even the usually pessimistic Johnson was confident that they could "put Hughes over." Consequently, on election night, they were surprised at the closeness of the vote in the state. But with Hughes leading they were still optimistic, and in the early morning hours of the following day, Chester Rowell joined with William H. Crocker in claiming the state by a majority of 40,000. The two national chairmen then sent their official congratulations to the Republican nominee. As Tuesday night turned into Wednesday morning, however, a noticeable tenseness grew in Republican headquarters at San Francisco and Los Angeles. By that time it was apparent that Hughes' brave start on the east coast that had seemed to assure him of the election was now being overturned by a slow but remorseless tide of Wilson votes from west of the Appalachians. By Wednesday evening it appeared likely that the outcome in California would decide the issue. Within California it was equally apparent by Wednesday noon that serious trouble was brewing. In the senatorial race, Johnson was walking away from his Democratic competitor, but Hughes, surprisingly, was lagging far behind and was in great danger of being overtaken.

At the start of the count, Hughes had amassed what seemed to be a comfortable majority in southern California. As later returns came in from San Francisco and the northern valleys, that lead dwindled, first to a few thousand and then to a paltry hundred votes. The state Republican headquarters at San Francisco frantically wired Meyer Lissner that unless Hughes had a greater lead in southern California than had been reported, the state was lost. Thursday noon that prediction was confirmed conclusively. San Francisco and the country precincts had given California to the Democratic electors and had reëlected Woodrow Wilson by a scant 4,000 votes. Ironically enough, the leading Wilson elector was Francis J. Heney, erstwhile Progressive.[34]

On Friday morning, after the fateful results were known, the Los Angeles *Times* appeared with a long front-page editorial denouncing Hiram Johnson and his Progressives for selling out the Republican party in California and the nation. In this and succeeding issues the *Times* specifically charged that Johnson and his followers had made a deal with the Democrats to support Wilson against Hughes in return for

Democratic support for Johnson against the democratic senatorial candidate, Curtin. Only this the *Times* declared, could account for the great disparity between Johnson's majority and Hughes' losing vote. It was a crime unparalleled in political history, the *Times* editorialized, "One which will long be remembered with awe and admiration by the whole tribe of Judas. . . ." Many regular papers followed the *Times'* lead and took up the charge against these "Benedict Arnolds," starting a national controversy that still occasionally rumbles throughout the state and nation.[35]

If there was any truth to the *Times'* charges that a "corrupt bargain" had been made between Johnson and the Democrats, none can be found. Unquestionably, thousands of California Progressives voted for Wilson and Johnson; but for this no deal was needed. Soon after Hughes left California, and before any such formal arrangement could possibly have been made, a private poll taken among the Progressives in one California district showed that only one out of every hundred intended to vote for the Republican candidate. Obviously, this sentiment was not the result of an organized campaign, but rather of the long series of events that wound through the Progressive and Republican conventions, and of the Hughes campaign in California.[36]

Had Hughes won back all or even a major part of the alienated former Progressives, he probably would have won California and the election. But the real question is whether any amount of work by Johnson and his associates could have won them back. Following in the footsteps of Fremont Older, Francis J. Heney, and William Kent, many of them had declared for Wilson as soon as Hughes was nominated. Presumably, the rest were not automatons to be shoved around as Johnson pleased. In fact many of them voted for Wilson, not because of Hughes' conduct in California, but rather because of real convictions they held on important national and state questions. Moreover, Hughes undoubtedly lost thousands of regular Republican votes on these same issues, votes that Johnson could not possibly have salvaged. Among the more important of such issues were labor and the peace.

For very obvious reasons, Wilson had had the official support of organized labor in all of California. Commenting upon the election, the official American Federation of Labor paper in the state described the results as an unqualified labor victory. Although labor did support Hiram Johnson, he could not deliver their vote to another candidate at will, as was attested by his failure to win San Francisco for Theodore Roosevelt in 1912. In that year the national Progressive ticket failed to carry a single district in the labor wards south of Market Street where Johnson regularly rolled up majorities. What Hiram Johnson could not deliver to Theodore Roosevelt in 1912, he certainly could not deliver to Charles Evans Hughes of San Francisco open-shop fame and a foe of the Adamson Act, precisely at the time that organized labor was fighting for its very life in northern California.[37]

Probably what carried even greater weight than the labor question in the election results was the war and peace issue. Since 1914 California had been subjected to an intensive peace campaign led by David Starr Jordan and most of the progressive journals. Johnson acknowledged the strong peace sentiment in the state by arguing in his campaign for social rather than military preparedness. Against this peace background of the state William Allen White, back in June, 1916, had written in the *California Outlook:* "The Republican party probably is the war party in this country, if there is one." During the campaign Theodore Roosevelt's connection with Hughes gave substance to the cry that a Republican vote was a vote for war. As one staunch California progressive Republican who voted for Wilson and Johnson put the matter after the election, Roosevelt had surrendered his liberal faith to secure the support of big business and had "tried to lead the people astray after the strange Gods of militarism." On the conservative side, the California journals may have been for preparedness, but they were strongly opposed to intervening in the European struggle. It is interesting to note that the official British propaganda agency was unable to list one large California paper in 1916 as pro-British. Instead, the San Francisco *Chronicle*, the San Francisco *Call*, and the Los Angeles *Times* were all labeled "unfriendly." A British agent traveling through California in the summer of 1916 repeatedly referred to the California press in his reports as "deplorable" and "execrable." It is little wonder that Senator Works noted that many of his conservative friends, particularly the women, were going to vote for Wilson because of the war issue.[38]

The Democratic slogan, "He kept us out of war," was particularly effective among California women, as was freely admitted by both conservative and progressive Republicans. When the belligerent Theodore Roosevelt offered to campaign the state, one of the two major objections to his coming was that he would lose more votes than he would win. The Wilson strength in California, Johnson replied to Roosevelt through an intermediary, lay in labor and women. The only effective speakers from outside the state would be those who could gain the sympathy of these two groups, something Johnson was sure that Roosevelt could not do.[39] Johnson was right not only for California but for the rest of the West. Woodrow Wilson carried nine of the twelve states all of them lying outside the solid South, where women voted in 1916.

The attempt to assign reasons for one candidate's defeat and another's victory in any historic election is an extremely hazardous occupation. The closer the election, the more the hazard. The very closeness gives play to thousands of minor factors, many of them probably unknown, and any one of which in conjunction with others might have been decisive. If there is some truth to the observation that Hughes lost California in 1916 because of Progressive defection, there is probably equal truth in the statement that his defeat was due in part to the loss of the labor vote, the peace votes, and the women's votes. It might also be argued that Wilson won because he appealed to the small towns and the countryside. In the six most populous counties of the state, which included every sizable city, Hughes had a majority of ten thousand votes. Consequently, it would seem that any single explanation of the 1916 California election must be false precisely because of its restrictive aspect.

Although the absolute truths about the election are buried in the darkness of the past, this much can clearly be said for Hiram Johnson. From the primary on he worked hard for the success of the national ticket, far harder than the California regular politicians worked for his success. And if Hughes lost California by a close vote he did better there than in Kansas and Washington, both traditionally Republican states and ones which in 1916 had elected former Progressives to the governorship and to the United States Senate. In neither of these states was there any charge that the Progressive candidates had sold the national ticket down the river. The truth was that the normal Republican West liked neither the cold, dignified-looking Hughes, nor the principles he stood for. As for California, it seems probable that Charles Evans Hughes lost the state not because of Hiram Johnson, but in general because of Charles Evans Hughes.

CHAPTER XI

The Downhill Years

✳

The election results of 1916 seemed to assure continued success for progressivism in California. In the August primary the old Lincoln-Roosevelt Republican League faction again dominated the Republican party. The following November Johnson was elected to the United States Senate, where he was to join the Wilson Democrat, James D. Phelan. Back home the progressive William D. Stephens was to become the new governor, and a majority of nominally progressive Republicans sat in both houses of the state legislature.

Yet within three years the California progressive movement had lost most of its cohesion and more of its reform zeal. The years from 1916 were downhill and presaged the eventual collapse and disappearance of the reform ideology that had been triumphant in the state since 1910. A partial explanation of this death of the reform spirit lay in the disintegrating effects of the great new national issues which came out of the war, and the effect of the peacemaking upon political creeds and parties. Another substantial explanation for the eclipse of progressivism lay in the more personal and local conflicts engendered among its leaders. Central to these struggles was the character, mentality, and ambition of Hiram Johnson.

When Johnson first seriously considered running for the Senate in 1914, he would have preferred to see John Eshleman his successor as governor. With 1916 in mind, Johnson personally selected Eshleman in 1914 to run for the lieutenant-governorship. Eshleman's death in the spring of 1916, however, left the office vacant, and Johnson was forced to choose another man to fill out the unexpired term, a man who would

274

automatically become governor if Johnson became senator. It was a most grave and perplexing decision for the governor. He had fought so hard to establish all that had been done for the state, he said, that he wanted a man who would be equally militant and obstinate in the defense of what had been accomplished. The heir-presumptive should have one further qualification—that of being a Johnson man in a peculiarly personal sense. This requirement, of course, was unstated; but it was fully implied in the governor's correspondence and in all of his later actions.[1]

Had Johnson acted upon his personal preferences alone, it is probable that H. L. Carnahan of Riverside would have been selected. Carnahan had many qualifications for the office. He was from southern California, and the new man had to be from that section of the state because if Johnson were elected both senators would come from the north. Carnahan was a man of considerable ability and had shown himself a thoroughgoing Johnson man as the state's Blue Sky commissioner. Unfortunately for the governor's peace of mind, however, other considerations were involved. An important election was in the offing. And since southern California regularly supplied an impressive total of votes for the progressive cause, southern California had to be consulted and given heed to. The hard truth was that the choice of the new man was not to be Johnson's; he was selected by a group of southern leaders, and expediency alone persuaded the governor most reluctantly to accept their choice.

For some time before 1916 a growing tension had existed between Johnson and his intimates and the Earl-Dickson faction of the Los Angeles Progressives. Perhaps it was first caused by Johnson's refusal to act upon Earl's advice on several important measures. Or perhaps the first faint rift came about because of Earl's feeling that he and his associates were not getting the proper recognition in Sacramento. Evident to many people was the fact that Rowell and Lissner were much closer to the throne than Earl and Dickson. The first serious open breach between the governor and the owner of the Los Angeles *Express* and the *Tribune* came shortly after the 1913 Los Angeles municipal elections. During the bitter controversy that developed over the 1913 election strategy between Lissner and Earl, Johnson had refused to take sides. But his ensuing show of confidence in Lissner, who was then chairman of the Progressive state committee, seemed like approval after the event. The following year Earl, Dickson, and Stimson supported Francis J. Heney for senator, and Lissner, with Johnson's blessings, gave backstage support to Rowell. The governor's cavalier treatment of Heney during the following campaign irritated Heney's Los Angeles friends. Thereafter, the influence of the Los Angeles Heney group rapidly diminished at the Statehouse. It is interesting to note, furthermore, that the once extremely cordial relations between Dickson and Lissner seemed to dry up after 1913. And according to Lissner, he and Earl never again exchanged a word, cordial or otherwise.

When Dickson heard of Johnson's intention to appoint Carnahan, he protested that the Riverside man was not well enough known in southern California to command widespread support, and he urged the governor to appoint Congressman William D. Stephens to the important vacancy. A successful Los Angeles businessman, Stephens had been president of the Chamber of Commerce and mayor of the city before he was elected to Congress. There he had served his district faithfully and well, obtaining among other things continued federal support for the development of the San Pedro harbor.

The governor was decidedly cool to Dickson's suggestion from the first. Only after many long discussions was it agreed that the issue be settled by the preference of a conference made up of forty of the more prominent progressive leaders in southern California. After the names of the forty men had been agreed to by Johnson, Lissner, and Dickson, the conference was held in Los Angeles. There Lissner proposed Carnahan, emphasizing that he was the governor's choice, and Dickson presented the name of Congressman Stephens. After a long discussion the results of a vote showed thirty-seven preferences cast for Stephens, as against three for Carnahan. Johnson received the results of the meeting bitterly, but finally salving his wounds, he wrote to Dickson that he would abide by the results of the conference.

Dickson left for Washington to attempt to persuade Stephens to accept the appointment if tendered to him. Stephens was disinclined to give up his seat in Congress, but later succumbed to Dickson's arguments and agreed to accept if the governor offered him the position. Returning to Los Angeles on Johnson's invitation, Stephens met the governor at the Alexandria Hotel. It was a strange meeting and a token of things to come. When Stephens came into the room, Johnson brusquely remarked: "So you want to be appointed lieutenant-governor! Is that correct?" Having been cautioned by Dickson not to give Johnson any reason for withdrawing the appointment, Stephens replied in a moderate tone: "I have come here, Governor, because I was given to understand from your letter that you wanted me to accept the office of lieutenant-governor. I am willing to accept the appointment if it is your pleasure." Johnson replied that Stephens had interpreted his letter correctly, and that he would issue a statement at once of Stephens' nomination. The meeting ended on this note. It had been short and to the point, and no one in the room was under any illusion as to where Johnson's heart lay. The bargain had been sealed principally because Johnson, faced with a critical election, needed support from the south and particularly from the Earl papers and the Earl, Dickson, Stimson group of southern Progressives. The subsequent newspaper talk that Earl had made Stephens governor against the wishes of Hiram Johnson was not entirely true. But it was near enough to the mark to make the prestige-conscious Johnson squirm.[2]

During the following campaign the Earl papers strongly supported Hiram Johnson. After the election, however, both sheets refused to carry Johnson's reply to the *Times'* charge that he had sold out Hughes in order to assure his own success. Johnson attributed the studied slight to the fact that he had refrained from praising the Earl papers during his speeches in Los Angeles and had refused to support an Earl-backed candidate in the local election. By the middle of November, 1916, the gulf had widened between the departing king and the new kingmaker.[3]

With Johnson's election to the Senate, most Californians assumed that he would immediately resign and turn the governorship over to Stephens. As November and December went by, it was clear that the governor had no such idea. In fact, he announced that he would continue in office at least until the legislature was organized. Otherwise, his friends explained, the governor was afraid that the newly elected legislature would get out of hand. Johnson's refusal to give up the office as he had agreed, as well as his bumptious reasons for staying, were taken by Stephens and his friends as studied insults. When the governor still retained his office in January and February, the Stephens group became downright hostile. Pointed remarks were made about the universal officeholder, and as the legislature came to its half-way point and recessed, public suggestions were made that a court suit be instituted to determine whether a man could legally be both governor and senator at once. Meanwhile, it was apparent in Sacramento that whatever relations existed between the Johnson and Stephens circles were extremely formal and increasingly more frigid.[4]

As pressure for his resignation mounted, Johnson became wrathful at his former supporters who were seeking to push him out of office. This inept group, now demanding that he turn over all that he held precious, he mourned to Lissner, were men without sufficient vision to know how or when to fight and had no intention of fighting the forces of reaction at all. Dickson, he was sure, was even now busily dividing the spoils with the full intention of reëlecting Stephens governor in two years and senator in four, and had not had the decency to call upon him. As for Stephens, Johnson had heard nothing from him since the legislature had recessed.[5]

By January, 1917, Hiram Johnson had completely identified

the California progressive movement with his own person. For any of his old supporters to dispute this was to him base ingratitude. Edward Dickson was asked by one of Johnson's official family whether he did not think that the governor should stay in office throughout the entire session of the legislature. When Dickson replied in the negative to the leading question, he was summoned to the governor's office. When the two old friends were alone, Johnson said nothing for a long time, but simply sat and smoked. Then, getting up and pacing the floor, he turned and abruptly asked, "So you want to be governor, Dickson?" To the newspaperman's query as to whether Johnson was joking, the governor replied it was obvious that Stephens was a man of putty and that Dickson, in making him governor, would own him body and soul. "Well," Johnson concluded, "so you want to be governor? At last you have found your ambition!" Dickson said goodbye, walked out of the office, and did not see Hiram Johnson again for years.[6]

How long Hiram Johnson would have remained governor of California had not America's entrance into the First World War intervened can only be a matter of speculation. In early March, Woodrow Wilson finally determined to call Congress into the special session that was to mark the beginning of his great international crusade. On March 15 Johnson made his farewell speech to the state. It was a curious speech, and one that clearly indicated Johnson's fundamental distrust of those he left behind in Sacramento. After recounting all the advances of the past six years, he confessed that his leaving the governorship was the most difficult act of his life. Scarcely a paragraph was interjected between that remark and the following ones entrusting his successor with the preservation of all the great reforms he had secured. "We do it," Johnson said, "with the full expectation that he has the will to do and the courage to protect, and the firmness uncompromisingly to maintain them. . . ." Johnson thus showed no strong confidence in Stephens, simply expectation. That same day the Earl papers ran a cordial editorial of welcome to the new governor. No hail-and-farewell appeared for the departing one.[7]

During the next two years the split between the Johnson and Stephens factions of the party steadily widened. Johnson, Lissner reported, became obsessed with the idea that Stephens and his friends were "bent upon destroying his political influence" and that as a matter of self-preservation he had to respond "to that challenge." Although Lissner did not agree with this estimate, he did join the senator in complaining that from the Earl papers one would never know that Johnson was in the Senate.[8]

During the late fall of 1917 the Johnson group formulated plans to defeat Stephens for governor in the next year's election. A conference of fifty leading Johnson Progressives was held in San Francisco in November, and Johnson suggested that the fifty meet and notify Stephens of their opposition to his candidacy. Then, according to the plan, the fifty would formally announce for Rowell with Johnson's authorized backing. If Rowell agreed to the scheme, the senator promised to return from Washington and campaign for the Fresno man. That the plan fell through was no fault of Johnson. Again and again he promised Rowell that he would stump the entire state for him if he would announce. But Rowell delayed in making up his mind until a serious illness forced him to curtail all his activities. To recuperate he sailed for Hawaii in April, 1918. Behind him he left a letter with Lissner announcing his candidacy which, he wrote, Lissner might use only "in the last extreme necessity." In Lissner's estimation that necessity never came, and when Rowell returned he offered the Stephens faction his support in 1918 if they would agree to back him for the senatorship in 1920. But these negotiations broke down and there was little for Johnson's supporters to do but accept the inevitable. After Stephens' victory in the fall election, the newspapers of the state noted that the governor was busy appointing anti-Johnson men to important state positions. If more was needed to point out Senator Johnson's impotence in the state administration, it was supplied by the appointment of a new railroad commissioner. Wanting and needing a state position, Lissner had set his heart on obtaining this post, but despite all the influence he could bring to bear, Brundige, the managing editor of Earl's Los Angeles *Express,* was selected. There were new kings in Egypt that knew not Joseph.[9]

If the split between Johnson and Governor Stephens was not enough finally to destroy all cohesiveness in the progressive movement, the events of the next two years all but completed the job. By the time the issues surrounding the war and the subsequent peace were settled, the progressive movement was finished in California, as well as in the United States, for the next twelve years. Perhaps Hiram Johnson was one of the first of the keener politicians to sense this sharp turn in the road ahead.

Following the death of Theodore Roosevelt, Johnson again was entranced with the possibility of becoming President of the United States. By February, 1919, he was already a candidate and by then he had chosen his main issue—not reform, but "Americanism." In the terms of 1919, that meant, among other things, being a zealous opponent of Woodrow Wilson's League of Nations. Johnson had not yet announced his position on the League in February, 1919, nor would he for some time. He had already, however, chosen his side, and in spite of Rowell and Lissner's pleas for moderation the senator from California became one of the most implacable foes of the League idea in the national Congress. Hiram Johnson had never been moderate on any issue. His position on the League was to be no exception. He saw behind it a gigantic scheme to sell out America to the British or Japanese. By its adoption he felt that the international bankers would inherit the world and make billions. The war itself, he believed, had really been no concern of ours, and neither was the peace. Ultimately, Johnson was not only opposed to Wilson's League; he was also against the League with the Lodge reservations, and in fact any international league. If partisanship were discounted, he was convinced that the Senate would not cast ten votes for the League, with or without reservations.[10]

Hiram Johnson's uncompromising opposition to the League should have been expected. It was consistent with his point of view and with his personality. Fundamentally, Johnson's attitudes were provincial. He was opposed to the entrance of the United States into the war; he was now opposed to any further international commitments. Beyond that, Johnson was usually orientated toward the negative in political questions. He had begun his political life in opposition, and he was never completely happy unless he played the role of critic. During his governorship, what positive contributions he had made had been largely formulated and initiated by other men. His intimate friends in California had early recognized this peculiar negative trait in his make-up and had been more than liberal with constructive suggestions. Rowell foresaw the difficulty Johnson would have in Washington without his alter egos, and tried to get him some competent advisors. But, he wrote later, the only ones available were some New York "highbrows," and as Johnson had an "instinctive aversion" to intellectuals, they were completely "ineffective." [11]

When the Johnson movement for President was first organized in June, 1919, there was no mistaking its position on the international question. From the first to the last day of its life, it was dedicated to the defeat of the League idea. All other issues were played down or forgotten. Perhaps the most heavily sacrificed principle that Johnson had stood for in the past was the central one of progressive government. The old progressive appeals, of course, were still used to gather votes. But the truest indicator of the way the wind was blowing was in the nature of Johnson's organization and support. Included among his new-found friends were Frank P. Flint, Michael H. de Young, William H. Crocker, Herbert Fleishhacker, and Joseph R. Knowland, names which three years before had been anathematized by every good Progressive in the state. Rowell and Lissner, it is true, were on the organizing committee, but both were greatly disturbed by Johnson's position on the League, and both were most uncomfortable with their new associates. Lissner lamented at the conclusion of the campaign that "nine out of ten of those recognized" in the Johnson organization were standpatters, and his Progressive friends all felt that they had been left "out in the cold." In Los Angeles, Lissner pointed out, the Johnson organization had been dominated by members of the Commercial Federation, an organization which spent half of its time boosting Americanism and the other half destroying organized labor. Lissner considered the Federation as "the greatest menace to progressive government in the state." [12]

While Hiram Johnson was finding these new friends, many of his old companions were deserting him. Marshall Stimson had been one of the chief organizers in southern California of the League to Enforce Peace. Eventually he, as well as Dickson and Brundige, opposed Johnson's presidential aspirations and announced for Herbert Hoover. The three men, Lissner wrote, had "hoodwinked many other Progressives in their campaign to destroy Johnson." Lissner thought that the senator was getting a very "raw deal from his former friends." [13]

In the north, the old progressive cohesion was also destroyed over the League issue. Rowell had been an ardent supporter of the League idea from the time it had first been proposed. Having failed to modify Johnson's extreme nationalistic views, he was now cruelly torn between supporting his old Progressive chief and his own international principles. His wife and practically everyone on his paper, the Fresno *Republican,* had already enrolled under the banner of Hoover and the League. He found himself in disagreement with Johnson "on almost every public issue that now comes up and with his methods and manners even on issues on which we take the same side." But eventually Rowell's loyalty to the past triumphed over his preferences for the future. Regretting Johnson's stand on the League, he nevertheless announced his support of the senator on the basis of his California record.

Even so, Rowell refused to attack Herbert Hoover and continued to print favorable accounts of Hoover throughout the campaign.[14]

It was not in Johnson's character to remain friends with a man who did not give him unqualified support. Early in August the senator wrote to Lissner that he and Rowell had come to the parting of the ways. He had allowed Rowell to write the last letter, he added in a tone of regret.[15]

During the rest of that fateful summer the progressive spirit seemed to wither. Johnson did manage to win the California delegates in the presidential primaries even though he lost southern California for the first time in his political life. But in the Republican national convention his hopes and those of all progressives were completely blighted by the nomination of Warren G. Harding. Johnson left the meeting a disgruntled and disillusioned man. In the midst of his bitterness he came home to lash out viciously at the League of Nations and to support Sam Shortridge for senator.

Johnson's vigorous support of Shortridge fully testified to the disintegration of the once powerful progressive movement. A conservative of conservatives and now a staunch foe of the League of Nations, Shortridge had the great advantage in the Republican primary of running against two Progressives, William Kent and A. J. Wallace. Even so, he just barely defeated Kent, and had it not been for Johnson's help the result probably would have been different. During the following presidential campaign Rowell and Stimson supported the Democrat Cox. Dickson was still loyal to the Republican party, but that loyalty did not include devotion either to the principles or the ambitions of Hiram Johnson. Asked why he did not plan to speak in Los Angeles during the campaign, Johnson replied that he had been warned by Dickson that if he came to Los Angeles and spoke against the League of Nations, the *Express* would no longer advocate the election of Warren G. Harding.[16]

Two years later the majority of the old progressive leadership was solidly opposed to the reëlection of Johnson to the

United States Senate. Both Rowell and William Kent toyed
with the idea of becoming candidates against Johnson themselves. Eventually both men combined with Dickson, Stimson,
and Pardee in supporting the unsuccessful candidacy of C. C.
Moore. In public and private they lashed out against the
triumvirate of "Hiram, Hearst, and Hate." To a man, they
were convinced that Johnson had sold his progressive birthright for the pottage of office. William Kent faithfully reflected
their attitude when he wired Mark Sullivan for publication
that Johnson was satisfactory to Fleishhacker and the big
power interests in domestic policy and to William Randolph
Hearst in "international Hell raising." [17]

Of the men most responsible for the birth of the California
progressive movement, Meyer Lissner by 1922 was one of the
very few who still remained loyal to the fortunes of Hiram
Johnson. Lasting loyalty, however, did not mean continuing
influence. On the contrary, Lissner's name was left off the list
of Johnson delegates to the national convention in 1920 and
was restored only after his personal protest to the candidate.
Moreover, he was not even consulted about local Los Angeles
affairs, he wrote, by the powers in the new Johnson organization. That fall, for the first time since 1910, his name was
absent from the state executive committee. By 1922 he was
little more than a personal friend of the senator, and the old
political magic had vanished from his name. [18]

Within the state government, meanwhile, the progressive
tradition was fighting for its life against an aroused and confident conservatism. In every session of the state legislature
from 1916 on, the influence of the state's great corporations
seemed to grow. Increasing opposition was directed against
the initiative and referendum, the direct primary, and the
labor legislation of the Johnson period, including the eight-
hour law for women. Laws incorporating a theory of "mob-
democracy" were "frightful sources of expense," a pamphlet
put out by the Farmers and Merchants' Bank of Los Angeles
charged, and should be repealed at the earliest opportunity. [19]

The new California conservatism was mainly interested in

lower taxes for corporations and in legislation granting long term franchises to electric power companies and other public utility corporations. Under the twin banners of Americanism and free enterprise such organizations as the California Taxpayers' Association, representing twelve of the largest corporations in the state, did effective work during the summer and fall of 1920. After defeating many progressive legislators in that year's elections, their representatives descended on Sacramento in force at the opening of the 1921 legislature. One veteran reporter observed, "It looks like old times around the corridors and hotel lobbies." No legislator, he wrote, needed to pay for meals; corporation money provided plentifully for all. "The old guard," the correspondent ended, "has come out of its hole at last." [20]

Against this conservative tide Governor Stephens struggled valiantly. During the debate over a new tax bill in 1921 he called upon the people of the state to support him in his fight against the "gigantic corporation lobby," the like of which, he said, had "never before been seen in Sacramento." But it was uphill work at best. Hiram Johnson's well-known hostility to the governor, the disintegration of the progressive organization throughout the state, the growing opposition of labor, and the governor's own rather colorless personality made any positive progressive achievements extremely difficult. Governor Stephens did manage to secure moderately progressive tax legislation, but most of his energy was spent in defending the reforms of the Johnson period—considering the times a mammoth achievement in itself. Clearly the progressive clock in California, as in the nation, was rapidly running down.

From 1922 to 1926, during the administration of Governor Friend Richardson, California progressivism was nothing more than a historical memory. As William Kent noted, the governor and like spirits in the legislature were successfully destroying many of the advances made under Johnson and Stephens. Once more the regulatory commissions of the state were "unduly responsive" to the corporations they were legally supposed to regulate. Once more the strength of the state's great corporations, especially that of the public power companies, "bulked overlarge" in the people's government.[21]

Even as late as the mid-twenties, however, enough vitality was left in the old progressivism to rise and meet this new challenge. Before Richardson's election in 1922, a state-wide movement had been organized to secure the state regulation of water and electrical power. Leading the movement were William Kent, Francis J. Heney, C. K. McClatchey, Rudolph Spreckels, John R. Haynes, William Mulholland, Franklin Hichborn, and Clyde L. Seavey, progressives all. Three years later, with the regulation of power companies still unachieved, the Progressive Voters' League of California made its appearance. Heading its executive committee were Chester Rowell, C. C. Young, Franklin Hichborn, and Clyde Seavey. The League's stated purpose, "to restore, maintain, and promote a progressive state government," was plainly an indictment of the Richardson administration and a call for its defeat in the 1926 elections. Thanks to the work of the League and the efforts of Hiram Johnson, Richardson was defeated in the Republican primaries, and C. C. Young was elected governor. Young temporarily reversed the conservative trend and left a record of having been one of the state's ablest administrators. But with the 1926 victory the last sands of the old progressivism seemed to run out. When the great depression came, the progressive answers were no longer adequate to the new problems. In 1934 Johnson resurrected the Progressive party to aid in his reëlection to the Senate, but the old magic name appealed to only four thousand registered voters, and Johnson dropped it. Nineteen-twelve progressivism was a thing of the past.[22]

An analysis of the progressive movement in California shows clearly that its strength and weakness in the state coincided with the rise and decline of the bipartisan reform movement nationally. A close study of the two developments, in fact, reveals striking parallels. In California, as in the nation, one of the more potent reasons for the decline of progressivism was the sharp personal conflicts among its leaders. If an average can be struck on such elusive matters, the national Progressive leader was extraordinarily individualistic and his character was marked by a pronounced ambitious and competitive strain. He was usually highly intolerant of opposition either from within or without his own ranks. After he had held his first important office he seemed to demand a fealty from his supporters which they were often unable or unwilling to give. Certainly many of these characteristics were found in Hiram Johnson. His opposition to Francis J. Heney and his shabby treatment of Governor Stephens were obviously expressive of his fear that they might become serious competitors for the acclaim of the voters. William Kent put the matter bluntly in 1922 when he stated publicly: "The Johnson machine recognizes but one 'all progressive' and one omnibus candidate for high office. To hold otherwise is heresy." To Chester Rowell, Johnson's insistence upon "a personal feudal or tribal loyalty" was too ridiculous to be taken seriously. But for the progressive movement that basic strain of character, not peculiar to Johnson alone, helped spell disaster.[23]

The extreme individualism of the progressive politician also played a part in disrupting the movement in other ways. United as a group in opposition to the old political system, their unity rapidly disappeared when once victory had been achieved. This was particularly true when the new issues which clustered around the First World War and the following peace appeared. Organized on the basis of attitudes toward domestic issues, the California progressive movement utterly disintegrated when it was faced with grave problems of foreign policy. Once split over such issues, there was no glue of party regularity or of tradition strong enough to hold the movement together.

The rise of radicalism and the counter witch-hunting spirit which characterized the postwar period also contributed to the decline of California progressivism. The years from 1916 to 1920 witnessed a militant stand by the International Workers of the World and the birth of internationally organized communism. They were also sharply punctuated in the United States by the Boston police strike, numerous bomb outrages, and other manifestations of lawless radicalism. The war and its aftermath had intensified patriotism as well as conservative fears for the future of property, and in this clash between a foolish radicalism and a hysterical conservatism little regard was given to democratic principles and individual freedom. When witch-hunters and reactionaries sought to stamp out all deviations from their creed they inevitably attacked Progressives and progressive principles. But even more disastrous to the reform movement was the tendency of progressive leaders to fall prey to the same spirit themselves.

After the conviction of Mooney and Billings for the San Francisco Preparedness Day bomb atrocity, Kent, Older, and Spreckels rose to their defense. The three firmly believed that the two radicals had been railroaded to prison on insufficient evidence by the aroused conservatives and nationalists. Although he agreed that Mooney was "a bad actor," Kent was also convinced that he had been "improperly convicted." Many Progressives, however, did not distinguish between this concern for preserving legal principles and an endorsement of violent radicalism. Like Theodore Roosevelt they believed that Kent, Older, and Spreckels had grown to be "downright sympathizers with anarchy and murder." [24]

The reaction of the progressive mind to the impact of radicalism is well illustrated in the political evolution of C. K. McClatchey, Sacramento newspaper owner and an ardent progressive. At the end of 1917 McClatchey still talked in the progressive idiom. Denouncing the government's wartime fiscal policy for letting Wall Street dominate it, he vehemently observed: "The patriotism of Wall Street in general and the bankers also is largely bunk. Everything they have done for the government has been paid, and repaid, and repaid over, and over, and over again. . . ." Eighteen months later McClatchey was engrossed in the new problems growing out of the war, and felt that what was most important to the public was "treating the I.W.W. with a stern hand, exterminating them, if possible, root and branch, horse, foot, and dragoons, male and female." [25] In his editorial columns McClatchey also marked for extermination the followers of communism, free love, internationalism, and atheism. He was particularly worried about their possible presence on the faculty of the state university and confidentially asked Lissner whether he could supply any relevant proof. McClatchey confessed that he did not have actual evidence on specific professors, but he was certain that such individuals were teaching at Berkeley. Since "free love episodes" had taken place there, the poison must have been "instilled somewhere around the class rooms." If this and the worshipful attitude of the university toward Great Britain went on, McClatchey expostulated, "The institution should be cut off from state taxes . . . and razed to the ground in the interest of the state of California and its citizenship in general." [26]

By 1920 the owner of the Sacramento *Bee* was spending much of his energy not in opposing Wall Street, but "Reds," "atheists," the supporters of the League of Nations, and the progressives and liberals who sought to give these groups at least a fair hearing. Nor was McClatchey an exception among progressives. Lincoln Steffens noted that even Heney "was slipping off the old point of view . . . and went right up in the air at the first breath of radicalism." Moved by such concerted criticism, President Barrows of the University of California prohibited Raymond Robbins from addressing the students of the University. Four years later Robbins was to join Chester Rowell in an attack upon Robert LaFollette and his presidential campaign. LaFollette was a "sinister enemy of democracy," and his platform was designed "to wreck the constitution of the United States," their combined statement read. Assaulted by its enemies and forgotten by its friends, California progressivism seemed doomed. William Kent had this fate in mind when he wrote, "The war and the radicals in Russia have set back the course of democratic progress at least twenty years." [27]

As important perhaps to the future of progressivism as

this assault on the free competition of ideas, was the relationship between progressivism and labor, both organized and unorganized. The relations between middle-class progressives in the state and the unions had always been anomalous from various viewpoints. In San Francisco, at least, progressivism had been sired by an attack upon labor's political pretensions. In Los Angeles, when a labor-supported Socialist campaign had apparently been on the road to success in 1911 a combination of Progressives and conservatives had defeated the movement. Two years later a like combination again defeated the labor movement and the city remained an open-shop town. It was a progressive city government, moreover, that passed and enforced the stringent Los Angeles antipicketing ordinance of 1911. Five years later much of the support for a similar ordinance in San Francisco came from middle-class Progressive wards.[28]

On the level of state government, however, the California Progressive appealed to labor for its support in 1910 and obtained it with promises of political reform and a limited program of legislation favorable to the laboring classes. During Hiram Johnson's first administration, labor scored not a few legislative victories. The advance in workmen's compensation legislation, the eight-hour day for women, the weekly pay law, and the statute requiring all employers confronted with a strike to advertise that fact when seeking strikebreakers, were all patent benefits to both union and nonunion men. In a more general way, so were many of the Progressives' political reforms. But beyond that program of legislation the Progressive majority in the California legislature refused to go. Defeated was organized labor's insistent demand for an anti-injunction bill, and defeated were measures designed to grant labor organizations immunities in strikes and on the picket line. As organized labor grew and increased its legislative demands, California progressivism stood pat on its past record, unwilling or unable to grant the workers any further legislative favors. It was not accidental that no representative of organized labor was included among its leaders. Neither was it merely fortuitous that one Progressive legislature after another in California refused to pass an income tax. The fact that of all the Progressive-controlled states Wisconsin alone had passed a graduated income tax by 1917, speaks volumes about the progressive movement nationally.[29]

The year 1914 was fateful for the relations between the progressive movement and labor in California. In the latter part of 1913 and well into the next year, the nation had suffered from what appeared to be the beginning of a great depression. With hunger stalking the streets of San Francisco and Los Angeles, and with unemployed armies ranging through the state, progressivism might well have broadened its appeal and cemented labor to its cause by caring for the unfortunates. But Governor Johnson approved a system of free labor exchange, after having vetoed a similar measure two years before, and this was the end for the worker. It was now plainer than ever that there was to be no lightening of labor's legal burdens and no state aid. Instead the governor, by his silence, acquiesced to the Sacramento solution of the unemployment problem by the use of the firehose and the club. More to the point, it was precisely in this year that Hiram Johnson announced to the newspapers that his legislative program had been accomplished. All that remained for the progressives to do, he concluded, was to "consolidate" the reforms already on the statute book. It was scarcely a coincidence that Woodrow Wilson and Theodore Roosevelt ran out of progressive issues the same year. Wilson's lone public reaction to the depression was to create an industrial commission to inquire into the causes of labor unrest. And Roosevelt opined in the fall of 1914 that the reform age had ended because the masses of people were no longer interested in "social and industrial justice" but rather in the "bread and butter" issue of how best to "shape conditions" so that they could make a living.[30] That unwillingness or inability of both Democratic and Republican progressives to connect social justice with the "bread and butter" issue was loaded with significance for the future.

Like many of their fellow ideologues elsewhere, California progressives had no more issues by 1914 and could not bring themselves to take that long, and to them radical, jump onto the new ground of socioeconomic legislation and direct cooperation with labor. Four years later, with progressivism decidedly on the defensive, a few California progressive leaders did depart radically from their old ideology. Both Rowell and Lissner, among a few others, objected to the proposals of Will H. Hays, the chairman of the Republican National Committee, for a 1920 Republican national platform. Their objections were focused particularly on Hays' blast against "the socialist tendency of the times." Rowell and Lissner now held for government operation of railroads, telephone and telegraph companies, steamship lines, and insurance firms; for extremely high income and inheritance taxes; and for legal encouragement to organized labor. They approved of the program of the British Labour Party, and defended it against Theodore Roosevelt's criticism that the "five to ten per cent pure communism" in British labor's proposals contaminated it just as a small percentage of sewage contaminated pure spring water. After reading the British program for the third time Lissner replied to Roosevelt that he regarded the document as "the most inspiring and suggestive piece of political writing published in many a year." If Bolshevism meant the appropriation of surplus wealth toward the goal of providing a comfortable life for every man, Lissner reasoned, then he was a Bolshevik. And Rowell wrote that he could not see any sharp demarcation between the progressive and the socialist movements.[31] This from the men who had believed just six years before that the only choice before the people was the one between socialism and progressivism, and that if socialism were chosen it would mean the end of democracy.

William Kent, who had consistently been more favorable to labor than either Rowell or Lissner, also moved to the left in the postwar years. Along with "trying to restore the almost forgotten ideals of freedom of speech and the right of men in a free country to discuss the terms under which they live," he was also, he wrote during his campaign of 1920, trying to protect the laboring man's "right for an adequate division of wealth production, and a voice in the processes of production." [32]

But Rowell, Lissner, and Kent's attempt to inject into the old movement a goodly portion of Fremont Older's "economic progressivism" came too late by at least four years. Progressivism had lost its cohesion and vitality since many of the leaders had deserted the old standards to crusade for isolationism, prohibition, and Red baiting. Both the prosperity of the war years and the rising threat of radicalism had served to convert onetime progressives into latter-day conservatives. Nationally, the old progressivism in these years seemed to organized labor its greatest enemy. The Bull Moose slogans had apparently been forgotten in the postwar period; Theodore Roosevelt's mind was on foreign policy almost exclusively. Albert J. Beveridge was openly consorting with an antiunion, strikebreaking crowd, and Henry Allen was soon to support a compulsory arbitration law in Kansas. On the other political side Woodrow Wilson's attorney general, A. Mitchell Palmer, was busy nullifying the once potent New Freedom with Red hunts and some of the most sweeping labor injunctions in American history. And even President Wilson had denounced the coal strike of November 1919 as "morally and legally wrong." In California, during three successive sessions of the legislature, the best that organized labor could do was to beat off the attacks of a determined opposition to the favorable legislation of the Johnson period. It is little wonder then that labor lost most of its enthusiasm for progressivism and Progressives. Late in 1920 Herbert Croly summed up the progressive attitude as having no understanding of the wage earner's problems and as being thoroughly unsympathetic to labor's needs and wants. At about the same time William Kent, possibly labor's best friend among the California Progressives, observed that he had lost his senatorial contest because he had been "betrayed by organized labor." [33]

Even if the Rowell-Lissner-Kent formula for a new economic progressivism had not been out of step with the times and had been accepted by their California colleagues, it probably would not have appealed to organized labor for long. Essentially it was still an expression of the old progressive desire to restore and preserve a uniformly middle-class state in which power would reside with the individualistic progressive politician. Although Rowell and Lissner praised the program of the British Labour Party, they abhorred the thought of direct political action by labor. Instead of a labor party and labor politicians they saw themselves as the dispensers of new social justice. They still believed what William Kent had expressed ten years before, that for the health of the state and the good of society as they conceived it, middle-class benevolence was preferable to labor self-help.

But that benevolence translated into specific issues was too class-consciously self-interested to have won labor's support over the years. Specifically attacking one of the paramount problems of modern society, Rowell and Lissner insisted that the solution to the labor-capital struggle on the industrial level lay in compulsory arbitration. They supported the Kansas compulsory arbitration law, firmly believing that the alternatives for society lay in "such tribunals or in the Prussianizing of the state." [34] To reënlist labor's support, progressivism had to await a new synthesis, a reformulation that was not to come until the great depression had made the middle class less secure and more willing to coöperate with the class they deemed below them.

If nothing succeeds like success, then the reverse is also true. The series of Progressive defeats from 1916 on helped materially in the bankruptcy of California progressivism. Within the state, it is true, no serious reverses occurred until the defeat of Kent by Shortridge in 1920. But the numerous defeats elsewhere had had considerable impact on California.

Certainly Roosevelt's failure in 1916, the return to the Republican party, and the control of that party by conservative elements, all helped to numb the progressive will to act, both inside and outside the state.

Perhaps the crowning blow to progressive self-esteem was the nomination of Warren G. Harding in 1920. "Of all the men who aspired to the presidency," Rowell later wrote, "Harding was the only impossible one." Hiram Johnson agreed. Moreover, he was certain that Harding's election cemented the old standpatters in power and signified the end of progressivism for his generation. Sometime in the future, Johnson thought, another generation with less fear and more fervor would upset conservative control. But for his age Johnson was sure that progressivism was through and that reform had ended.[35]

Discouraged by these costly defeats and by the national sloughing off of ideals, many progressives lost all hope of concerted action and were ready to withdraw from the reform crusade. Rowell felt that he could no longer subscribe to parties, only to individuals, and that even faith in them had to be qualified by time. Older was sure that "Politics is hopeless." And George W. Norris considered quitting the game to see if he could accomplish more for his beliefs by coming at them "from a different angle." "I have not been able to do much while I have been in public life," the great Nebraska liberal wrote plaintively to Kent. "I would like to see if I could not do something outside." [36]

Some progressives were willing to make their peace with the new national ethics. When Hiram Johnson outdid even his standpat colleague, Shortridge, in getting skyhigh tariff protection for California products in 1922, Rowell offered an explanation for his actions. He was sure, he wrote, that Johnson was more disgusted with his own tariff performance than any of his critics, and that the senator knew perfectly well the whole Fordney-McCumber proceedings were just one great "farcical game of grab." But Johnson was also aware, Rowell asserted, that his continued stay in the Senate depended upon his acting as "attorney for the California bunch of grabbers," and he was determined to see that he came out of the debates with the biggest fistful of loot.[37]

Rowell's cynical explanation of Johnson's actions was a significant comment on the almost complete collapse of progressive morale. In 1908 Kent had written to a friend that the vision of expanding morality and democracy was enough to make a man optimistic and "to make him realize that there is some use in and a reason for struggle." Now, fourteen years later, Kent saw the age as characterized by "a complete mental and moral breakdown." Surrounded by new and strange attitudes, Kent, in the words of Mark Twain, felt like "murdering his conscience as a useless handicap." [38]

As despair succeeded hope in the progressives, their fine progressive rationale of a decade earlier eroded. Gone was their firm belief in the ultimate success of moral values. Gone was their complete faith in democracy, and thus their confidence in politics. Gone was their once tenaciously held conviction of the essential goodness of man and his capacity to improve. But losing his trust in the ability of man to change very much, Fremont Older wrote in his memoirs, did not mean that he had become cynical. Rather it had made him more compassionate toward all mankind. He had come to the belief that most men do the best they are capable of at any one moment, a thought which Older confessed had led him to the position that he could not "blame anyone for anything." [39]

The best illustration of the decline in the progressives' faith in man, however, came in the preface to Older's book. There in a few paragraphs, William Allen White traced the disintegration of the progressive creed. Ten years ago, White wrote, he and his fellows had all been sure that "In the hearts of man a divine fire smoldered"; that men were fundamentally decent, that given a chance the great majority of them would be "honest, aspiring, neighborly, and affectionately helpful. . . ." But now he and his colleagues knew, "Much was futile in that earlier vision which sought to give men freedom while they still carried servile hearts." "Men who were mean in a mean environment," White reasoned, were still mean in a better one. Political power handed over to the masses was of little benefit to them "except to make them responsible for their own mistakes." Therefore, nothing was left but to lead the masses "in a slow and tedious process of education." "But," White concluded despondently, "we can no longer be sure that they are capable of political education." [40]

However true or false White's historical analysis was, it constitutes an extremely significant commentary upon the collapse of the progressive mind. White, along with many of his fellow progressives, sought to lay the blame for society's ills in the 1920's not upon his own associates, but upon the stupidity of the masses reared "in a mean environment." Aside from the group conceit expressed, this judgment betokened the end of the reform atmosphere of the past. When coupled with the doubt that the masses could ever learn even by a "slow and tedious process of education," 1910 progressivism became a thing for aging memories and for history.

Looking back over the twenty years that comprised the rise and fall of the California progressive movement, one is tempted to ask what was accomplished by all the furious sound, the social friction, and the great expenditure of human energy that went into the progressive crusade. The cynic would probably answer that very little came of it all, that it was just another long, drawn-out tale, signifying nothing. To document his view he might cite the recent statement of a San Francisco journalist: "California is still controlled body and soul by such great corporations as the Southern Pacific Railroad. . . ." [41] In further support of his argument he might point to the fact that the Speaker of the California Assembly in 1933 was the railroad's chief lobbyist from 1935 to 1941. As speaker he was paid $1,200 per year; his annual salary as a lobbyist has been estimated as more than $20,000. [42] From such testimony it might be argued that the Progressive never really accomplished the most concrete of his aims, the removal of corporation domination from government.

One might also argue with some effectiveness that the California progressive also failed in some of his even more significant ambitions. In 1934 William Allen White suggested that the fundamental progressive end was to enlarge the middle class. It sought to do this, White recorded, "by beating down the ears of the big crooks who were robbing us all by pennypinching dishonest devices of corporate financing . . . and . . . by making the way up easier for what might be called the underprivileged." White thought the movement had succeeded in providing more opportunity for the man below and thus in enlarging the middle class. Where it had failed, he maintained, was in curbing the pretensions of the very powerful. "We did not knock down the ears of the big crooks," he wrote in the midst of the great depression, "and they played hell with our civilization in the third decade, and here we are." [43] The historian might agree in general with White's comment on the ineffective curbing of the powerful, but question if the progressives, especially on the state level, did much in any real sense to assist the man on the bottom to climb upward. The progressive reforms largely dealt with the machinery of government, and it is difficult to see how the movement effectively widened economic opportunity for the masses within the boundaries of California.

From the vantage point of the present, one would have to agree that progressivism did not stop the growth of class consciousness in society and certainly did not reverse the time drift toward collectivism. Also, in recent years the people have turned their backs upon some of the progressive concepts of public morality. Like many other states, California has repealed its prohibitions against prize fighting, horse racing, and the liquor traffic.

Was the progressive's only accomplishment then that he held office for so many years? Not at all. The progressive political reforms were basic advances. They were, and are, the people's tools for the control of their government. If the great corporations do control the state of California today, which is extremely debatable, it is by the people's sanction.

As long as democratic government exists, the people, if they are concerned enough, can claim their own by effective use of the primary, the initiative, the referendum, the recall, and the free and honest ballot. Corporation influence, the power of the press, public opinion polls, and all the paraphernalia of minority pressure groups to the contrary, the people still rule in the United States and in California. A series of recent national elections constitutes good evidence of this.

Admittedly, the progressive did not solve the problems that center in the conflict of interests between capital, labor, and the public. One might ask, who has? Even labor governments have had considerable difficulties with the labor unions that helped elect them. But this much can be said for the progressive politician. He was representative of a group which, for the first time in recent American history, approached the industrial problem without all its loyalties foresworn either to capital or to labor. His objectivity, however partial, was important. If the progressive answers were incomplete and unsatisfactory, this group at least raised some important and hitherto unvoiced questions which constituted the essential first step toward any solution of the exceedingly complex labor problem.

The history of the progressive years is free from a major scandal. If the progressive did nothing else, he did give California honest and decent government. That in itself, in the light of the state's history, was a major achievement. But beyond that, the California progressive restored two words to the political language of the state. Instead of persistently talking in the idiom of crude power and the swap of self-interested groups, he frequently mentioned and often considered the words "ought" and "should." Much of the time, of course, he measured his actions in the light of self-interest, but more frequently than the casual observer would suppose, he squared his public deeds with an ethical yardstick. His ethics might not have been so precisely suited to the needs of his times as he thought, but public ethics he had. Can as much be said for those who preceded him?

In attempting to evaluate the place of the progressive in the life of California, the historian must ask one final question: What would California society have been like without him? The answer to this question can, of course, only be highly speculative. When one measures the Progressive against the Walter Parkers and the Abraham Ruefs, however, the general outlines of the answer are clear. The Progressive supplied an honest and decent middle way between a corrupt labor party and a corrupt corporation-dominated government. If he did not answer many of the pressing questions of his time in completely satisfactory terms, he at least answered them better than the generation before him and the one which followed.

Lincoln Steffens once said that no reform group is ever completely successful in all it hopes to do, for the people are fickle and self-interest is a constant. Steffens' remark might be modified and applied to the broader canvas of all history. Society apparently matches its impulse toward the settlement of existing problems with an equal propensity for creating new ones. At best, most generations are like the man who through his life borrows money on expected income to pay back old debts. But when the last balance sheet is drawn up on the progressive generation it will probably show that it paid back much more to the past than it borrowed on the future. In the broad history of human affairs, that is a worthy epitaph.

Notes for Chapter I

[1] Benjamin Ide Wheeler, "Forecast for California," *Outlook*, 99:167.

[2] Phil Townsend Hanna, *California Through Four Centuries* (New York, 1935), p. 175; California Bureau of Labor Statistics Fourteenth Biennial *Report*, p. 368.

[3] California State Water Commission, *Annual Report*, 1917, pp. 59 ff.

[4] *Thirteenth Census of the United States*, 6:141; California Bureau of Labor Statistics Tenth Biennial *Report* (Sacramento, 1902), 10.

[5] William W. Cumberland, *Coöperative Marketing, Its Advantages as Exemplified in the California Fruit Growers' Exchange* (Princeton, New Jersey, 1917), pp. 22 ff.

[6] "Federal Trade Commission re California Associated Raisin Company," Nov. 20, 1919, typescript, University of California, Berkeley.

[7] California Bureau of Labor Statistics Fourteenth Biennial *Report*, 87; *Thirteenth Census of the United States*, 11:53 ff.; H. T. Griswold, "Oil Boom," *Current Literature*, 30:167–168.

[8] Robert Glass Cleland, *California in Our Time* (New York, 1947), p. 266.

[9] G. W. Bemis, "Sectionalism and Representation in the California State Legislature, 1911–1913" (unpublished doctoral thesis, University of California, Berkeley, 1933), p. 19 *et passim*.

[10] The figures are taken from Bemis, *op. cit.*, p. 23, and from *Thirteenth Census of the United States, Population*, 1:760; 2:157 ff.

[11] United States Bureau of Census, *Special Reports*, 1906, "Religious Bodies," pt. 1, Summary Tables.

[12] California Bureau of Labor Statistics, Fifteenth Biennial *Report* (Sacramento, 1911), p. 310.

[13] John W. Caughey, *California* (New York, 1940), p. 442; Oscar Lewis, *The Big Four* (New York, 1938), p. 279; Stuart Daggett, *Chapters on the History of the Southern Pacific* (New York, 1926), p. 266.

[14] Dr. George C. Pardee, "Political Reminiscences," typescript in Borel Collection, Stanford University, p. 2; see also Lewis *op. cit.*, pp. 371 ff.

[15] Second Annual *Report* (Sacramento, 1916), pp. 325 ff.

[16] Fresno *Republican*, May 29, 1912.

[17] Fremont Older, *My Own Story* (New York, 1926), pp. 15 ff.

[18] Lewis, *op. cit.*, p. 311.

[19] San Francisco *Chronicle*, April 18, 1885.

[20] Dr. John R. Haynes, "Birth of Democracy in California," MSS, 3, Haynes Foundation, Los Angeles.

[21] San Francisco *Examiner*, April 10, 1890, as cited in Alice Rose, "The Rise of California Insurgency" (unpublished doctoral thesis, Stanford University, 1942), pp. 14–15.

Students of the California progressive movement will always be obligated to Miss Alice Rose for her extensive pioneer work on the subject. Her doctor's thesis is a veritable mine of information on the early phases of the movement. In addition, her scrupulously kept records of interviews with scores of progressive leaders, deposited in the Borel Collection at Stanford, constitute a priceless source of information for the entire period.

[22] Lincoln Steffens, *Autobiography* (New York, 1931), p. 567.

[23] Franklin Hichborn, *Story of the Session of the California Legislature of 1921* (San Francisco, 1922), p. 9.

[24] Haynes, *op. cit.*, p. 1.

[25] Statement of Dr. George C. Pardee to Alice Rose, typescript, Borel Collection, Stanford University, p. 5.

[26] Alice Rose, *op. cit.*, p. 76.

[27] Cumberland, *op. cit.*, p. 205; Charles Edward Russell, *Story of Great Railroads* (Chicago, 1912), p. 296.

[28] S. F. Moffett, "The Railroad Commission of California," *Annals of the American Academy*, 6:469–477; Commonwealth Club of California *Proceedings*, 3:354.

[29] *Arthur McEwen's Letter*, Feb. 17, 1894.

Notes for Chapter II

THE STRUGGLE FOR THE CITIES

[1] James D. Phelan, "Municipal Conditions and the New Charter," *Overland*, 28:104–111.

[2] Thomas W. Page, "San Francisco Labor Movement," *Political Science Quarterly*, 17:664–688; Ira B. Cross, *A History of the Labor Movement in California* (Berkeley, 1935), p. 229; Walton E. Bean, "Boss Ruef, the Union Labor Party, and the Graft Prosecution in San Francisco, 1901–1911," *Pacific Historical Review*, 17:443–455.

[3] Eugene E. Schmitz, "The San Francisco Election," *Independent*, 54:2867; Leight H. Irvine, "Union Labor Mayor," *Arena*, 27:150–156.

[4] San Francisco *Labor Clarion*, May 2, 1902.

[5] Ray Stannard Baker, "Corner in Labor," *McClure's* 22:366; San Francisco *Bulletin*, Jan. 1–19, 1905.

[6] San Francisco *Chronicle*, Nov. 5, 1905; Fremont Older, *My Own Story* (New York, 1926), pp. 57 ff.; Franklin Hichborn, *The System* (San Francisco, 1915), p. 17.

[7] Quoted in Robert Glass Cleland, *California in Our Time* (New York, 1947), p. 14. The supervisors were equivalent to councilmen in other cities.

[8] Stockton *Record*, July 13, 1906, cited in Alice Rose, "Rise of California Insurgency" (unpublished doctoral thesis, Stanford University, 1942), p. 131.

[9] Hichborn, *System*, pp. 73 ff.

[10] San Francisco *Call*, Oct. 14–26, 1906. At this time the *Call* was leading the demand for reform.

[11] Lincoln Steffens, "The Making of a Fighter," *American Magazine*, 64:339–356; *California Weekly*, 1:785.

[12] Quoted in Hichborn, *System*, p. 149.

[13] San Francisco *Labor Clarion*, March 22, 29, 1907; see the San Francisco *Chronicle*, the Los Angeles *Times*, and the San Francisco *Argonaut*, Dec. 1906 and Jan. 1907.

[14] Frederic C. Howe, *The Confessions of a Reformer* (New York, 1925), pp. 130–131; William Inglis, "Patrick Calhoun," *Harper's Weekly*, 52:25–26; Arno Dosch, "The Uplift in San Francisco," *Pacific Monthly* 18:374–380. See Theodore Bonnet, *The Regenerators* (San Francisco, 1911), p. 53, for a pro-Calhoun approach.

[15] Oakland *Tribune*, May 23, Oct. 24, 1907; *Argonaut*, June 29, 1907, Jan. 18, 1908; see also the Los Angeles *Times*, the San Francisco *Examiner*, and *Chronicle*, and even the San Francisco *Call*, one of the early staunch supporters of the prosecution.

[16] *California Weekly*, 1:785; Johnson to Theodore Roosevelt, Nov. 18, 1910, Roosevelt MSS.

[17] San Francisco *Bulletin*, Dec. 7, 1909.

[18] Frederick L. Bird and Frances M. Ryan, *Recall of Public Officers* (New York, 1930), p. 23.

[19] Los Angeles *Express*, March 27–April 2, 1906; *California Outlook*, 10:2.

[20] The *Record*, March 29, 1906, bluntly editorialized, "The Southern Pacific owns the council"; Dickson interview with author, June 25, 1948.

[21] Dickson interview with author, June 25, 1948; Stimson interview with author, June 23, 1948; Marshall Stimson "Autobiography," unpaged MSS in his possession; interview, Alice Rose with Russ Avery, Dec. 30, 1937, Borel Collection, Stanford University.

[22] Los Angeles *Express*, July 3, 1906; newspaper clipping in John Randolph Haynes Collection, John Randolph and Dora Haynes Foundation, Los Angeles.

[23] Edward A. Dickson, "Lincoln-Roosevelt League," p. 2, unpublished MSS in his possession.

[24] Los Angeles *Herald*, Oct. 5, 1906.

[25] *Union Labor News*, Oct. 12, 1906.

[26] Los Angeles *Express*, Nov. 30, 1906.

[27] Dr. John R. Haynes to W. B. Taylor, May 11, 1928, Haynes MSS, Haynes Foundation, Los Angeles; Lissner interview with Ida Tarbell, April 29, 1911, Borel Collection, Stanford University; Los Angeles *Record*, April 29, 1911.

[28] See the Los Angeles *Herald*, Jan. 25, 1909, for a summary of the graft articles.

[29] Meyer Lissner to Francis J. Heney, Feb. 2, 1909; Heney to Lissner, March 6, 1909, Lissner MSS, Borel Collection, Stanford University.

³⁰ Los Angeles *Times,* Jan. 14, Aug. 31, Oct. 24, Nov. 27, 1909; Los Angeles *Herald,* Dec. 7, 1909; Los Angeles *Express,* Nov. 16, 1909.

³¹ *Overland Magazine,* 51:288; P. C. McFarlane, "What is the Matter with Los Angeles?" *Collier's,* 48:28.

³² Commission on Industrial Relations, *Report,* 64th Cong., 1st. sess., Senate Doc. 415, 6:5526, 5535.

³³ *Ibid.,* 6:5501, 5569, 5571, 5596, 5682.

³⁴ *Ibid.,* 6:5497–5499.

³⁵ Commission on Industrial Relations, *op. cit.,* 6:5501; H. G. Otis, "Long, Winning Fight Against the Closed Shop," *World's Work,* 15:9675.

³⁶ Commission on Industrial Relations, *op. cit.;* San Francisco *Labor Clarion,* 9:8, and following weekly issues.

³⁷ E. T. Earl to Hiram Johnson, Nov. 23, 1911, Lissner MSS; Los Angeles *Times,* Nov. 1, 1911; Los Angeles *Examiner,* Nov. 20, 1911; Stimson interview with author June 24, 1948; Fresno *Republican,* Nov. 20, 1911.

³⁸ San Francisco *Labor Clarion,* 10:10.

³⁹ Undated memorandum, Lissner MSS; see the San Francisco *Bulletin,* Dec. 2–7, 1911, for Steffens' complete series of articles on the incident and his *Autobiography* (New York, 1931), 2:676 ff.

⁴⁰ San Francisco *Bulletin,* Dec. 7, 1911.

⁴¹ R. L. Green, typewritten statement, R. L. Green MSS, Borel Collection, Stanford University; *Pacific Outlook,* 11:11; Rose, *op. cit.,* pp. 29, 375.

Notes for Chapter III

AND THEN, THE STATE

¹ Frank P. Flint to Pardee, Oct. 20, 1904, Pardee MSS, Bancroft Library, University of California; Pardee, "Political Reminiscences," typescript, Borel Collection, Stanford University.

² Rowell to Mark Sullivan, May 27, 1910, Rowell MSS. The major part of the Rowell papers have now been deposited in the Bancroft Library, University of California, Berkeley.

³ See Senator Perkins' story of the banquet in the Oakland *Enquirer,* Oct. 26, 1906. A notorious servant of the railroad, the senator wrote to deny the story that Gillett had been chosen by the Southern Pacific at this gathering; Fresno *Republican,* July 24, 1906.

⁴ San Francisco *Call,* Sept. 6–8, 1906.

⁵ *Ibid.,* Sept. 10, 1906; *Everybody's,* 26:298.

⁶ Thomas Flint to Thomas R. Bard, Oct. 22, 1906, copy, Thomas R. Bard MSS, Borel Collection, Stanford University. Frank Short to J. D. Works, Feb. 3, 1914, Works MSS, Bancroft Library, University of California, Berkeley; George C. Pardee to E. T. Earl, Sept. 27, 1906, Pardee MSS, Bancroft Library.

[7] Dickson interview with author, June 25, 1948.

[8] San Francisco *Examiner*, Sept. 7, 1906; Sacramento *Bee* and Los Angeles *Express*, Sept. 11, 1906; Dickson interview with author, June 25, 1948; H. W. Brundige to Dickson, Sept. 8, 1906, Dickson MSS.

[9] Fresno *Republican*, Oct. 31, 1906. The final vote stood Gillett, 125,887; Bell, 117,645; Langdon, 45,008; Lewis (Socialist) 16,036.

[10] Bell to Judge Waldo M. York, July 20, 1907, Lissner MSS.

[11] San Francisco *Bulletin*, Feb. 5, 1907; San Francisco *Call*, March 9, 1907.

[12] San Francisco *Call*, Jan. 9, 1907; Fresno *Republican*, Jan. 14, 1907, San Francisco *Bulletin*, Feb. 28, 1907.

[13] Rowell to Ida Tarbell, Nov. 9, 1911, Rowell MSS; Dickson interview with author, June 25, 1948; San Francisco *Chronicle*, March 9, 1907.

[14] San Francisco *Call*, March 1–2, 1907.

[15] Fresno *Republican*, March 13, 1907; Los Angeles *Times*, March 15, 1907.

[16] Rowell to Mark Sullivan, May 27, 1910, Rowell to J. C. Forkner, April 23, 1914, Rowell MSS; Pardee, "Reminiscences," pp. 4–5. Pardee remembered the manifesto but not what it contained. Weight is given to the story, however, by an editorial in the Fresno *Republican* urging Pardee to revolt against the Southern Pacific and dated April 11, 1906.

[17] Statement of Rowell to Ida Tarbell, March 24, 1911, Borel Collection, Stanford University; Rowell interview with author, April 3, 1944.

[18] Dickson interview with author, June 25, 1948; Ida Tarbell interview with Meyer Lissner, April 29, 1911, Lissner MSS, p. 4; Rose interview with George B. Anderson, Dec. 27, 1937, Borel Collection; Rose, *op. cit.*, p. 400; Horace McPhee to Rowell, March 5, 1907, Rowell MSS. The editor of the Santa Ana *Blade* also wrote the editors of the Sacramento *Bee* and the Sacramento *Union* in the same vein.

[19] Edward A. Dickson, "The Lincoln-Roosevelt League," p. 7, unpublished MSS in his possession.

[20] Dickson to Lissner, Feb. 10, 1907, Lissner MSS; Dickson interview with author, June 25, 1948; Rowell to J. C. Forkner, April 23, 1914, Rowell MSS; Fresno *Republican*, August 27, 1907; Rowell interview with author, April 13, 1944; Fresno *Republican*, March 13, 1907.

[21] The invitation and the replies are to be found in the Dickson papers. Among those attending the meeting were Dickson, Rowell, Lissner, Stimson, Avery, A. B. Nye, R. B. Bulla, H. W. Brundige, Ed. Fletcher, E. A. Forbes, Dr. John R. Haynes, G. B. Daniels, A. J. Pillsbury, T. C. Hocking, and S. C. Graham. Lissner to H. Weinstock, April 25, 1907, Lissner MSS; Robert A. Waring to author, Nov. 14, 1949.

[22] Dickson, "The Lincoln-Roosevelt League," pp. 10–11; A. J. Pillsbury to Rowell, May 26, 1907, Rowell MSS. Pillsbury acted as the temporary secretary of the infant organization.

[23] Dickson, "The Lincoln-Roosevelt League," p. 11; Dickson to Rowell, July 20, 1907, Rowell MSS; Marshall Stimson, "Autobiography."

[24] Rowell remembered that Steffens proposed Roosevelt; Dickson said it was Heney. Dickson obtained his information from Winston Churchill, who had organized Lincoln Clubs in New Hampshire.

[25] Thomas R. Bard to L. C. Gates, Aug. 26, 1907, Bard MSS (copy); Sacramento *Union*, Aug. 7, 1907.

[26] Within a month after its founding, the League had enlisted the support of the entire chain of Scripps papers, the Los Angeles *Express*, San Francisco *Call*, San Francisco *Bulletin*, Sacramento *Bee*, Sacramento *Union*, Oakland *Enquirer*, Berkeley *Gazette*, Fresno *Republican*, Stockton *Record*, Modesto *Herald*, Tulare *Register*, Bakersfield *Echo*, San Diego *Sun*.

[27] Dickson, "The Lincoln-Roosevelt League," pt. 2, p. 1; Rowell interview with author, April 13, 1944; undated memorandum in Lissner MSS; Rowell to Dickson, Aug. 10, 1908, Dickson MSS.

[28] Rowell to Dickson, Aug. 12, 1908, Dickson MSS.

[29] Rowell to Lissner, Jan. 14, 1908; Lissner to Earl, June 9, 1908, Lissner MSS; Rowell to Steffens, June 17, 1908, Rowell MSS; Lincoln Steffens, *Upbuilders* (New York, 1909), p. 274.

[30] Rowell to Dr. Chester Rowell, April 28, 1908, Rowell MSS.

[31] Rowell to Lissner, March 12, 1908, Lissner MSS; Rowell to Spreckels, Nov. 28, Oct. 2, 1908, Rowell to Francis Heney, Oct. 31, 1908, all in Rowell MSS.

[32] Rowell to ———— (?), 1907; Rowell to Spreckels, Feb. 19, 1908, Rowell to Dr. Chester Rowell, March 18, 1908, Rowell MSS; Heney to Lissner, Oct. 11, 1907; Lissner to Heney, Jan. 4, 1908, Lissner MSS; Fresno *Republican*, March 29, 1908.

[33] Fresno *Republican*, May 3, 1908.

[34] San Francisco *Bulletin*, May 6, 1908; Los Angeles *Express*, July 23, 1908.

[35] Oakland *Tribune*, Aug. 9, 1908; Los Angeles *Times*, Aug. 10, 1908; San Francisco *Argonaut*, 58:1638.

[36] Los Angeles *Express*, Aug. 26, 1908; Fresno *Republican*, Nov. 2, 1908.

[37] Dispatches of the People's Lobby may be seen in the Hichborn MSS, Haynes Foundation, Los Angeles; Fresno *Republican*, Jan. 26, 1909.

[38] Miguel Estudillo to Franklin Hichborn, Sept. 6, 1909, Hichborn MSS, Haynes Foundation, Los Angeles. See also Hichborn, *Story of the California Legislature of 1909* (San Francisco, 1909), pp. 68 ff.

[39] Fresno *Republican*, Feb. 28, 1909.

[40] *Ibid.*, Nov. 24, 1909.

[41] Rowell to Spreckels, July 23, 1908, Hichborn MSS; E. T. Earl to Lissner, June 22, 1908, Lissner MSS.

[42] Fresno *Republican*, July 30, 1909.

[43] *California Weekly*, Aug. 13, 1909; Fresno *Republican*, Sept. 16, 1909; see also Los Angeles *Express* and San Francisco *Bulletin* for Sept. and Oct. 1909.

44 San Francisco *Bulletin,* Sept. 30, Oct. 18, 1909.

45 Fresno *Republican,* Sept. 8, Nov. 20, 1909.

Notes for Chapter IV

WHAT MANNER OF MEN: THE PROGRESSIVE MIND

1 Rowell interview with Ida Tarbell, March 24, 1911, typescript, Rowell MSS. Some of the material in this chapter has appeared in the *Mississippi Valley Historical Review* for September, 1949. The author wishes to thank the editors of the *Review* for their kind permission to reprint.

2 In 1910 the average age of ten of the most prominent Progressives was thirty-eight. These and the following figures were taken from biographical data found in the standard reference works, including *Who's Who in California* (San Francisco, 1929), in county histories, letters, and newspapers.

3 Of the 46 available places of birth, 24 were in the Middle West, 17 in California.

4 Five Catholics, three Methodists, and one Lutheran made up the total twenty-two.

5 The total is more than the original forty-seven because some men listed two occupations. Many of the others, of course, speculated in real estate.

6 Like McKinley, many conservative California Republicans had been for free silver until Hanna spoke.

7 Speech of Marshall Stimson preserved in Dr. John R. Haynes, "Personal Clippings," Haynes Collection; San Francisco *Call,* Oct. 28, 1906.

8 William Kent to George W. Douglas, Nov. 15, 1910, Kent MSS.

9 Fresno *Republican,* Aug. 23, 1911, March 26, 1907; Kent to E. W. Scripps, Sept. 9, 1911, Kent MSS.

10 Fresno *Republican,* Aug. 23, 1911; Lissner to Johnson, March 23, 1911, Lissner MSS.

11 Lissner to Dickson, April 11, 1908, Lissner MSS.

12 San Francisco *Labor Clarion,* April 25, 1905; Fresno *Republican,* Aug. 23, 1911; *Report,* Commission on Industrial Relations, 64th Cong., 1st sess., Senate Doc. 415, 5:4868; *Notes* of Dr. John R. Haynes on San Francisco, Haynes Collection.

13 John D. Works, "Significance of the Lincoln-Roosevelt Movement in California," *Arena,* 40:438–441.

14 San Francisco *Bulletin,* June 14, 1910: see also the almost identical words of Joseph Fels, the millionaire soap manufacturer, in the San Francisco *Bulletin,* Feb. 11, 1911.

15 Los Angeles *Express,* July 31, 1907.

16 Fresno *Republican,* March 10, 1907.

17 Jackson (Michigan) *Industrial News*, March 8, 1894, cited in Seymour Lutzky, "Survey of the Conflict of Labor, Progressive, and Radical Newspapers, 1890–1896" (unpublished master's thesis, State University of Iowa, 1948), p. 90.

18 *California Weekly*, Dec. 18, 1908, p. 51.

19 San Francisco *Bulletin*, March 2, 1912.

20 Oakland *Herald*, Aug. 21, 1903.

21 Fremont Older, *My Own Story* (New York, 1926), p. 9.

22 Kent to John Phillipps, May 26, 1908, Kent MSS.

23 This paragraph was written and delivered in a paper before the author examined the William Kent manuscripts. It was extremely interesting to note, therefore, Kent's remarks about the nature of his own religion. He knew "so little about the characteristics of the Divinity," he wrote, that he did not wish even "by implication to express a preference between the people who by different roads are seeking the same thing." Kent had written in an earlier memorandum that although he was a member of no denomination, his strongest affiliation in Chicago had been with All Souls' Church, which he had helped to pay off its obligations to the Unitarians, "for the specific purpose of making the church a part of a social institution known as the Abraham Lincoln Center where all, of every denomination, were equally welcome. We held that matters of creed were the peculiar business of the individual and that the ethics we sought and the helpfulness we gave and received from each other were not to be bounded by either race or creed." Kent to Samuel A. Eliot, Jan. 9, 1922; Kent memorandum dated April 19, 1920, Kent MSS.

24 San Francisco *Bulletin*, May 11, 1914.

25 Rowell to Lincoln Steffens, Aug. 1, 1908, Steffens MSS, Bancroft Library, Berkeley.

26 Fresno *Republican*, May 18, 1911.

27 See, for example, William F. Herrin's defense of "representative government" in the Oakland *Tribune*, June 15, 1910, also the San Francisco *Argonaut*, 68:161; Frank Short to Works, Feb. 3, 1914, Works MSS, Bancroft.

28 Fresno *Republican*, May 21, 1909. Joseph Fels felt that even the single tax issue was not a political, but rather a moral issue. "It is," he wrote, "if you please, somewhat of a religious question," Fels to Kent, Sept. 5, 1912, Kent MSS.

29 Steffens to Heney, June 1, 1908, Steffens MSS, Bancroft.

30 Willard to Theodore Roosevelt, (?) 1911, Roosevelt MSS, Library of Congress.

31 San Francisco *Bulletin*, Aug. 12, 1912.

32 C. K. McClatchey to Hichborn, Dec. 25, 1915, Hichborn MSS, Haynes Foundation, Los Angeles.

33 San Francisco *Bulletin*, Sept. 8, 1911, April 17, 1909.

34 *Ibid.*, Aug. 18, 1910.

35 Fresno *Republican*, Jan. 10, 1912.

³⁶ *Ibid.*, Aug. 14, 1911. The paraphrase of Macaulay was used by a progressive editor.

³⁷ Copy of open letter in Kent MSS, undated; San Francisco *Bulletin,* Sept. 8, 1911.

Notes for Chapter V

REBELLION BECOMES REVOLUTION

¹ Frank Devlin to Lissner, Nov. (?), 1909, Lissner MSS; Fresno *Republican,* July 28, 1907; Rowell to A. J. Pillsbury, Oct. 16, 1909, Rowell MSS; Dickson to Guy C. Earl, Aug. 4, 1909, Dickson MSS.

² Dr. John R. Haynes, "Notes on the Progressive Movement," unpaged MSS, Haynes Collection; Older to Rowell, Feb. 2, 1910, Rowell to Hiram Johnson, Jan. 31, 1910, Rowell MSS; Franklin Hichborn to C. K. McClatchey, Jan. 17, 1910, Hichborn MSS; Stimson interview with author, June 24, 1948; Dickson, "The Lincoln-Roosevelt League."

³ Rowell to Johnson, Feb. 2, 1910, Rowell MSS; Hichborn to McClatchey, Jan. 31, 1910, Hichborn MSS; Belshaw to Dickson, May 14, 1909, Dickson MSS.

⁴ *California Weekly,* 2:137; Rowell to Johnson, Jan. 20, 1910, Rowell to Dickson, Jan. 20, 1910, Rowell to W. R. Davis, Jan. 31, 1910, Rowell MSS.

⁵ Hichborn to McClatchey, Jan. 17, 1910, Hichborn MSS; Rowell to Older, Feb. 1, 1910; Rowell to C. C. Young, Feb. 2, 1910, Rowell MSS.

⁶ Rowell to Heney, Feb. 2, 1910, Rowell MSS; Fresno *Republican,* Feb. 3, 1910.

⁷ For second preferences the vote stood Johnson 3, Belshaw 5, Mott 7, and Heney 1; for third choice Johnson 1, Belshaw 3, Mott 6 and Heney 0. Tabulation in the Bard MSS, Borel Collection, Stanford University.

⁸ San Francisco *Bulletin,* Feb. 14, 1910; Rowell interview with Ida Tarbell, March 24, 1911, Rowell MSS; Marshall Stimson, "Autobiography," unpaged; Rowell interview with author, April 13, 1944; Fresno *Republican,* Feb. 20, 1910; Lissner to Dickson, Feb. 11, 1910, Dickson MSS; Dickson, "The Lincoln-Roosevelt League," p. 5.

⁹ Los Angeles *Times,* March 6, 1910; Rowell to Lissner, Jan. 31, 1910, Rowell to W. R. Davis, Jan. 31, 1910, Rowell MSS; *Grizzly Bear,* 6:6; San Francisco *Argonaut,* Feb. 26, 1910.

¹⁰ San Francisco *Bulletin,* Jan. 18, 1907.

¹¹ Rowell interview with Ida Tarbell, April 28, 1911, typescript in Rowell MSS.

¹² San Francisco *Bulletin,* Sept. 30, 1909; Rowell to Rolla V. Watt, Dec. 2, 1909, Rowell MSS.

¹³ Rowell to Ida Tarbell, ?, 1910, Rowell MSS; Steffens to Heney, Dec. 13, 1910, Steffens MSS.

NOTES

[14] Rowell to W. B. Taylor, undated, Rowell MSS.

[15] Cited in Cleland, *California in Our Time* (New York, 1947), p. 40.

[16] Works to McClatchey, Oct. 18, 1923, Works MSS, Borel Collection; Rowell to Lissner, April 11, 1914, Lissner MSS.

[17] Confidential source in possession of the author.

[18] Cleland, *op. cit.*, p. 40.

[19] William Allen White to Harold Ickes, May 23, 1933, cited in *Selected Letters of William Allen White*, Walter Johnson, ed. (New York, 1947), p. 334.

[20] Rowell to Edgar A. Forbes, Nov. 28, 1918, Rowell MSS.

[21] Works to Rowell, June 23, 1910, Rowell to Steffens, June 30, 1910, Rowell MSS; Rowell to Works, April 23, 1914, Works MSS, Bancroft.

[22] Fresno *Republican,* April 12, 1910; San Francisco *Bulletin,* Aug. 12, 1910.

[23] Fresno *Republican,* April 12, 1910; San Francisco *Bulletin,* Aug. 12, 1910; Los Angeles *Express,* Aug. 6, 1910.

[24] Kent to McKinley, July 6, 1910, Kent MSS.

[25] George E. Mowry, *Theodore Roosevelt and the Progressive Movement* (Madison, Wisconsin, 1946), pp. 98–115.

[26] Theodore Roosevelt to Theodore Roosevelt, Jr., Aug. 10, 1910, Roosevelt MSS, Library of Congress; Marshall Stimson, "Autobiography"; Los Angeles *Times,* March 13, 1910.

[27] Thomas R. Bard to Rowell, March 21, 1910, Bard MSS; Johnson to Rowell, April 19, May 20, May 29, 1910, Rowell MSS; Dickson, "The Lincoln-Roosevelt League," pt. 5, p. 1.

[28] Stimson, "Autobiography"; Lissner to Dickson, Oct. 23, 1907, Lissner to Heney, Oct. 5, 1910, Lissner MSS.

[29] Los Angeles *Times,* July 27, 28, 29, 1910; Los Angeles *Express,* Aug. 6, 1910; Stimson interview with author, June 24, 1948.

[30] Stimson, "Autobiography"; See San Francisco *Bulletin,* Oct. 18–19, for two other versions of the story.

[31] San Francisco *Bulletin,* June 12, 1910; Los Angeles *Times,* June 21, 26, July 17, 1910.

[32] Aug. 1, 1910. See also Oakland *Tribune,* July 31, Aug. 11, 1910.

[33] For tabulation of votes see *Congressional Record,* XLIV, pt. 5, pp. 4792–4818.

[34] San Francisco *Post,* Aug. 17, 1910; San Francisco *Argonaut,* Nov. 5, 1910, San Pedro *News,* Nov. 8, 1910; Fresno *Republican,* Oct. 3, 15, 1910.

[35] Milton U'Ren to Heney, Oct. 5, 1910; Kent to Older, July 18, 1910; Kent to Johnson, Aug. 22, 1910, Kent MSS; Steffens to Heney, Oct. 2, 1910, Steffens MSS; Johnson to Lissner, Oct. 24, 1910, Lissner MSS.

[36] "Some Reminiscences of Hiram Johnson," unpaged typescript in the Kent MSS.

Notes for Chapter VI

HARVEST TIME

1 Dickson interview with author, June 25, 1948; Rowell interview with Ida Tarbell, March 24, 1911, Rowell MSS.

2 Lissner to Johnson, Nov. 25, 1910, Johnson to Lissner, Jan. 14, 1911, Lissner MSS; Oakland *Tribune*, Jan. 8, 1911.

3 Johnson to Lissner, Feb. 12, 1911, Lissner MSS.

4 San Francisco *Argonaut*, 63:67; Johnson to Lissner, June 27, 1911, June 5, 1912, Lissner MSS.

5 Lissner to Martin Madsen, Aug. 7, 1916, Lissner MSS; Los Angeles *Times*, Jan. 17, 1911.

6 Dickson to Lissner, Feb. 11, 1911, Lissner MSS; Rose interview with Rowell, Nov. 17, 1937, Borel Collection.

7 San Francisco *Labor Clarion*, 9:1.

8 San Francisco *Argonaut*, 64:33, 65; Los Angeles *Times*, Jan. 20, March 8, 1911.

9 Roosevelt to Charles D. Willard, Feb. 27, 1911, Roosevelt MSS; Kent to David J. Thompson, Oct. 18, 1911, Kent MSS.

10 Two opposing views of the Henshaw incident are to be found in the Fresno *Republican*, March 1, 1911, and the San Francisco *Argonaut*, 63:130.

11 Johnson to Hichborn, June 26, 1911, Hichborn MSS.

12 Commission on Industrial Relations, *Report*, 64th Cong., 1st sess., Senate Doc. 415, 6:5505. This and succeeding pages of this chapter dealing with legislative activities are largely based upon the excellent volumes of the progressively minded Franklin Hichborn, which cover the California legislatures, save for the 1917 session from 1909 to 1921.

13 Dr. John R. Haynes, "Notes," typescript, Haynes MSS; Fresno *Republican*, Sept. 27, 1914.

14 Lissner to Dickson, Jan. 17, 1911, Lissner MSS.

15 California State Federation of Labor, *Report on Labor Legislation*, 1913, p. 99; Los Angeles *Times*, March 9, 1911.

16 Los Angeles *Times*, Feb. 22, 24, March 16, 18, 25, 1911; San Francisco *Chronicle*, March 18, 1911, San Francisco *Argonaut*, 68:179.

17 San Francisco *Bulletin*, March 10, 1911; Lissner to Johnson, March 23, 1911, Lissner MSS; Fresno *Republican*, March 23, 1911.

18 San Francisco *Labor Clarion*, 10:9.

19 San Francisco *Bulletin*, Oct. 6, 1911; San Francisco *Chronicle*, Oct. 9, 1911; San Diego *Union*, Oct. 8, 1911; Los Angeles *Times*, Oct. 11, 1911.

20 San Francisco *Bulletin*, Sept. 2, 26, 1911; Bird and Ryan, *op. cit.*, p. 53.

21 Cleland, *California in Our Times* (New York, 1947), p. 45.

22 Dewey Anderson, *California State Government* (Palo Alto, 1942), p. 199.

23 Fresno *Republican*, Dec. 26, 1911.

[24] According to their own count the Progressives claimed 26 of the 39 senators and 51 of the 79 assemblymen in the 1913 legislature.

[25] Rowell to Lissner, Nov. 29, 1911, Johnson to Lissner, Dec. 3, 1912, Lissner MSS.

[26] San Francisco *Bulletin*, April 11, 1913; Los Angeles *Times*, March 2, 1913.

[27] *California Weekly*, Jan. 29, 1909.

[28] California Superintendent of State Banks, Second Annual *Report* (Sacramento, 1911), pp. 4 ff.

[29] California Bureau of Labor Statistics Sixteenth Biennial *Report* (Sacramento, 1914), p. 10; George Creel, "What About Hiram Johnson of California?" *Everybody's Magazine*, 31:448–460.

Notes for Chapter VII

GOODBYE, MY PARTY, GOODBYE!

[1] See, for example, Fresno *Republican*, April 4, Dec. 5, 1910.

[2] Benjamin I. Wheeler to Roosevelt, Oct. 7, 1910, Roosevelt MSS.

[3] Fresno *Republican*, Dec. 30, 1910.

[4] Marshall Stimson, "Autobiography," unpaged typescript.

[5] Kent to Spreckels, May 10, 1911, Kent MSS; Johnson to Roosevelt, Oct. 20, 1911, Roosevelt MSS; Fresno *Republican*, Oct. 19, 1911.

[6] Lissner to W. L. Hauser, Oct. 17, 1911, Lissner MSS; San Francisco *Bulletin*, Oct. 16, 1911.

[7] Johnson to Roosevelt, Oct. 20, 1911, Roosevelt MSS; Fresno *Republican*, Nov. 19, 1911.

[8] Johnson to Lissner, Nov. 1, 1911, Rowell to Lissner (telegram) Nov. 5, 1911, Lissner to Rowell (telegram) Nov. 5, 1911, Lissner MSS; Rowell to Ralph H. White, Nov. 8, 1911, Rowell MSS.

[9] Lissner to LaFollette, Nov. 10, 1911, LaFollette to Lissner, Nov. 21, 1911, Lissner MSS.

[10] Lissner to Johnson, Nov. 20, 1911, Lissner MSS.

[11] Rowell to Spreckels, Nov. 29, Dec. 5, 1911, Rowell MSS.

[12] Roosevelt to Johnson, Oct. 27, 1911, Roosevelt to Judge Ben Lindsey, Dec. 5, 1911, Roosevelt MSS; see Mowry, *op. cit.*, pp. 188 ff., for extended account of Roosevelt's changing attitude.

[13] Roosevelt to Johnson, Jan. 14, 18, 1912, Roosevelt MSS; Johnson to Lissner, Jan. 16, 19, 1912, Lissner MSS; San Francisco *Bulletin*, Jan. 23, 1912.

[14] Rowell to Hauser, Jan. 30, 1912, Rowell to Leo S. Robinson, Jan. 30, 1912, Rowell MSS.

[15] According to the two Pinchots, William Kent, Medill McCormick, and

Gilson Gardner's later testimony, Hauser had made the same remarks early in December, 1911. Signed statement of Amos and Gifford Pinchot, William Kent, Medill McCormick, March 27, 1912, Johnson MSS. Gilson Gardner, who read the statement a day later, wired Johnson on March 29, "That statement is correct in all particulars."

16 Johnson to Lissner, Feb. 3, 1912 (telegram), Lissner to Rowell, Feb. 6, 1912 (telegram), Lissner MSS.

17 The senator was apparently guilty of some inexactitude here. According to Amos Pinchot, LaFollette himself prepared a draft of a letter to Theodore Roosevelt at the end of December, promising to withdraw from the race and to turn over all of his support provided Roosevelt agreed to accept a Progressive nomination "under any circumstance." After considering it, Pinchot remembered, the senator then refused to send the letter. The account of events from Jan. 30 to Feb. 6 has been pieced out from statements collected by Hiram Johnson from the individuals concerned, copies of which are to be found in the Chester Rowell MSS. They include letters from the two Pinchots, William Kent, Gilson Gardner, Medill McCormick, and John D. Fackler, all dated from March 27 to April 5, 1912. Johnson's own account of the happenings is recorded in a signed statement to Chester Rowell dated April 3, 1912, in the Rowell MSS. See also Rowell's published account in the Fresno *Republican*, April 5, 1912.

18 Lissner to Rowell, Feb. 12, 1912, Rowell to Lissner, Feb. 12, 1912 (telegrams), Lissner MSS.

19 Lissner to Dickson, Jan. 30, 1912, Rowell to Lissner, Feb. 6, 1912, Lissner to Rowell, Feb. 6, 1912, Lissner MSS; Johnson to Lissner, Feb. 13, 18, 1912 (telegrams), Lissner to Rowell Feb. 18, 1921, Lissner MSS. See *California Outlook*, March 23, 1912, for extended defense of the group's actions.

20 Oakland *Tribune*, Jan. 31, 1912.

21 Lissner to Johnson, March 29, 1912, Johnson to Lissner, April 17, 1912, Lissner MSS.

22 Kent to Norman Hopgood, May 17, 1912, Kent MSS; San Francisco *Bulletin*, April 20, 1912; Johnson to Lissner, April 1, 17, 1912, Lissner MSS; Johnson to Hichborn, April 4, 1912, Hichborn MSS.

23 Fresno *Republican*, Feb. 20, 1912; New York *Times*, March 2, 1912; Lissner to Rowell, May 27, 1912, Lissner MSS.

24 June 1, 1912.

25 Los Angeles *Tribune*, June 11, 13, 1912; Los Angeles *Times*, June 16, 1912.

26 New York *Times*, June 13, 1912.

27 Los Angeles *Express* and *Tribune*, June 12, 1912; Kansas City *Star*, June 15, 1912; Johnson to Lissner, June 9, 1912, Lissner MSS.

28 Los Angeles *Express*, June 18, 1912.

29 Los Angeles *Times*, June 22, 1912.

30 Johnson to Roosevelt, July 8, 1912, Roosevelt MSS.

[31] Rowell to William Allen White, Nov. 29, 1919, Rowell MSS.

[32] Rowell to White, Nov. 29, 1919, Rowell MSS; Progressive National Committee, Minutes, typescript, Aug. 8, 1912, in Roosevelt MSS.

[33] Rowell to White, Nov. 29, 1919, Rowell MSS.

[34] Johnson to Lissner, July 29, 1912; Lissner MSS.

[35] San Francisco *Bulletin*, July 7, 27, 1912; Los Angeles *Times*, July 13, 1912; San Francisco *Call*, July 18, 1912.

[36] San Francisco *Bulletin*, May 16, 1911; Johnson to Roosevelt, July 8, 1912, Roosevelt MSS; Lissner to Johnson, July 3, 1912, Lissner to Hichborn, July 30, 1912, Lissner MSS.

[37] San Francisco *Chronicle*, Aug. 8, 1912; Fresno *Republican*, Oct. 8, 1912.

[38] San Francisco *Bulletin*, Aug. 31, 1912.

[39] Davis MSS (scrapbooks), pp. 344, 399; Johnson to Lissner, Sept. 15, Oct. 13, 1912, Lissner MSS; Johnson to Perkins, Oct. 1, 1912, copy, Roosevelt to Henry F. Cochem, Nov. 19, 1912, Roosevelt MSS.

[40] Johnson to Lissner, Oct. 13, Nov. 1, 1912, Lissner MSS.

[41] Lissner to Philip Bancroft, Nov. 9, 1912, Johnson to Lissner, Nov. 16, 1912, Lissner MSS.

[42] Johnson to Lissner, Dec. 29, 1912, Lissner to Perkins, Nov. 18, 1912, Lissner to Roosevelt, Nov. 26, 1912, Lissner MSS; Roosevelt to Heney, Dec. 13, 1912, Progressive National Committee, Minutes, typescript, Dec. 11, 1912, Roosevelt MSS.

[43] Lissner to Johnson, July 2, 1913, Lissner MSS.

[44] Roosevelt to Johnson, Jan. 28, 1913, Roosevelt MSS.

[45] Kent to Heney, Aug. 18, Sept. 6, 1913, Heney to Kent, Sept. 10, 1913, Kent MSS; Rowell to H. E. Davies, Rowell MSS; *California Outlook*, Nov. 8, 1913.

[46] Lissner to Dixon, Nov. 18, 1913, Johnson to Lissner, Nov. 12, 1913, Lissner MSS.

[47] Rowell to Kent, Dec. 7, 1913, Rowell MSS; Lissner to Dickson, Dec. 21, 1913, Lissner to Albert J. Beveridge, Nov. (?), 1913, Lissner MSS.

Notes for Chapter VIII

DEPRESSION AND DIVISION

[1] C. H. Parker, "The California Casual and His Revolt," *Quarterly Journal of Economics*, 30:110; Inez H. Gilmore, "Marysville Strike," *Harper's Weekly*, April 4, 1914; Woodrow C. Whitten, "The Wheatland Episode," *Pacific Historical Review*, 17:37–42.

[2] San Francisco *Bulletin*, May 18, 1912.

[3] Fresno *Republican*, June 3, 1914.

[4] *Ibid.*, March 7, 8, 9, 1914.

[5] San Francisco *Bulletin*, Aug. 29, 1914.

[6] Commission on Industrial Relations, *Report,* 61st Cong., 1st sess., Senate Doc. 415, 5:4812–2818; hereafter cited as Commission on Industrial Relations.

[7] Commission on Industrial Relations, *Report,* 5:4868; Martin to Hichborn, Aug. 3, 1914, Hichborn MSS.

[8] Commission on Industrial Relations, *Report,* 64th Cong., 1st sess., Doc. 415, 5:4877 ff.

[9] Kent to Heney, Oct. 12, 1911, Kent to Johnson, Feb. 12, 1912, Kent to Milton T. U'Ren, Aug. 16, 1912, Kent MSS; Kent to Hichborn, Aug. 3, 1912, McClatchey to Hichborn, Nov. 24, 1913, Hichborn MSS.

[10] White to Perkins, June 5, 1913, Roosevelt MSS; San Francisco *Bulletin,* July 8, 1914.

[11] Los Angeles *Times,* March 20, 26, 27, 1913; Los Angeles *Express,* March 29, 1913.

[12] Lissner to Earl, March 6, 1913, Earl to Lissner, March 8, 1913, Lissner MSS.

[13] Los Angeles *Tribune,* March 29, April 26, 1913; Los Angeles *Express,* March 29, April 23, 26, May 5, 1913.

[14] Los Angeles *Times,* May 2, 4, 1913; Los Angeles *Express,* May 3, 1917.

[15] Avery to Lissner, June 25, 1913, Lissner MSS.

[16] Lissner to Dickson, May 7, 1913, Lissner MSS; Rowell to Works, July 19, 1916, Works MSS, Bancroft Library.

[17] Rowell to Lissner, July 2, 1913, Lissner MSS.

[18] Johnson to Haynes, Oct. 24, 1911, Haynes MSS; Johnson to Lissner, April 18, 1912, July 1, 1913, Lissner MSS; Johnson to Kent, March 22, 1912, Kent MSS.

[19] Kent to Hichborn, Aug. 3, 1912, Hichborn MSS.

[20] Johnson to Lissner, Jan. 6, 1914, Lissner MSS.

[21] The 1913 legislature had conveniently passed a resolution amending the constitution to permit such an act. But that provision could not be ratified by the people until November, 1914.

[22] Heney to Roosevelt, Sept. 26, 1914, Roosevelt MSS; Lincoln Steffens to Laura Steffens, Dec. 1913, in Steffens, *Letters,* 2:331; Johnson to Lissner, Dec. 20, 1913, Lissner MSS.

[23] Rowell to Lissner, Dec. 19, 1913, Rowell MSS; Lissner to Johnson, Dec. 19, 1913, Lissner MSS.

[24] Heney to Kent, Dec. 30, 1913, Kent MSS.

[25] Rowell to Lissner, Nov. 27, 1913, Rowell MSS.

[26] Johnson to Lissner, Jan. 6, 1914, Lissner MSS.

[27] Rowell to Avery, Oct. 17, 1913, Lissner MSS.

[28] Dickson interview with author, June 25, 1948.

[29] Rowell to Lissner, Dec. 19, 26, 1913, Lissner MSS.

[30] Rowell to Lissner (copy to Johnson) Dec. 19, 1913, Rowell to Lissner, Dec. 26, 1913, Lissner MSS.

[31] Rowell to Lissner, Jan. 14, 28, 1914, Lissner MSS; Rowell interview with Alice Rose, Dec. 8, 1937, Borel Collection. See also Fresno *Republican,* Aug. 29, 1914.

[32] Roosevelt to Johnson, July 30, 1914, Roosevelt MSS. The California registration totals were: Republicans, 388,000; Democrats, 206,000; Progressives, 184,000.

[33] Fresno *Republican,* Sept. 17, 1914.

[34] San Bernardino *Index,* Sept. 29, 1914; J. D. Works to A. M. Drew, Feb. 9, 1914, Works MSS, Bancroft; Los Angeles *Express,* Oct. 26, 1914; San Francisco *Labor Clarion,* Nov. 6, 1914.

[35] Stimson interview with author, June 24, 1948; Heney to Johnson, Aug. 29, 1914, Johnson to Heney, Aug. 31, Sept. 1, 1914, all copies in Roosevelt MSS.

[36] *Sunset Magazine,* 33:654–655; Los Angeles *Examiner,* Nov. 3, 1914.

[37] Approved also were measures providing for a state regulatory water commission, legislative control of irrigation districts, the abolition of the poll tax, and the prohibition of prize fighting. A prohibition amendment was defeated.

[38] See, for example, Ray W. Ryder, *Harper's Weekly,* 59:560; *Argonaut,* 75:289; Los Angeles *Times,* Nov. 4, 1914. The final vote in San Francisco Co. stood: for governor, Johnson, 72,000, Fredericks, 36,000, Curtin, 16,000; for senator, Phelan, 60,000, Knowland, 31,000, Heney, 29,000.

[39] Roosevelt to Lissner, Nov. 16, 1914, Roosevelt MSS.

[40] Guido Marx to Hichborn, Dec. 28, 1914, Hichborn MSS; Stimson, "Autobiography"; Dickson interview with author, June 25, 1948; Kent, "Some Reminiscences of Hiram Johnson," Kent MSS.

[41] Heney to Roosevelt, Dec. 7, 1914, Roosevelt MSS; Lissner to White, July 29, 1915, Lissner MSS.

[42] Roosevelt to Charles J. Bonaparte, Nov. 7, 1914, to Johnson, Nov. 6, 1914, to Earl, Nov. 12, 1914, Roosevelt MSS.

[43] San Francisco *Bulletin,* May 3, 1915.

[44] Significantly, Wisconsin was the only progressive state among the nine states that had adopted income taxes by 1917. California State Tax Commission, *Report,* 1917, p. 9.

[45] Fresno *Republican,* March 11, 1915.

[46] May 11, 1915.

[47] Geddes Smith, "California Progressivism," *Independent,* 83:296; San Francisco *Bulletin,* May 7, 1915.

Notes for Chapter IX

NATIONAL POLITICS

1 Johnson to Roosevelt, Nov. 30, 1914, Roosevelt MSS.

2 Executive Committee Progressive party, Minutes, typescript, Dec. 2, 1914; Dwight B. Heard to Matthew Hale, Jan. 15, 1915, Roosevelt MSS.

3 New York *Times*, Oct. 13, 1915. See Roosevelt's articles in the *Metropolitan*, March, April, and May, 1915.

4 Heard to Roosevelt, April 2, 1915, Roosevelt MSS.

5 Fresno *Republican*, Aug. 12, 1913; San Francisco *Bulletin*, May 2, 1914; Kent to A. J. Waterhouse, Oct. 20, 1915, Kent MSS.

6 *California Outlook*, June 12, 1915, p. 3; Roosevelt to Lodge, Feb. 4, 1916, Roosevelt MSS; San Francisco *Bulletin*, Sept. 29, 1915; Fresno *Republican*, April 22, 1915.

7 Lissner to Rowell, Dec. 28, 1915, Lissner MSS.

8 Roosevelt to Johnson, July 26, 1914, Roosevelt MSS.

9 Johnson to Roosevelt, Aug. 20, 1914, Roosevelt MSS; *Everybody's Magazine*, 31:457; Fresno *Republican*, Dec. 2, 1914.

10 Roosevelt to George E. Miller, Dec. 27, 1915; Oakland *Enquirer*, Feb. 26, 1916.

11 Heard to Roosevelt, April 2, 1915, Roosevelt MSS.

12 Lissner to White, July 29, 1915, Lissner to Heard, Dec. 27, 1915, Lissner MSS.

13 Johnson to Rowell, Jan. 22, 1916 (telegram), Rowell MSS.

14 San Francisco *Examiner*, Feb. 6, 1916; San Francisco *Bulletin*, Feb. 7, 1916.

15 Lissner kept more than a hundred newspaper clippings of the Progressive offer, among which was one from the Eureka *Standard*, Feb. 23, 1916, across which was written in longhand, "The Real Thing." See also San Francisco *Chronicle* and Oakland *Tribune*, Feb. 21, 1916.

16 Lissner to Roosevelt, April 15, 1916, Roosevelt MSS; Fresno *Republican*, Feb. 27, 1916.

17 Lissner to Johnson, Feb. 21, 1916, Lissner MSS; San Francisco *Examiner*, Feb. 27, 1916; Los Angeles *Times*, Feb. 27, 1916.

18 *California Outlook*, May, 1916, p. 30.

19 Johnson to Roosevelt, March 27, 1916, Roosevelt to Johnson, April 8, 1916, Roosevelt MSS.

20 Oakland *Tribune*, Los Angeles *Times*; San Francisco *Chronicle*, May 2–7, 1916.

21 San Francisco *Bulletin*, April 24, May 4, 22, 1916.

22 Johnson to Lissner (telegram), June 3, 1916, Lissner MSS; Chicago *Tribune*, June 4, 1916.

23 Chicago *Tribune*, June 9, 1916.

[24] New York *Times,* June 10, 1916; Bonaparte to Roosevelt, June 13, 1916, Bonaparte MSS, Library of Congress.

[25] Nicholas Murray Butler, *Across The Busy Years* (New York, 1939), pp. 269–271.

[26] San Francisco *Bulletin,* June 10, 1916.

[27] Fresno *Republican,* June 11, 1916.

[28] *Ibid.,* July 6, 1916; New York *Times,* June 12, 1916.

[29] Rowell to Lissner, June 15, 18, 1916, Lissner MSS; Roosevelt to Lissner, Sept. 14, 1916, Roosevelt MSS; Rowell to Lissner, Nov. 18, 1916, Rowell MSS.

[30] Rowell to Lissner, June 18, 21, 1916, Lissner MSS.

[31] Rowell to Lissner, June 21, 1916, Perkins to Rowell, June (?), 1916, Rowell MSS; Rowell to Roosevelt, Aug. 23, 1916, Roosevelt MSS.

[32] Progressive National Committee, Minutes, typescript, June 26, 1916, Heard to Roosevelt, June 27, 1916, Roosevelt MSS; San Francisco *Bulletin,* June 27–28, 1916.

Notes for Chapter X

1916 AND THE LOST ELECTION

[1] San Francisco *Examiner,* July 9, 1916; Fresno *Republican,* July 9, 1916.

[2] Lissner to Johnson (telegram), July (?), 1916, Lissner MSS; San Francisco *Bulletin,* July 3, 1916. Rowell was so sure that Heney would run in the Democratic primary that he announced it as fact in his paper, the Fresno *Republican,* July 10, 1916.

[3] Los Angeles *Times,* June 15, 1916; Oakland *Tribune,* July 2, 1916; Works to Rowell, July 11, 1916, Works MSS, Bancroft Library; San Francisco *Argonaut,* 68:414.

[4] Perkins to Rowell, July 7, 1916, Willcox to William H. Crocker (copy), July 8, 1916, Rowell MSS.

[5] Rowell to Perkins, July 12, 1916, Perkins to Rowell, July 13, 1916, King to Rowell, July 13, 1916, Rowell MSS.

[6] Rowell to Crocker and to Perkins, July 14, 1916, Rowell MSS.

[7] Willcox to Keesling, July 18, 19, 1916, Crocker to Willcox, July 19, 1916 (copies), Rowell MSS; San Francisco *Argonaut,* July 22, 1916.

[8] Rowell to Perkins, July (?), 1916, Perkins to Rowell, July 22, 1916, Rowell MSS.

[9] Rowell to Willcox, July 29, 1916, Rowell MSS.

[10] Los Angeles *Times,* July 28, 30, 1916; San Francisco *Bulletin,* Aug. 24, 1916.

[11] Rowell to Willcox, July (?), 1916, Rowell to Crocker, July (?), 1916, Rowell to Perkins, July (?), 1916, all copies in Rowell MSS. The last intended to be shown to Willcox has been transposed.

12 Rowell to Perkins, July 27, 1916, Perkins to Rowell, July 27, 1916 (telegrams), Rowell MSS; *Argonaut*, 79:131; Oakland *Tribune*, Aug. 26, 1916.

13 Rowell to Willcox, July 28, 1916, Willcox to Rowell and Crocker, July 30, 1916, Willcox to Crocker, July 30, 1916, Crocker to Willcox, July 31, 1916, Rowell MSS.

14 Rowell to Perkins, July (?), 1916, Rowell to Willcox, July 31, 1916, Crocker to Willcox, July 31, 1916, Keesling to Rowell, Aug. 8, 1916 (open letter), Crocker to Willcox, Aug. 11, 1916, Rowell MSS.

15 Rowell to Lissner, Aug. 7, 1916, Crocker to Willcox, Aug. 9, 1916, Willcox to Crocker and Keesling, Aug. 12, 1916, San Francisco *Bulletin*, Aug. 15, 1916; *California Outlook*, 20:198.

16 San Francisco *Bulletin*, Aug. 15, 17, 1916; Oakland *Tribune*, Aug. 18, 1916.

17 Rowell to Roosevelt, Aug. 23, 1916, Rowell to Willcox, Aug. 19, 1916, Rowell MSS.

18 San Francisco *Bulletin*, Aug. 18–19, 1916; San Francisco *Chronicle*, Aug. 18, 19, 1916; Works to Hughes, Nov. 13, 1916, Works MSS, Bancroft; John Hays Hammond, *Autobiography*, p. 663; San Francisco *Argonaut*, 69:131; Rowell to Willcox, Aug. 19, 1916, Rowell MSS.

19 San Francisco *Argonaut*, 79:1, 33; San Francisco *Bulletin*, July 11, 1916; San Francisco *Labor Clarion*, 15:8, 25.

20 Henry F. Grady, "Open Shop Campaign in San Francisco," *Survey*, 37:192.

21 San Francisco *Bulletin*, July 21–25, 1916; San Francisco *Labor Clarion*, July 28, Aug. 18, 1916; San Francisco *Chronicle*, July 21–25, 1916.

22 Hugo Ernst to Keesling, Aug. 17, 1916, Keesling to Ernst, Aug. 17, 1916, San Francisco *Bulletin*, Aug. 17–18, 1916.

23 San Francisco *Labor Clarion*, Aug. 25, 1916. The fact that on August 19, the Commercial Club asked the union to supply sixty-five waiters for the banquet suggests that some pressure was applied to compromise the issue. When the union refused to supply the men until the open-shop card was taken down, the negotiations ended.

24 Rowell to Roosevelt, Aug. 26, 1916, Roosevelt MSS; Marshall Stimson, "Autobiography."

25 Dickson interview with author, June 25, 1948. Statement of Dickson in Cleland, *California in Our Time*, pp. 60–63.

26 This account of the Johnson-Farnham negotiations was mainly based upon a statement drawn up by Rowell in January, 1917, which Hiram Johnson obviously approved; a long Johnson letter to Roosevelt dated Nov. 20, 1916, in the Roosevelt MSS; and a copy of Johnson's telegram to Farnham, in the Rowell MSS. It is thus a one-sided account and should be treated as such.

27 Lissner to Perkins (telegram), Aug. 27, 1916, Lissner MSS.

28 San Francisco *Bulletin*, July 28, Aug. 12, 28, 1916.

[29] Oakland *Tribune*, Aug. 24, 26, 1916.

[30] Rowell to Willcox, Sept. 1, 1916, Rowell MSS; *California Outlook,* 114:413.

[31] Cleland, *op. cit.,* p. 59.

[32] Fresno *Republican*, Sept. 24, Oct. 7, 1916; San Francisco *Bulletin,* Nov. 4, 1916; Los Angeles *Tribune,* Oct. 28, 1916; Oakland *Tribune,* Nov. 5, 1916; New York *Times,* Sept. 7, 1916.

[33] San Francisco *Argonaut,* 69:145; Los Angeles *Times,* Sept. 21–Nov. 4, 1916; Oakland *Tribune,* Nov. 6, 1916; San Francisco *Chronicle,* Nov. 6, 1916.

[34] Johnson to Harold Ickes, Oct. 7, 1916 (copy), Rowell MSS; Fresno *Republican*, Nov. 8, 1916; Stimson, "Autobiography."

[35] Los Angeles *Times,* Nov. 10–12, 1916. It is interesting to note that even before the election rumors of such a "deal" were circulated and believed. See Los Angeles *Times,* Oct. 23, 1916, Oakland *Tribune,* Oct. 8, 1916; John D. Works to John W. Weeks, Sept. 25, 1916, Works MSS, Bancroft.

[36] Rowell to Raymond Robbins, Aug. 24, 1916, Rowell MSS.

[37] San Francisco *Labor Clarion,* Nov. 10, 1916.

[38] William Allen White, *California Outlook,* 20:51; Haynes to Johnson, Dec. 17, 1916, Haynes MSS; Horace C. Peterson, *Propaganda For War* (Norman, Oklahoma, 1939), p. 164; Works to W. H. Booth, Sept. 18, 1916, Works MSS, Bancroft.

[39] Lissner to Perkins, July 27, 1916, Lissner MSS; Roosevelt to Earl, Nov. 1, 1917, Roosevelt MSS; Johnson to Ickes, Oct. 7, 1916, Rowell MSS.

Notes for Chapter XI

THE DOWNHILL YEARS

[1] Johnson to Haynes, April 14, 1916, Haynes MSS.

[2] The account of the Johnson-Stephens conference is based upon a confidential source in possession of the author. See the San Francisco *Argonaut,* 80:130, and Los Angeles *Examiner,* Nov. 7, 1918, for newspaper accounts of the event.

[3] Johnson to Lissner, Nov. 25, 1916, Lissner MSS; San Francisco *Bulletin,* Dec. 2, 1916.

[4] Stimson, "Autobiography"; Los Angeles *Examiner,* Feb. 25, 1917; Los Angeles *Times,* March 4, 1917.

[5] Johnson to Lissner, Feb. 18, 1917, Lissner MSS.

[6] Dickson interview with author, June 25, 1948.

[7] Los Angeles *Express,* March 15, 1917.

[8] Lissner to Arthur Arlett, Sept. 27, 1917, Lissner MSS; Johnson to Haynes, June 6, July 5, 1917, Haynes MSS.

⁹ Rowell to Lissner, Nov. 24, 1917, March 30, April 19, May 23, 28, June 27, July 2, 1918, Rowell MSS; Los Angeles *Examiner,* Nov. 7, 1918.

¹⁰ Lissner to Johnson, Feb. 23, 1919, Lissner MSS; Johnson to Haynes, May 15, 1919, Haynes MSS; Johnson to Hichborn, Aug. 16, 1919, Hichborn MSS.

¹¹ Rowell to Kent, July (?), 1922, Kent MSS.

¹² Lissner to McClatchey, March 27, 1920, Lissner to Johnson, Nov. 15, 1920, Lissner MSS.

¹³ Lissner to Rowell, Feb. 17, 1920, Lissner MSS.

¹⁴ Rowell to Lissner, Feb. 9, May 2, 1920, Rowell MSS; Fresno *Republican,* May 1, 1920.

¹⁵ Johnson to Lissner, Aug. 20, 1920, Lissner MSS.

¹⁶ Johnson to Elmer Dover, Sept. 28, 1920 (copy), Lissner MSS.

¹⁷ Kent to Haynes, March 11, 1922, Haynes MSS; Kent to Rowell, Jan. 13, March 14, 1922, Kent to Mark Sullivan, Aug. 26, 1922 (telegram), Kent MSS; Oakland *Tribune,* Aug. 25, 1922.

¹⁸ Lissner to Johnson, Feb. 9, Sept. 1, Nov. 15, 1920, Lissner MSS.

¹⁹ As cited in Dewey Anderson, *California State Government* (Palo Alto, 1942), p. 213.

²⁰ San Francisco *Examiner,* Jan. 18, 1921, cited in Hichborn, *Story of the Session of the California Legislature of 1921* (San Francisco, 1922), p. 51.

²¹ Kent to Leon Haynes, Jan. 12, 1925, Kent MSS; Rowell to Hichborn, July 11, 1923, Hichborn MSS.

²² The inside story of the Progressive Voters' League and the organization for public power can be obtained from the manuscripts of Rowell, Kent, and Hichborn.

²³ Copy of public statement in Kent MSS; Rowell to Kent, June 24, 1922, Kent MSS.

²⁴ Kent to Heney, July 8, 1918, Kent MSS; Roosevelt to Rowell, Dec. 12, 1917, Rowell MSS.

²⁵ McClatchey to Kent, Dec. 3, 1917, Aug. 4, 1919, Kent MSS.

²⁶ McClatchey to Lissner, July 23, 1920, Lissner MSS. Lissner replied to this letter that he was for the discussion of all "isms."

²⁷ Steffens to Laura Steffens, Oct. 23, 1917, cited in Steffens, *Letters,* 1:411; San Francisco *Argonaut,* 86:129; copy of statement attacking LaFollette, Sept. 15, 1924, Rowell MSS; Kent to Hichborn, Nov. 10, 1924, Kent MSS.

²⁸ San Francisco *Bulletin,* Nov. 1–15, 1916.

²⁹ By that time Wisconsin, Massachusetts, Connecticut, West Virginia, Oklahoma, Mississippi, Nebraska, and North and South Carolina had passed such state taxes.

³⁰ Roosevelt to Charles J. Bonaparte, Nov. 7, 1914, Roosevelt MSS.

³¹ Rowell to Hays, July 18, 1918 (copy), Roosevelt MSS; Lissner to Hays,

June 27, Aug. 19, 1918, Roosevelt to Lissner, April 19, 1918, Lissner to Roosevelt, May 24, 1918, Lissner MSS.

[32] Kent to S. D. Thatcher, (?), 1920, Kent MSS.

[33] Hichborn, *op. cit.*, p. 297; Croly, "The Eclipse of Progressivism," *New Republic*, 24:210; Kent to Louis F. Post, Jan. 31, 1921, Kent MSS.

[34] Rowell to Will Hays, June 18, 1918, copy in Lissner MSS. As a solution to the same problem Kent prophetically advanced the idea that government, while guaranteeing labor's right to strike, must have the power to seize and operate nation-wide industries during the course of a prolonged labor dispute, Kent to George P. West, Dec. 7, 1919, Kent MSS.

[35] Rowell to Johnson, April 4, 1921, Rowell MSS; Johnson to Lissner, Nov. 8, 1920, Lissner MSS.

[36] Rowell to Kent, June 24, 1922, Norris to Kent, Jan. 6, 1924, Kent MSS; Older, *My Own Story*, p. 350.

[37] Rowell to Kent, June 24, 1922, Kent MSS.

[38] Kent to John S. Phillips, Oct. 16, 1908, Kent to Lynn T. Haines, July 13, 1922, Kent MSS.

[39] Older, *op. cit.*, pp. 339–340.

[40] *Ibid.*, preface, ix ff.

[41] Robert S. Allen, ed., *Our Fair City* (New York, 1947), p. 358.

[42] Anderson, *op. cit.*, p. 136.

[43] White to Henry Allen, Jan. 28, 1934, *Selected Letters of William Allen White, 1893–1943*, Walter Johnson, ed. (New York, 1947), p. 348.

BIBLIOGRAPHICAL NOTE

Fortunately for the historian, the California Progressives were both highly literate and aware of history. Consequently, their carefully preserved manuscripts constitute the best raw sources for the history of the period. Of these manuscript collections six are particularly rich, both because of their size and because of the importance of their author to the movement. Perhaps the best single manuscript collection is the Meyer Lissner papers in the Borel Collection at Stanford University. The letters of Chester H. Rowell, in the Bancroft Library of the University of California at Berkeley, of Edward A. Dickson in his possession in Los Angeles, of William Kent in the Yale University Library, and of Franklin Hichborn in the John Randolph and Dora Haynes Foundation, Los Angeles, are also of exceptional value. The voluminous Theodore Roosevelt manuscripts in the Library of Congress contain many letters to and from the California Progressives, in particular Hiram Johnson, Chester Rowell, Meyer Lissner, E. T. Earl, Francis J. Heney, and William Kent. They also contain the typewritten minutes of the governing bodies of the national Progressive party, and thus throw much light on the connection of the Californians with national politics.

Of almost equal significance to the history of the period are the personal papers of George C. Pardee, Lincoln Steffens, and John D. Works, all in the Bancroft Library, a second collection of John D. Works' papers in the Borel Collection at Stanford, and the manuscripts of John Randolph Haynes in the Haynes Foundation. The Pardee collection deals largely with his term as governor, and most of the Steffens letters were written either to or by Francis J. Heney.

The manuscripts of Thomas A. Bard, some copies of which are to be found in the Borel Collection, and of John C. Needham and Rufus L. Green, both in the Stanford University Library, are of less importance. The original papers of Thomas

R. Bard are in possession of his son at Huleneme, California. A few letters of William R. Davis may be found in his scrapbooks in the Bancroft Library. Three very important unpublished sources are the diary of Arthur Judson Pillsbury, in possession of his son, Warren H. Pillsbury of Berkeley, "The Lincoln-Roosevelt League," by Edward A. Dickson, and the "Autobiography" of Marshall Stimson. Two minor unpublished sources, "The Political Reminiscences of Dr. George C. Pardee" and J. D. Works', "Some of My Experiences in Political and Official Life," are to be found in the Borel Collection at Stanford University.

Much valuable material of a personal nature was gathered for this work by interviewing some of the more important progressive leaders still alive. The late Chester Rowell, Edward A. Dickson, and Marshall Stimson were all extremely gracious in giving their time and memory to a bothersome historical inquisitor. The student of the California progressive movement cannot afford to overlook the invaluable work of Miss Alice Rose, during the late 'thirties, in recording her interviews with at least twenty-four surviving progressive leaders and placing them in the Borel Collection at Stanford University.

Since many leading Progressives were editors, the newspapers of the day are extremely rich in source material. This is particularly true of Chester Rowell's Fresno *Morning Republican*, E. T. Earl's Los Angeles *Express*, for which Edward A. Dickson wrote many of the editorials, Fremont Older's San Francisco *Bulletin*, and George C. Pardee's Oakland *Enquirer*. Of the regular Republican conservative papers the most useful are perhaps the Los Angeles *Times*, the San Francisco *Chronicle*, and the Oakland *Tribune*. For a Democratic view as influenced by William Randolph Hearst, the Los Angeles *Examiner* and the San Francisco *Examiner* were used. The best labor paper of the period and the most comprehensive in its coverage is the *Labor Clarion*, the official journal of the California State Federation of Labor, published weekly by the San Francisco Labor Council.

Two extremely useful periodicals are the *California Outlook* and the San Francisco *Argonaut*. The *Outlook*, formed in 1911 by the fusion of the old progressive magazines, the *California Weekly* and the *Pacific Outlook*, became the official organ of the California progressive movement. Among its editors and trustees were Chester Rowell, Edward A. Dickson, Meyer Lissner, C. D. Willard, and A. J. Pillsbury. The *Argonaut* faithfully reflected the opinion of San Francisco's Montgomery Street and high Republicanism as few other news sources did in the period. A wealth of material is also to be found in the national magazines of the times, particularly in the articles by Lincoln Steffens, Ray Stannard Baker, and Charles E. Russell appearing in the so-called muckrake press. For accounts of California's industrial and technological development, the files of the *Scientific American* are laden with valuable material.

In a more formal and statistical way, the official reports of many state agencies are excellent sources of information. The reports of the California Bureau of Labor Statistics, later incorporated in the Department of Industrial Relations, of the State Tax Commission, and of the Commission of Immigration and Housing, may be cited in particular.

Among the many unpublished doctoral and master's theses about the progressive period, that of Alice M. Rose, "Rise of California Insurgency, Origins of the League of Lincoln-Roosevelt Republican Clubs, 1900–1907" (unpublished doctoral thesis, Stanford University, 1942), makes by far the most important contribution to the history of the subject.

Without the volumes of Franklin Hichborn on the sessions of the California legislatures from 1909 to 1921, excluding the war years, the historian would be put to almost endless work in tracing developments in the state's legislative body. This book has leaned heavily upon those volumes, as it has upon Hichborn's *The System* (San Francisco, 1915), an invaluable account of the San Francisco graft trials. Among the many other books which should be consulted for an understanding of the state in the period, perhaps the few most important are Robert G. Cleland, *California in Our Time* (New York, 1947), Stuart Daggett, *Chapters on the History of the Southern Pacific* (New York, 1932), Ira B. Cross, *A History of the Labor Movement in California* (Berkeley, 1935), Oscar Lewis, *The Big Four* (New York, 1938), and Carey McWilliams, *Southern California Country* (New York, 1946).

As the footnotes partly indicate, the author borrowed heavily from numerous other works in the preparation of this book. Those listed in the present section represent but a small part of his total obligation to the historical and literary world. Limitations of space alone preclude a further accounting of that great unacknowledged debt.

INDEX

Initiative (*continued*)
 barely passes, 149; increasing opposition to, 285. *See also* Recall of
 judges
Industrial Welfare Commission, 153
I.W.W.: at Durst Ranch, 195–196;
 talk of conspiracy, 198; postwar
 militant stand, 288–289
Interstate Commerce Commission,
 adjusts railroad charges to citrus
 growers, 17
Irrigation and Rural Credits Commission, 152–153
Irwin, Wallace, 1

Jess, Stoddard, 202
Johnson, Albert M., 112
Johnson, Grove, 63; five antirailroad
 bills, 64; temporary rebellion
 against Southern Pacific, 64; leads
 Southern Pacific machine to defeat bills to amend legal procedure, 82; political career, 111; objections to initiative, referendum,
 and recall, 140
Johnson, Hiram: Langdon favors as
 graft prosecutor, 30; succeeds
 Heney, 36, 112; speaks for Lincoln-Republican League, 78; supports unions, 93; refuses to run for
 governor, 107–109; consents, 110;
 life, 111–117; 1910 campaigning,
 119 ff.; attacks Southern Pacific,
 119–120; aligns with Roosevelt,
 121–122; pessimistic about campaign, 123–124; strength in 1910
 primary, 129; tension between
 Heney and, 132–133; elected, 133;
 advises with Eastern Progressives,
 135; resents San Francisco conference, 136; advisors, 136; ideas on
 patronage, 137–138; tight political
 organization, 138–139; asks 1911
 legislature for amendatory legislation, 139–140; for recall of judges,
 141; signs eight-hour day for
 women, 144–145; compromises
 on employers' liability, 145; de-
 clares self an insurgent, 158;

Roosevelt invites, 166; conference
 with Rowell, Brundige, and Lissner, 166; wires that Roosevelt a
 candidate, 167; answers LaFollette
 speeches, 176; contender for vice-
 presidential nomination, 177; refuses to attend Chicago meeting,
 178; letter to Lissner on Progressive party, 180; demands founding
 of new party, 180; leads Californians out of Chicago convention, 181; chairman of national
 organizing committee, 182; fights
 Perkins, 182, 183, 190; Roosevelt
 selects for vice-president, 183–
 184; speech at Dreamland Rink,
 187–188; irritability on cross-
 country tour, 188–189; cited on
 near-progressives, 193–194; relations with Heney, 201, 206 ff.; irritation at Kent, 201; and Earl-
 Lissner quarrel, 205; wish to run
 for Senate, 207–208; wavers, 209;
 final rupture with Heney, 209–
 210; seeks second term, 209;
 wrath at Heney's backers, 210;
 Fredericks' campaign against,
 212–213; attacks Otis, Spreckels,
 and de Young, 213; refuses to
 campaign with Heney, 214; re-
 elected, 214; charges against, 215;
 and 1915 legislature, 218–219;
 Weinstock opens campaign to
 nominate, for presidency, 220;
 national aspirations, 221; attitude
 toward national party, 221, 223;
 nonpartisan plan for elections defeated, 224, 244; Roosevelt suggests presidency to, 225–226;
 Hughes-Johnson slate proposed,
 226–227; refuses to enter out-of-
 state primaries, 228; letter to Republican party, 231–232; at Chicago convention, 233 ff.; speech,
 235–236; seconds Roosevelt's
 nomination, 237; to New York,
 239; announces for Hughes, 241,
 244; determines to run for senatorial nomination, 243; power

mittee (1910), 131, 136, 274; appoints committee to investigate reform proposals, 136; lukewarm on recall, 141; asks governor to defeat eight-hour day for women, 144; appeals for defeat of labor injunction bill, 146–147; quoted on separation from Republican party, 159; urges LaFollette to speak in California, 162; conference with Johnson on visit to Roosevelt, 166; opposes Roosevelt-LaFollette poll, 173; fights Perkins' influence, 182, 183–190; resignation as chairman demanded, 185; determined to break away from state Republican party, 193, 194; heads 1913 Los Angeles campaign committee, 202; feud with Earl, 202–204; overtures to Otis-Republicans, 203; 1915 letter to Progressive chairmen, 224; for Hughes-Johnson slate, 227; proposes joint delegation to Republican National Convention, 229; wants railroad commissionership, 281; disturbed by Johnson's stand on League of Nations, 283; still loyal to Johnson, 285; loses political influence, 285; approves program of British Labour Party, 293

Lodge, Henry Cabot, 236–237

London, Jack, 1

Los Angeles: largest city, 7–8; difference in social attitudes from San Francisco, 8; Protestant, 8; middle-class respectability, 38; charter of 1903, 39; initiative, referendum, and recall, 39; franchise to Gillmore, 39; closing of gambling houses and saloons, 38; Parker's municipal machine, 38–39; antiunion ships, 48, 91

Los Angeles Chamber of Commerce: encourages mass immigration into state, 6; forges powerful social group, 22; recall proceedings against mayor, 45; 1910 resolution to admit Oriental fruit pickers,

154; ex-officio meeting "to expel McCarthyism," 202

Los Angeles Examiner: supports 1911 Good Government candidate, 51; supports Knowland, 214

Los Angeles Express: editorials against Southern Pacific, 40, 67; charges Times with ballot forgery, 42–43; urges caution in blame for Times bombing, 50; supports Bell, 61, 62; opposed to eight-hour day, 144; in municipal campaign, 203–204; supports Heney, 214

Los Angeles Herald: investigations of Harper and joint-stock companies, 45

Los Angeles Times: supports Bard, 16; denounces Southern Pacific, 20; assails city nonpartisan movement, 42, 46; accused of forgery and fraudulent ballots, 42–43; attacks Lissner, 46, 127; in 1909 campaign, 46; printers' strike, 48; building dynamited, 50; pledges support to Good Government candidate, 51; blasts Johnson, 124–126 passim, 146; opposes recall of judges, 141; against labor injunction bill, 146; Lissner's letter to Dickson in, 204; quoted on proposal for joint delegation, 230; on refusal to permit Progressive leaders to return to Republican party, 245; attacks Republican party, 268; continues to attack Johnson, 269–270; accuses Johnson of deal with Democrats, 269–270; anti-British, 272

Los Angeles Tribune: Earl-controlled, 180; on Progressive party, 180; in Los Angeles municipal campaign, 203

Los Angeles Union League Club, 52

Los Angeles Voters' League, 40

Luce, Edgar, 123

McCabe, Al, 229

McClatchey, C. K.: protests "holier-

nor, 105, 110; arbitration bill, 143–144; opens campaign to nominate Johnson for President in 1916, 220

Wells Fargo Express Company, earnings reduced, 156

Western Pacific Railroad: first train from East to Oakland, 3; Sacramento city council defeats franchise, 17; referendum on grant, 17–18; bankruptcy, 229; movement for state purchase, 219

Wheat, 4

Wheatland outbreak, 196; Johnson's intervention, 196; reflects class tensions, 198

Wheeler, Benjamin Ide, 2

Wheeler, Charles S.: protests overhead trolley system, 29; organizes Municipal Street Railroad Company, 29; in state-wide revolt, 38; speaks for Lincoln-Republican League, 78; opposes recall of judges, 141; at Chicago convention, 180

Wheeler, Fred, 46

White, Clinton L., 74, 78

White, William Allen: estimate of Johnson, 116; traces disintegration of progressive creed, 297–299

Wickersham, George W., sues Southern Pacific for government oil lands, 11

Willard, C. D., quoted on democracy, 99

Willcox, William R., 246; repudiates

agreement to support Johnson, 247–248, 251; Rowell's wire to, 252–253; suggests Johnson preside at Hughes meeting, 254; entreats Rowell not to resign, 255; tries to break deadlock, 255, 256

Wilson, Woodrow: nomination blow to Progressive hopes in California, 186; cited on Progressives, 187; re-elected, 269; support of California labor, 271; peace issue, 271; strength in labor and women's votes, 272

Woman suffrage: 1896 defeat, 8; Johnson dodges issue, 132; 1911 issue, 148; opposition of Catholic San Francisco, 149; Heney endorses, 213

Wood, Leonard, 236

Woolwine, Thomas L.: law enforcement campaign, 44; uncovers Harper's graft, 44; dismissed, 44–45

Works, John D.: quoted on older progressive leaders, 94; doubts efficacy of democracy, 99; candidacy for Senate, 117–118; for Roosevelt, 122; majority in 1910 primary, 129; opposes recall of judges, 141; refuses to leave Republican party, 186; asked to resign, 186

Young, C. C., 287

Zeehandelaar, F. J., cited on antilabor practices, 49